Paul Deats   *Carol Robb*

The editors of this volume, Paul
Deats and Carol Robb, are, respectively,
third- and fourth-generation Boston Personalists. Paul Deats is Walter G.
Muelder Professor of Social Ethics and
chairs the Division of Theological and
Religious Studies in Boston University
Graduate School. Carol Robb is assistant
professor of Christian social ethics at San
Francisco Theological Seminary. The
authors in this volume include the most
prominent figures among the third generation of Boston Personalists.

D1565699

The Boston
Personalist Tradition
in Philosophy,
Social Ethics,
and Theology

The Boston Personalist Tradition in Philosophy, Social Ethics, and Theology

edited by
    Paul Deats and Carol Robb

ISBN 0-86554-177-9

B
828.5
.B65
1986

The Boston Personalist Tradition
Copyright © 1986 by
Mercer University Press
Macon, Georgia 31207
All rights reserved
Produced in the United States of America

The paper used in this publication meets the minimum requirements
of American National Standard for Information Sciences—
Permanence of Paper for Printed Library Materials, ANSI Z39.48-1984.   ∞ ™

Library of Congress Cataloging-in-Publication Data

Main entry under title:

The Boston personalist tradition in philosophy,
    social ethics, and theology.

    Includes index.
    1. Personalism—Addresses, essays, lectures.
2. Boston University—Addresses, essays, lectures.
I. Deats, Paul. II. Robb, Carol, 1945–
B828.5.B65   1986   141'.5'0974461   85-25863
ISBN 0-86554-177-9 (alk. paper)

JESUIT - KRAUSS - McCORMICK - LIBRARY
1100 EAST 55th STREET
CHICAGO, ILLINOIS 60615

Contents

Dedication

This volume is dedicated to those who will carry on the explorations begun in this tradition, working critically in university, church, and society at the tasks of philosophy, theology, and ethics.

Acknowledgments

To Julius S. Scott, Jr. and Donald H. Treese, Associate General Secretaries, respectively, of the Divisions of Higher Education and of Ordained Ministry, Board of Higher Education and Ministry of the United Methodist Church, for a grant that made possible the lectures in the spring of 1984 on which this volume is based.

To Richard D. Nesmith and the Boston University School of Theology for grants to cover videotaping the lectures and typing the manuscripts in final form.

To Robert Watts Thornburg, Dean of Marsh Chapel at Boston University, for counsel, encouragement, and technical assistance in videotaping the lectures.

To Ruthlyn Glover Palmer and Margaret Craddock Huff, friends and colleagues, who with patience and skill transformed edited manuscripts into a document ready for the publisher.

To the staff of Mercer University Press for their interest and assistance in bringing the idea of publication to fruition.

To the lecturers for devotion beyond the call of duty in providing manuscripts, accepting editorial suggestions, and agreeing in some cases to shorter chapters.

Contributors

PETER ANTHONY BERTOCCI received the Ph.D. in Philosophy from Boston University in 1935, under Edgar S. Brightman. He taught at Boston University from 1945 until his retirement in 1975, from 1953 as the Borden Parker Bowne Professor of Philosophy.

DIANNE E. S. CARPENTER received the M.S.M. from Boston University in 1978 and the M.Div. from Andover Newton Theological School in 1985. She is a candidate for the Ph.D. in Social Ethics at Boston University, under Paul Deats and Walter G. Muelder, and is pastor of the East Natick, Massachusetts, United Methodist Church.

PAUL DEATS received the Ph.D. in Social Ethics from Boston University in 1954, under Walter G. Muelder, and has taught there since, from 1979 as the Walter G. Muelder Professor of Social Ethics.

L. HAROLD DEWOLF received the Ph.D. in Philosophy from Boston University in 1935, under Edgar S. Brightman. He taught there as Professor of Philosophy and later Systematic Theology until 1965, then serving as Dean and Professor of Systematic Theology at Wesley Theological Seminary in Washington, D.C., until his retirement in 1972.

ROLAINE M. FRANZ received the Ph.D. in English Literature from Brown University in 1978. She is an M.Div. candidate in the Boston University School of Theology and pastor of the Holbrook, Massachusetts, United Methodist Church.

JOHN H. LAVELY received the Ph.D. in Philosophy from Boston University in 1950, under Edgar S. Brightman, and has been Professor of Philosophy there since 1951.

WALTER G. MUELDER received the Ph.D. in Philosophy from Boston University in 1933, under Edgar S. Brightman. He was Dean and Professor of Social Ethics at the Boston University School of Theology until his retirement in 1972. He has since taught at Berea College, Garrett-Evangelical Theological Seminary, and Andover Newton Theological School.

CAROL S. ROBB received the Ph.D. in Social Ethics from Boston University in 1978, under Paul Deats. She is the Assistant Professor of Christian Social Ethics at San Francisco Theological Seminary, San Anselmo, California.

S. PAUL SCHILLING received the Ph.D. in Philosophy from Boston University in 1934, under Edgar S. Brightman. He was Professor of Systematic Theology there from 1953 until his retirement in 1969. He has taught since at Union Theological Seminary in Manila, Wesley Theological Seminary, Garrett-Evangelical Theological Seminary, and Andover Newton Theological School.

F. THOMAS TROTTER received the Ph.D. in Systematic Theology from Boston University in 1958, under S. Paul Schilling and L. Harold DeWolf. He was Professor of Theology and the Arts and Dean at Claremont, California, School of Theology until 1973. Since then he has been the General Secretary of the Board of Higher Education and Ministry of the United Methodist Church.

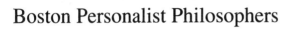

Boston Personalist Philosophers

Borden Parker Bowne

Edgar S. Brightman

Albert C. Knudson

Francis J. McConnell

Georgia Harkness

F. Thomas Trotter

John H. Lavely

Walter G. Muelder

Peter A. Bertocci

S. Paul Schilling

L. Harold DeWolf

Introduction
to Boston Personalism

Paul Deats

These essays, first given as lectures in the spring of 1984,[1] trace how the theories and explanations of the first three generations of Boston Personalists grew out of their life experiences in university, church, and world. One essay traces Borden Parker Bowne's life and thought from a second-hand point of view; the others are firsthand remembrances or first-person stories.

This introduction will provide a brief working definition of Boston Personalism, explore some of its intellectual roots in the history of philosophy and in the historical settings of selected figures, distinguish Boston Personalism from other varieties of personalism, and present certain themes that will be more fully explored in the remaining essays.

---

[1]The lectures were set in a course, "Ethics and Theology of Personalism," developed by John H. Lavely and Paul Deats in 1980 and taught for the third time in 1984. The lectures and videotaping were made possible by a grant from the Divisions of Higher Education and of Ordained Ministry of the United Methodist General Board of Higher Education and Ministry.

WHAT IS BOSTON PERSONALISM?

Clarifying terms was the first step of philosophical method for Edgar Brightman,[2] for whom definitions were not finalities but guides to facilitate exploration. Personalism is a philosophical perspective for which the person is the ontological ultimate and for which personality is the fundamental explanatory principle.[3] Walter Mueder has expressed its essence as holding that truth is *of, by,* and *for* persons. More precisely, human persons (not isolated but in community) are the clues to reality with the Divine Person. Borden Parker Bowne, the founder of Boston Personalism, introduced his important chapter entitled ''The Failure of Impersonalism'' with this report:

> In all our thinking, when critically scrutinized, we find self-conscious and active intelligence the presupposition not only of our knowledge but of the world of objects as well.[4]

William Ernest Hocking, himself an absolute idealist, wrote in 1922,

> It is unequivocal insistence upon the attribute of personality in all that is real which marks Bowne off from most of his idealistic colleagues.

Humans are not identical to God, nor absorbed into God; instead, they share God's purposes even as they are distinct selves. Personality ''cannot be explained by anything else, but everything else can be explained by it.'' Hocking concluded,

> There is no more powerful and convincing chapter in American philo-

---

[2]Edgar S. Brightman, *An Introduction to Philosophy,* rev. ed. (New York: Henry Holt and Co., 1925, 1951) 25.

[3]See especially John H. Lavely, ''Personalism,'' in *Encyclopedia of Philosophy* (New York and London: Collier-Macmillan, 1967, 1972) 5:107-110. Other sources used here include A. C. Knudson, *The Philosophy of Personalism* (Boston: Boston University Press, 1949); Edgar S. Brightman, ''Personalism,'' in Vergilius Ferm, ed., *A History of Philosophical Systems* (New York: The Philosophical Library, 1950) 340-52; L. H. DeWolf, ''Personalism in the History of Western Philosophy,'' *The Philosophical Forum* 12 (1954): 29-51.

[4]Borden Parker Bowne, *Personalism* (Norwood MA: The Plimpton Press, 1908, 1936) 217.

sophical writing than that of Bowne "on the failure of impersonalism".[5]

Personalism is a species of Personal Idealism (as distinguished from Realism). Persons experience self-identity in change (memory), are active in knowing and choosing, are purposive and value-seeking, and are at least potentially rational.[6] Personalist methodology is empirical in consulting human experience as a whole. Personalist epistemology is dualistic, postulating an objective order that we find and do not construct (situation-experienced as distinct from situation believed in); on this basis it is hypothetical. Boston Personalists are metaphysical pluralists, to account for the facts of error, evil, and ignorance. In social philosophy, the interpersonal focus typically becomes democratic and reformist.

WHAT ARE ITS ROOTS?

W. H. Werkmeister has called Bowne's Personalism "the first complete and comprehensive system of philosophy developed in America which has had lasting influence."[7] Even so, it had ancient intellectual roots, and many of the first three generations of Boston Personalists studied philosophy in Germany.

Knudson closed his *The Philosophy of Personalism* with a section entitled "The Development of Personalism," in which he listed a "personalistic Hall of Fame."[8] He began with Plato, stressing the superiority of thought over sense and the objectivity of ideals. Aristotle is credited with emphasizing the concrete character of reality, as opposed to Plato's abstract universalism, and with substituting a Prime Mover for Plato's Eternal Ideas. Plotinus introduced the active character of self-consciousness, while Augustine wrote of the role of self-knowledge in metaphysics and of the significance of the will. Aquinas gave a more personalistic cast to

---

[5]Quoted from *The Methodist Review*, 374, in Knudson, *The Philosophy of Personalism*, 16.

[6]Brightman, "Personalism," 341, with following material from pages 345-50.

[7]W. H. Werkmeister, *A History of Philosophical Ideas in America* (New York: Ronald Press, 1949) 103.

[8]Knudson, *The Philosophy of Personalism*, 428ff.

Aristotle. Descartes introduced the primacy of self-certainty, and Leibniz formulated the principle of individuality. Berkeley was the first philosophical personal idealist. Kant, Hegel, and Lotze will be dealt with in later essays for their influence on Bowne and other personalists. Bowne himself is the twelfth member of the Hall of Fame.

Obviously, there is a certain eclectic character to a system with such a diverse heritage, but Knudson claimed that Boston Personalism is not simply a sum of the previous parts. It is a dialectical reconstruction. Bowne held that when views are accepted after scrutiny they bear the marks of their handling and reworking. He is quoted by Knudson thus:

> It is hard to classify me with accuracy. I am a theistic idealist, a Personalist, a transcendental empiricist; an idealistic realist, and a realistic idealist; but all these phrases need to be interpreted. They cannot well be made out from the dictionary. Neither can I be called a disciple of any one. I largely agree with Lotze, but I transcend him, I hold half of Kant's system, but sharply dissent from the rest. There is a strong smack of Berkeley's philosophy, with a complete rejection of his theory of knowledge. I am a *Personalist,* the first of the clan in any thoroughgoing sense.[9]

It is not only Bowne, the founder, whom we will seek to understand, but also later generations of the clan. The second generation includes not only Edgar S. Brightman, Albert C. Knudson, and Francis J. McConnell, to whom we devote chapters, but also George Albert Coe, in religious education, and Ralph T. Flewelling, who taught at the University of Southern California and edited *The Personalist.* The third generation includes a number of our authors and one of our subjects: Peter Bertocci, Harold DeWolf, Georgia Harkness, John Lavely, Walter Muelder, and S. Paul Schilling. Others who should be mentioned are Paul E. Johnson, Jannette E. Newhall, Robert Beck, Richard M. Millard, Arthur W. Munk, and Warren Steinkraus.

The fourth generation is just discovering itself, but at least one name should be lifted up, that of Martin Luther King, Jr., who came to Boston University Graduate School to study philosophy and theology with Edgar Brightman and L. Harold DeWolf, but who also worked with Walter Muelder and S. Paul Schilling. In *Stride toward Freedom* he wrote that the

---

[9]Ibid., 16.

personal idealism of these teachers "remains today my basic philosophic position."[10] Muelder holds that this orientation "influenced his role in the civil rights struggle, the method of non-violence, and the extension of the struggle to issues of peace and economics."[11]

BOSTON PERSONALISM AND OTHER PERSONALISMS

Bowne began his career with an interest in physics. He early read Darwin's *Origin of Species* and could accept critical evolution theory and interpret it to the fundamentalists in the churches. But he reacted strongly against *un*critical Evolutionism (with a capital *E*) and wrote a continuing polemic against Herbert Spencer. He was vigorous in his criticism of some late-nineteenth-century science and philosophy, especially that which presupposed a crude materialism (matter is all there is) or sensationalism (our only evidence is from sense data). He also did battle against pragmatism and positivism, against any impersonalism.

In this regard a letter to Bowne from William James, written from Holland in 1908, is intriguing, as indicated in the following excerpts.

> It seems to me that you and I are now aiming at exactly the same end, though . . . we often express ourselves so differently. . . . The common foe of both of us is the dogmatist-rationalist-abstractionist. Our common desire is to redeem the concrete personal life . . . from fastidious (and really preposterous) dialectical contradictions, impossibilities, and vetoes. But whereas your "transcendental empiricism" assumes that the essential discontinuity of the sensible flux has to be overcome by high intellectual operations on it, quite *a la* Kant, Green, Caird, etc., my "radical" empiricism denies the flux's discontinuity, making conjunctive relations essential members of it as given, and charging the conceptual function with being the creator of factitious incoherencies.

---

[10]Martin Luther King, Jr., *Stride toward Freedom* (New York: Harper & Brothers, 1958) 100.

[11]Muelder, "Philosophical and Theological Influences in the Thought and Action of Martin Luther King, Jr.," *Debate and Understanding* (King Afro-American Cultural Center at Boston University, 1977) vol. 1, no. 3, 179-89. See also John J. Ansbro, *Martin Luther King, Jr.: The Making of a Mind* (Maryknoll NY: Orbis Books, 1982).

> You don't stop with the abstract syntheses of the intellect, however; you restore concreteness by the "will," etc.; whereas I *keep* the full personal concreteness which I find in time and the immediate particulars that fill it.

James concluded the letter,

> But the essential thing is not these differences, it is that our emphatic footsteps fall on the *same spot.* You, starting near the rationalist pole, and boxing the compass, and I traversing the diameter from the empiricist pole, reach practically very similar positions and attitudes. It seems to me that this is full of promise for the future of philosophy.

James wrote that there was no need to reply—by letter;[12] he had to go with his wife to hear the organ at church.

We have already noted that Personalism has roots, and Knudson wrote that it is a new name for old ways of thinking, a new emphasis, a new approach. But not all personalisms are the same. Walt Whitman was probably the first to use the term in American published print in an article entitled "Democracy" in 1867, with a later article entitled "Personalism" in 1868.[13] Then, between 1903 and 1908 the term appeared three times, the third in Bowne's book. Charles Renouvier's *Le Personalisme* appeared in 1903, and William Stern's *Person und Sache* came out in 1906.

Lavely distinguishes realistic personalism from three types of idealistic personalism. For realistic personalists ultimate reality is a spiritual, supernatural being, a God who has created a natural order that is not intrinsically spiritual or personal. This group includes not only such Neo-Thomists as Etienne Gilson, Jacques Maritain, and Emmanuel Mounier, but also Nicholas Berdyaev and Georgia Harkness. There are three types of idealism. Absolute idealism (or absolutistic personalism) is monistic, holding that all reality is one, with finite beings as manifestations of the absolute mind. Josiah Royce and W. E. Hocking are mentioned here. Panpsychic idealism stems from Leibniz and is expressed through process philosophy and theology, with A. N. Whitehead and Charles Hartshorne as exponents, along with John Cobb and David Griffin. This school, as

---

[12]Quoted in *Representative Essays of Borden Parker Bowne,* ed. Warren E. Steinkraus (Utica NY: Meridian Publishing Co., 1980) 189-90.

[13]DeWolf, "Personalism in the History of Western Philosophy."

will be noted later, is closer to personalistic theism than to traditional theism. Personalistic idealism holds that all reality is personal, that reality is pluralistic—a society of persons, with God as the source and ground of all being.[14]

Knudson criticized "the atheistic, pantheistic, absolutistic, relativistic, and purely teleological forms of personalism."[15] J. M. E. McTaggart was rejected as atheistic, William Stern as pantheistic, and Josiah Royce as absolutistic. G. H. Howison was seen as a purely ethical or teleological personalist. Charles Renouvier was labeled as relativistic, is said to have influenced William James's pragmatism, and was criticized by Knudson because his "finitistic conception of God seems to us unduly anthropomorphic."

The debate over the finite-infinite God will be a continuing theme in these essays. Other persistent points of divergence include the "body-mind problem," the relation of nature to God, and the relation of the individual to community. Later personalists, such as Walter Muelder, report that Brightman took his body seriously in practice but tended to focus on the mind when he wrote theory. Muelder also notes that personalists have tended to neglect nature, and some personalists have been preoccupied with psychology, neglecting the communitarian dimensions of personality. These are unresolved problems.

RECURRENT THEMES IN BOSTON PERSONALISM

In Boston Personalism, philosophy is not an isolated discipline but an integrating one. Bowne's concern was with the sciences, physics, and Darwinian evolutionary theory. Bertocci, Brightman, and Paul Johnson have maintained a continuity of interest in psychology, while Lavely has worked on the philosophy of religion. DeWolf's attention has turned increasingly to criminal justice, and Schilling has devoted research and writing to Marxism and atheism. Muelder's studies in Ernst Troeltsch and Max

---

[14]This section has drawn heavily from Lavely, "Personalism."

[15]The following section relies on Knudson, *The Philosophy of Personalism*, 17-87; the quotation is from page 61.

Weber, Robert M. MacIver and Gunnar Myrdal, and the Social Gospel in America were influential in the developing thought of Martin Luther King, Jr.[16]

A second theme is the integral relationship between philosophy, philosophy of religion, and philosophical theology. These have been treated neither as contradictory—mutually exclusive—nor susceptible to conflation into a single discipline, but as requiring critical interaction of method and substance. Philosophy's task is critical and synoptic reflection on all of human experience, while theology focuses its critical reflection on the experience of the Christian community.[17]

Lavely notes that personalism in almost all its forms has been integrally related to theism. Still, it has usually considered itself a system defensible on the grounds of philosophy, not based solely on theological presuppositions. In his introduction to Bowne's *Representative Essays,* Herbert W. Schneider wrote, ''Thus theism has the task of guiding beliefs which in their origin are non-logical until they become norms that are accountable.''[18] This stance has meant that personalists have typically been in critical dialogue with elements in the church that were conservative both theologically and ethically. It has probably also contributed to the mainline character of its exponents, who were not easily drawn into such fads as the ''Death of God'' theology.

In response to questions, Muelder has commented that for Boston Personalists all philosophical positions are hypothetical, subject to reassessment and revision, not taken as dogmas or final statements. Brightman has also made a helpful distinction between faith and reason that does not set the two modes (or their content) in basic conflict. Faith is defined as confidence, opposed not to reason but to distrust. Reason is interpreted as

---

[16]See Muelder, ''Philosophical and Theological Influences,'' and Brightman, ''Personalism.''

[17]DeWolf, *A Theology of the Living Church* (New York: Harper & Brothers, 1953) esp. 18.

[18]Herbert W. Schneider, ''Bowne's Radical Empiricism,'' in *Representative Essays of Borden Parker Bowne,* xiii.

coherence, with its contrary as incoherence and irrationalism rather than faith.[19]

A third theme, then, concerns the relationship of reason, as critical rationality, and experience, as more inclusive than sense experience. Reason is typically seen as being reasonable, as thinking and drawing inferences. Bowne took it as a compliment when one critic charged that he had thought more widely than he had read.[20] This may have been due to his lack of footnoting, but it probably also reflects his refusal to limit learning to book learning. Muelder argues in his essay that Brightman's view is more empirical, more temporalist, and more inherently historical than was Hegel's. Lavely characterizes personalism, as noted, as metaphysically pluralistic and epistemologically dualistic, postulating an objective order that we find and do not construct; but that finding is an active process, not passive. Our immediate experience is our starting point, but it always points beyond itself (self-transcendence) from the "shining present" of the situation experienced to the "illuminating absent" of the situation believed in. And Muelder comments that there is always a gap between these situations, thus always an element of mystery.[21]

Here we should at least note Brightman's understanding of metaphysics as "orientation."

> Wonder is the beginning of metaphysics. No one without curiosity can enter.
>
> Metaphysical wonder is a wonder about how everything hangs together. The metaphysician is a synoptic man . . .
>
> Abstraction is omission. Temporary omissions enable thought to start; permanent omissions compel thought to falsify . . .

---

[19]Brightman, *Introduction to Philosophy,* 170. The similarity to H. Richard Niebuhr's understanding of faith as trust and loyalty is illuminating: Faith "is the attitude and action of confidence in, and fidelity to, certain realities as the sources of values and the objects of loyalty." *Radical Monotheism and Western Culture* (New York: Harper & Brothers, 1960) 16.

[20]Francis J. McConnell, *Borden Parker Bowne* (New York: Abingdon Press, 1929) 31.

[21]Lavely, "Personalism," 109.

> . . . reason is more than logic. . . . The practical reason has the
> primacy over the theoretical; but nothing has the primacy over reason.
> We cannot start without presuppositions, but we can discover our
> presuppositions and then test them.[22]

Brightman then goes on to outline the radical empirical metaphysical method of his personalism. It is empirical, considering all experience without arbitrary limits. It is experimental, forming and testing hypotheses. These focus attention on the unity of consciousness characteristic of persons. The method is, further, both analytic and synoptic. The continuing test is coherence, which treats consistency as a presupposed necessity (but not a sufficient test in itself), systematic ordering of hypotheses, inclusiveness of all the data of experience, and a dialectic of hypothesis-testing-revision.[23]

A fourth theme of Boston Personalism is the Kantian postulate of freedom—of the person, not of the will. Freedom is not only a matter of experienced choice, but a necessary presupposition for rationality, as well as for choice and thus for morality and ethics. Brightman wrote, ''There is no moral situation where there is no choice.''[24]

Purpose is another persistent theme. Bowne defined persons in terms of self-consciousness and self-direction. For him purpose was the clue to understanding evolution, and axiology was the clue to ethics. There is continuing and rigorous attention to values and theory of values in philosophy, ethics, and the social sciences.

Almost every Boston Personalist gives attention to ethics, and for one stream it is a preoccupation. Bowne had an early essay on ''Morals and Life.''

> Abstract ethics is good as far as it goes. It lays down some general forms
> for moral thinking, but it really does not give very much practical guid-

---

[22]Brightman, *Person and Reality: An Introduction to Metaphysics,* ed. P. A. Bertocci, J. E. Newhall, and R. E. Brightman (New York: The Ronald Press Co., 1958) 15. The authors of these essays attempt to use inclusive language in their own writing but do not revise the language in quoted material.

[23]Ibid., 23-33. See also Brightman's ''The Presuppositions of Experiment,'' *The Personalist* 19 (1938): 136-43.

[24]Brightman, *Moral Laws,* (New York: Abingdon Press, 1933) 74.

ance. . . . we are insisting that ethics shall concern itself more with practice. . . . Life must be moralized by being brought under the control of moral principles, and morals must be vitalized by being brought into connection with our everyday human life in the world that now is.

Here is at least the germ of the moral law tradition. But Bowne warned against legalism.

The claim that life must be moralized and rationalized must not be understood to mean that life must lose all spontaneity and be reduced to a body of rules. This would be worse than the wilderness of nature itself. Our claim is only that free rational beings should not live mechanically or at random, but should aim to direct and mold their lives so that right reason and goodwill should bear rule in them.[25]

The ethical themes will be spelled out in most of the lectures that follow, especially two by Muelder and two by Deats. But here let us trace briefly the engagement with ethical issues and causes. Bowne was committed to women's suffrage. He was dean of the Boston University Graduate School, which awarded the first Ph.D. to a woman in American higher education. Bowne expressed no sympathy for the ''deliberate criminal.'' Knudson wrote on war and peace issues and was concerned with racism as it found expression in the union of Methodist churches.

Francis J. McConnell led the Boston Personalists in international and ecumenical concerns, from his lecturing in India and his studies of Latin America to his leadership in the ecumenical ''Social Creed'' of 1908 and 1912. Muelder followed, from the university situation but as an active ecumenical church leader, bringing together his experience in the labor movement, his commitments to racial justice, socialism, and non-violence. He, along with Deats and Schilling, was part of the team selected to do the research and writing for the MESTA volumes—Methodist Social Thought and Action. Other colleagues included Richard Cameron, Nils Ehrenstrom, and Herbert Stotts. The project issued four volumes, all published by Abingdon Press: *Methodism and Society in Historical Perspective* (Cameron, 1961), *Methodism and Society in the Twentieth Century* (Muelder, 1961), *Methodism and Society in Theological Perspective* (Schilling, 1960), and *Methodism and Society: Guidelines for Strategy* (Deats and Stotts, 1962).

---

[25]*Representative Essays,* 79, 84.

DeWolf, though not a pacifist as were many other of the Boston Personalists, gave vigorous leadership in peace work and in civil rights, where he was close to King, before turning his attention to criminal justice.

Edward Leroy Long, Jr., in his *A Survey of Christian Ethics*,[26] labels Muelder an "institutionalist" in ethics, misinterpreting Muelder's positive appreciation of power as expressed in structures of justice and order, especially the state. Personalists were all institutionalists in seeking to deal critically and constructively with the institutions of church and university in which they had membership, as well as with economic and political institutions in the Social Gospel tradition.[27]

This ethical sensitivity, as well as the personal experience of tragedy, led Boston Personalists, almost without exception, to deal resolutely with human suffering and anguish, the problem of good-and-evil. They worked out a theodicy that sought to do justice to both the goodness and the power of God, as well as the human experience of anguish and of redemption. With few exceptions, the priority was given to God's goodness, sacrificing the idea of omnipotence, but actually redeeming the idea of power. Here there is no party line. There are genuine even though subtle differences in how this shift has had an impact on the worship of God, who is not conceived as omnipotent.

The eighth theme is the self-corrective note in the tradition. There is a unique methodological self-consciousness, most fully expressed in Brightman, and a refusal to close the door to further insight. Brightman closed his chapter on "Ethics as a Science" by setting forth a method "which renders subsequent criticisms and improvement possible."[28] Later essays will show how this criticism and attempted improvement have been applied to Brightman's formulation of the moral laws.

---

[26]Edward Leroy Long, Jr., *A Survey of Christian Ethics* (New York: Oxford University Press, 1967) 168, 213-15, 301.

[27]See Paul Deats, Jr., ed., *Toward a Discipline of Social Ethics: Essays in Honor of W. G. Muelder* (Boston: Boston University Press, 1972) 7-8; and his "Protestant Social Ethics and Pacifism," comparing Muelder, Reinhold Niebuhr, and Yoder on concepts of the state, in Thomas A. Shannon, ed., *War or Peace? The Search for New Answers* (Maryknoll NY: Orbis Books, 1980).

[28]Brightman, *Moral Laws*, 31.

In the essays that follow, we will deal with the Boston Personalists as persons as well as Personalists, with their lives as well as with their thoughts, with their questions as well as with their answers. Most were persons of deep piety; all were Methodists; some were mystics. They gave persistent attention to the Bible and were early involved in controversy over the critical approach to the Scriptures. McConnell quoted Bowne in an interesting aside on the use of the Bible, concerning the gloss in the Gospel of John on the story of the woman taken in adultery: "The passage is perfect, no matter who said it."[29] This expresses loyalty to the tradition, confidence in the unity of truth, trust in one's own experience and rationality.

---

[29]McConnell, *Bowne,* 187-88.

Boston Personalism's Contributions to Faith and Learning

F. Thomas Trotter

The contribution of Boston Personalism to higher education in America is a subject sometimes discussed but infrequently analyzed. Commentators have noted the extraordinary influence of the university in locating its alumni in influential positions in higher education over the years, in both public and church-related sectors. Is there a sufficient cause for this phenomenon and can a case be made for that to include the influence of the dominant philosophical position of the faculty over most of the last century?

There are three elements that must be noted when one surveys the matter under discussion. First, we need to discuss the place of Borden Parker Bowne and the university in the intellectual climate of the late nineteenth century. Second, we need to analyze the philosophical style of personalism and its sympathy for the purposes of the university. Third, we need to look at the history of higher education in the Methodist movement. Each of these elements intersects to form a pattern that will enable us to assess the questions of the influence of personalism on faith and learning.

PERSONALISM IN THE LATE NINETEENTH CENTURY

The intellectual climate in American philosophy and religion in the late nineteenth century was problematic. It was one of the more desperate periods for intellectuals in the church. The onslaught of post-Darwinian derivatives was in full tide. Thoughtful religion was in retreat. The nineteenth century was a time in which successive religious revivals were, in Gabriel Vahanian's phrase, "revivals of less and less." Popularizers of evolutionary thought such as Herbert Spencer and Chauncey Wright are not exactly household names today, but they were immensely popular in their times. Borden Parker Bowne's first published book (1874) was an attack on Spencer, who typified the sublime confidence of a generation of commentators after Darwin. The issue was not the scientific value of the work of Darwin, but the philosophical generalizations that flowed from that fount. Of Spencer, Bowne wrote,

> His work began about the same time as the great naturalistic revival of the generation just past, and he became the official philosopher of the movement. In this way he acquired a prestige beyond what his speculative work deserves. It was a time of loose and yeasty thinking, with great evolution of speculative gas. Bubbles covered with prismatic colors looked solid. It was just the time for the philosophical impressionist, and Mr. Spencer, with his big canvas and big brushes, was just the man for the time. But works of art produced in this way suffer from close inspection. Grandiosity must be viewed at a distance.

Of Chauncey Wright, Bowne wrote that "the empiricist never feels the same need of historical study as other thinkers and he rarely resists the tendency to become oracular on the subjects of which he knows nothing."[1]

Philosophy after Hegel, already in an idealistic swamp, was sideswiped by Darwin, and suddenly materialism and naturalism became the popular philosophical positions of the time. Exhausted by the idealistic debates, German philosophy had already turned toward subjectivism in Schopenhauer, Schleiermacher, and Fichte, but now a powerful alternative in materialism was available. As Sydney E. Ahlstrom has noted, in that period "greater metaphysical and logical sophistication was required of theology. . . . [As] at no other time in American history, philosophy was hewing wood and drawing water for the Church."[2] Bowne's program,

---

[1]Bowne, in Warren E. Steinkraus, ed., *Representative Essays of Borden Parker Bowne* (Utica NY: Meridian Publishing Co., 1980) 121, 107.

[2]Sydney E. Ahlstrom, "Theology in America: A Historical Survey," in *The Shaping of American Life,* ed. James Ward Smith and A. Leland Jamison (Princeton NJ: Princeton University Press, 1961) 288.

in one sense, was an attempt to make it possible for the thoughtful religious person not to be abandoned either to the solipsism of extreme subjectivity or to the nihilism of total mechanism. In the religious community, the issue was joined at other levels, of course. Generally it took the form of a retreat into scriptural literalness and a profound resistance to learning of all types.

Bowne's "solution" to this dilemma was what came to be called "personal idealism" and, later, "personalism." In essence, he affirmed the world of things in space as phenomenal, a world that has its existence only in intelligence. Because that world does not depend upon our intelligence, it surely must be affirmed that there is a cosmic intelligence as the abiding seat and condition of the world. Bowne was a realist in affirming the objective existence of the world independent of finite thinking. He was an idealist in maintaining that this system is essentially phenomenal and exists only in and for intelligence. Against the materialist, he affirmed the existence of the world but asserted its phenomenological essence. Against the subjective idealist, he asserted the independence of other consciousness and the practical certainty of the objective world. Because of the rejection of a private or solipsistic epistemology, Bowne derived a moral theory from ethical rather than merely speculative philosophical work. It is this final assertion that became central for personalism: the cause of phenomena is not spatial or mechanical, but rational and spiritual.

Bowne is misunderstood if he is thought of merely as a speculative philosopher. Commentators (William James, Herbert Schneider) have noted that Bowne moved across his productive years from a "snappish," disciplined, and logical style to a more "patient" and pious style. He came to express himself in more traditionally religious language. His later reflection turned toward theological issues, and he was increasingly influential in directing attention toward renewal of religious intellectual life. Cosmic consciousness became God in his vocabulary. It may be no coincidence that the motto of Boston University rather fully expresses the Bownian trinity: Learning, Virtue, and Piety. But his vocation had not changed. His public vocation was making religion intellectually possible in a time when all the classical supports for religion seemed to be cracking. His shift from the technical language of philosophy to the more direct language of piety is described in his interesting essay entitled "Religion and Theology." One thinks of the myth of Kant, finding his housekeeper weeping after reading his *Critique of Pure Reason* and then writing his

Critique of Practical Reason to make faith possible again. Bowne seems to have had a similar journey.

Recently, commentators have captured more fully the enormous religious problem of the nineteenth century. The problem was the loss of God. To understand Bowne properly, one must have considered Melville and Hawthorne, understood Kierkegaard's attack on absolute idealism, and sensed the tragic optimism of the century against overwhelming nihilism. In this context one may account for the systematic treatment in Bowne of such questions as theism versus mechanism, logic and faith, theology and religion. Some critics have accused personalism of suffering from the "apodictic fallacy," that is, being predisposed to theism before completing the evidence. To that charge, Bowne would have reacted strongly since it was his contention that the theism was the logical consequence of his epistemology. To the faithful for whom Bowne's philosophical arguments may not have been available, the fact that one could affirm an intellectual structure for faith was itself salvific. Harry Emerson Fosdick, in his autobiography *The Living of These Days,* asserted that reading Bowne saved his intellectual life.

PERSONALISM AND THE UNIVERSITY

This attempt to restate for modern persons a possible philosophical basis for a religiously sound and philosophically consistent intellectual and moral life provides a practical structure for the understanding of the role of the university. Personalism in Bowne and his followers emphasizes the basic rationality of the world. This knowable and understandable world makes possible the structures of intellectual life. For a world in which there was no causality but only randomness, there would be no need for intelligence, much less of moral purpose.

It would be absurd to suggest that the modern university is only the product of idealistic philosophy. One may suggest, however, that the model of a research university out of the German tradition owes a great deal to the nineteenth-century world view of idealism. But one may suggest that the confidence in a rational world and the sustenance of values in such a world is sufficient logical ground for justifying the purposes of the university.

The university in the West evolved out of Christian theological foundations. The religious affirmation consisted of the claim that the world was knowable and good. Unlike some non-Western religious traditions, the Christian West asserted the revelatory character of the world. While mystery remains, there is the promise of full knowledge. All things are made new. Providence overwhelms nescience. Note that Herbert Spencer's cosmic mover was called "The Unknowable." Bowne's personal idealism was a restatement of the classical rationality of Christian personalism and a positive description of the purposes of learning itself. In this statement, Bowne was adamant about the tools of discourse, and here he affirms another important principle about the university. That is, the university in the West is a scientific as well as a humanistic institution. This sense of a need for clarity of method was characteristic of Bowne. With others, he established the American habit of doing philosophy of religion instead of dogmatics. This was due in part to the need for methodological clarity. Spencer was busy making a religion out of philosophy, and Strauss was making philosophy out of religion. Bowne was offended by romantic and careless method, and his writings abound in acid critiques of such carelessness.

To know the world, in all its intricacies, its glory, and its misery, is to respond to the gracious invitation of God. To know the truth inevitably carries with it the responsibility to do the truth. Knowledge is not indifferent to its moral uses in the Christian tradition. One of our most profound social problems today is the apparent collapse of the tradition of the university as a moral agent.

Implied in this understanding of the university, besides rationality and moral responsibility, is the precondition of freedom for the investigator. Bowne wrote an important essay entitled "The Speculative Significance of Freedom."[3] The immunities of a university person are not privileges of status but guarantees of the independence of investigation, sanctioned by God's radical gift of freedom, subject only to the interactions of academic debate and investigation. Bowne, in a somewhat dramatic gesture of solidarity with faculty colleagues and certainly in sight of this important principle, agreed to stand trial for heresy in 1904. The charges of heresy specified deviation from the Articles of Religion of the Methodist Episcopal Church; they specified "unitarianism," denial of biblical "inspiration," and an "erroneous" view of the Atonement. The charges were

---

[3]*Methodist Review* 77 (September 1895): 681-97.

rejected unanimously. His criticism of the episcopacy and church leadership in general was consistently bitter. Although exonerated, the philosopher lost some of his verve and continued to despair of the church's understanding his role.

HIGHER EDUCATION AND METHODISM

The Methodist movement in America has been characterized by its rage for education. The first action of the Baltimore Conference in 1784 was the establishment of a college—Cokesbury College of Maryland. Subsequently, more than 1,000 colleges were founded by Methodist people. Today, the group has been compressed to a much more modest number, but the system of schools is the largest Protestant system of colleges in the world and represents ten percent of all independent colleges in the nation.

The theological reasons for founding these schools lie deep in the history of learning in Christendom itself. A prominent element in the motivation of the Wesleyans was social. Providing access to learning was originally, and has continued to be, the most powerful element in the church's commitment. But the religious motivation persisted. In the famous Kingswood hymn, Charles Wesley asserted the Methodist program for overcoming the antinomies: "Unite the two so long disjoined, / Knowledge and vital piety / learning and holiness combined, / and truth and love let all men see." The passion for wholeness in learning and faith has been a Methodist characteristic and can be illustrated in a variety of ways.

The special role of personalism in higher education in the church has more to do with the role of Boston University itself than with other factors. One must note the prominent national role that the university has played over the last century to assess this contribution adequately. Bowne's students and others influenced by Bowne have had a profound influence in American higher education. This influence is much wider than Boston University, although Boston University was the institutional center of this significant system.

The significance of the leadership of Boston Personalism in higher education can be measured by the extent of Boston graduates serving as university presidents, professors of philosophy and religion, and church leaders. The network of persons supplied successive generations of students who would graduate from Ohio Wesleyan, Millsaps, Baker University, Nebraska Wesleyan, or DePauw and go on to graduate school at Boston University. (When I entered the School of Theology at Boston University in 1950, there were twenty Californians in the student body.) The impact of personalism through this school can be measured when one notes that teachers and religious leaders like Francis J. McConnell, G. Bromley Oxnam, Ralph Tyler Flewelling, George Albert Coe, Albert C. Knudson, Edgar S. Brightman, Walter G. Muelder, L. Harold DeWolf, S. Paul Schilling, Peter A. Bertocci, and John H. Lavely have taught hundreds of theological students and graduate students. Personalism was the dominant philosophical position in scores of colleges across the land. Ministerial students flocked to Boston University.

In the late nineteenth century, there was a movement in the Northern and Southern branches of Methodism to systematize education, from the preparatory schools to the university. This was the expression of the Methodist "connectional system" applied to higher education. For some years in the South there was an active debate over this issue. Vanderbilt University was established partly with the view that it would be the university for a system of four-year colleges and preparatory schools, linked together into a comprehensive church educational system. In the North, this plan was less articulated, but one of the stated expectations for the founding of The American University in Washington was that it would become the university for a Northern system of four-year colleges related to the church. The idea never fully caught on. However, Boston University, especially its School of Theology and its Graduate School, has fulfilled this role for most of the last century. It was to the university that colleges turned for instructors in religion and for academic leadership in philosophy.

At Boston University there is a continuing tradition of vitality, based on the philosophical assumptions of a liberal world view, profoundly conscious of the role of a university in clarifying the nature of intellectually informed religion, and operating as a national institution. This tradition has always guarded, as Bowne did, the intellectual life in religion, but has also clung to the Wesleyan insistence on the practice of vital piety. In season and out, this coherence has provided a tradition of religious power in America that is worthy of continued support and appreciation.

Boston University, shaped by personalism, has been a remarkable university in terms of social change. Bowne himself was an outspoken advocate of women's rights and published articles and letters in the cause.

Later the university took the lead in developing prototypes of affirmative action programs for blacks who were systematically being deprived of adequate higher education through racist policies in the accrediting practices. The university's development of schools of social work and Christian education provided impetus to those professions. Personalism has provided a model of wholeness in learning. Brightman's phrase "growing comprehensive coherence" is an appropriate description of the proper goal of a university in its quest for knowledge. This philosophical program encouraged openness and comprehensiveness in its students. Many were drawn to teaching and to university administration. Most valued that spirit so much that Boston University became an acknowledged center for preparation for academic careers, especially careers in church-related colleges.

Personalism's Debt to Kant

John H. Lavely

To understand the roots of personalism, one must recognize the importance of Immanuel Kant. Unfortunately, the task of understanding personalism's debt to Kant is complicated. Kant's thought, like that of most great thinkers, is not easy to grasp and is subject to various interpretations. Furthermore, although personalism has a certain continuity (at least in the Boston tradition) and some recurrent themes, it is by no means homogeneous. Bowne's debt to Kant may not be shared by Brightman. Bertocci's debt to Kant may not coincide with Muelder's. Perhaps, then, the easiest way (at least for me) to get into the topic is through personal and particular intimations of the Kantian impact on personalism, the personalism that I was first and directly exposed to in my study at Boston University.

EARLY INTIMATIONS
OF PERSONALISM'S DEBT TO KANT

During my second year as a student at the School of Theology (1939-1940), I took my first graduate seminar from Edgar S. Brightman, his "Twenty-First Annual Seminar in Philosophy." The entire year was devoted to a close reading of Kant's *Kritik der Urteilskraft (The Critique of Judgment)*. Near the end of that year I wrote a report for the seminar entitled "Various Interpretations of the *Critique of Judgment* by Kant Scholars." In it I referred to a book by Bowne on Kant and Spencer, a book little known even among those who study Bowne. *Kant and Spencer* makes no mention of Kant's third critique. Otherwise, about all I remember about the book was that it was definitely pro-Kant and anti-Spencer. Bowne's more important works give us a better basis for knowing how Kant influenced him.

Another indication of the Kantian presence was brought home to me through the Boston University Philosophical Club, which was very active during my years as a graduate student. I recall that Dr. Brightman always spoke of the Philosophical Club as a branch of the Kant-*Gesellschaft,* that is, the Kant Society. I confirmed this by finding the following entry in some note cards compiled by Richard Schlagel (Ph.D. in the early 1950s), the Bowne Fellow serving Brightman at that time. It reads,

> An amendment to Article I Section II of the Constitution (of the club) was passed at its meeting on Feb. 23, 1927 (identifying the club as) Boston University Local Group of the Kant-*Gesellschaft.*

In fact, if I am not mistaken, during the bad days in Germany, the Boston University branch became the only Kant-*Gesellschaft* in existence. The German Kant-*Gesellschaft* was totally disbanded in 1939. It was not until after World War II that it was reorganized in Germany.

I cannot resist mentioning that Dr. Brightman kept a collection of German postcards, which I have inherited. These cards show six likenesses of Kant, representing different images of him by artists in Germany who were his contemporaries. These cards were printed by the Kant-*Gesellschaft* to mark the two hundredth anniversary of Kant's birth in 1924. This collection is further evidence of Brightman's Kant connection. I prize, especially, Brightman's card written from Berlin to Dean Wm. Marshall Warren of the College of Liberal Arts, on 7 November 1931.

> Greetings from the land of Kant, even if it is divided by the Polish corridor. I feel strongly that the Versailles Treaty should be revised. Next month I am to give a lecture on Behaviorism at the University.
>> Best regards,
>> Edgar S. Brightman

It may not, therefore, be a surprise that soon after I returned to teach in the department in 1951, I was teaching courses and seminars on Kant. I have taught more courses and seminars on Kant than on any other single figure in the history of philosophy. Even though I follow Brightman in counting myself more of a Hegelian than a Kantian (in fact, I think I am more Hegelian than my teacher, as I will try to show later in this book), I nonetheless owe an immense debt to Kant. I consider the *Critique of Pure Reason* the greatest single work in philosophy for pedagogical purposes and for personal reflection in dealing with the fundamental problems of knowledge and reality. It is fascinating; it is frustrating. It is opaque; it is illuminating. To probe its pages is endlessly provocative. It forces one into the arena of hand to hand mental combat and mental companionship. It is, as Kant himself said of philosophy, *"eine unendliche Aufgabe,"* an endless task.

It is time now to ask what all these anecdotal intimations of personalism's debt to Kant amount to. How specifically is personalism indebted to Kant?

EVERYBODY PHILOSOPHICAL IS INDEBTED TO KANT

Before we can turn to that question, however, there is one other point that needs to be made, namely, that everyone is indebted to Kant. His philosophy is a gold mine. A very generous man, he loaned money to everybody. To some he gave one talent, to some he gave three talents, and to some he gave five talents. Some have repaid what they borrowed with interest. Whether his largess fell more generously on personalism remains to be seen. Whether personalism has made profitable investments also remains to be seen. At any rate, I repeat, personalism is no exception in its indebtedness to Kant and cannot per se claim any merit for its position on that ground alone.

If this is the case, then it is important to see Kant in context. We can't begin to appreciate personalism's debt to Kant unless we have some sense about how his philosophical thought produced the monumental impact it has had on all subsequent philosophy. To do this we must first look backward from Kant and then look forward, both briefly.

LOOKING BACKWARD

When Kant came on the philosophical scene, philosophy, and particularly metaphysics, had been almost totally discredited. The scandal of philosophy had reached its zenith. Metaphysics was discredited by what

Kant spoke of as the antinomies, two conflicting contradictory positions, both of which were maintained with unyielding ideological intensity. A political analogy is instructive. The present impasse between the Soviet Union and the United States is a pretty good indication of the sort of situation that prevailed in the intellectual life of Europe at that time. There were two basic perspectives so disparate, so separated from each other, that the possibility of communication was hardly there. One eventuated in an utterly dogmatic stance, and the other eventuated in an utterly skeptical stance. Kant faced an intellectual schizophrenia.

This was the situation that emerged from the development of the Continental Rationalists on one side—Descartes, Spinoza, Leibniz—and the British Empiricists—Locke, Berkeley, Hume—on the other. The rationalists and the empiricists emphasized different facets of the mind in such a way and so exclusively that they tended to sever the mind into warring camps.

The rationalists, as the name suggests, maintained that the source and validity of knowledge was to be found in reason alone. Mathematics was the ideal of knowledge. They were attempting to account for the power of scientific knowledge in terms of the mathematical abstraction that was central to it, the rationalistic apparatus, the relation of ideas. They de-emphasized the place of experience, so the validity of knowledge had virtually nothing to do with the empirical input of experience. That position was worked out to its limits, and in Spinoza we have the epitome of rationalism. We have a kind of "block universe" where everything is rigidly necessary and follows from the principles of reality with the same validity and strength that comes in syllogistic argument. Reality was a logical system. It was all ideas; one had no way to account for the concrete facts of experience.

The British Empiricists, on the other hand, emphasized that experience, usually meaning sense experience, was the source and validity of knowledge. If one could not trace any belief to its origins in sense experience, one could not validate it. Consequently, the appeal was to sense experience. Now there is no question that there is rational thought as well as sense experience. The question is, can we explain the validity of scientific knowledge, of knowledge in general, by exclusively emphasizing one side or the other? The consequence of so doing was to jeopardize the validity of scientific knowledge, as is shown by Hume's critique of the concept of causality, on the basis of experience alone. He maintained that there is no necessary connection among events that we can discover by an appeal to experience. Indeed, on Hume's terms there is no metaphysical reality, no notion of substance, nor even the personal identity of human selves, that can be warranted by an appeal to experience alone.

Thus, the rationalists advocated a rigid, unchanging universe where everything was necessary, logical. And the empiricists ended up with nothing but the fleeting passage of perceptions. As a result the philosophic enterprise, especially the possibility of metaphysics, was discredited.

It was this situation that confronted Kant. He had been trained in the tradition of Leibnizian rationalism. He was fairly well along in his career before he read David Hume. As anyone familiar with the history of modern philosophy knows, it was Hume who, as Kant says, "woke me from my dogmatic slumbers." For ten years he gave himself fully to an effort to reconstruct philosophy. He probed the relationship between the activity of the mind in reason and the passive input of sense experience. Was there any way in which one could coordinate reason and experience and thus achieve a compelling and comprehensive account not only of the validity of scientific knowledge but of the cogency of human thought in general?

The system in which Kant sought to answer this question is often spoken of as a synthesis. He attempted to put together the insights of two different traditions and make them compatible. The amazing thing, the thing that differentiates him from his predecessors, is that he really grasped how serious the problem was. Neither the rationalist nor the empiricist could get beyond his own suppositions. But Kant raised the question as to how the mind could constitute itself so that it could achieve valid knowledge without sacrificing important aspects of the knowing process. The Kantian synthesis was consciously constructed. He knew what he was doing. He intended to bridge the gap between reason and experience. Knowledge was for him, then, a joint product. Sense and reason were both required in order to ground the possibility and the validity of knowledge. Reason, through the activity of thought, gave form to the passive content of experience. Sense could not produce the form. Reason could not produce the content. Thus Kant was conscious of what he set out to do. He set out to do a new thing, a monumental thing. Whether he was successful in doing it is another question. It is not even so important as the tremendous achievement of seeking to overcome this hiatus in the mind.

In my judgment Kant's solution to the problem of knowledge, laudable as it is, is still more of a compromise than a synthesis. It was, of course, a very subtle compromise. Much of the philosophy after him was a response to the compromise between science and morals. Science deals with the phenomenal world, which we can know but which has no grounding in reality that we can know. Morality gives us a practical justification for belief in ourselves, in freedom, and reality; it is not a theoretical justification. That is the compromise. Most personalists have tried to get beyond the Kantian compromise by repudiating the separation between the phenomenal and the noumenal. Most personalists, however, have not been very good at showing how they have the right to go beyond Kant in this respect.

To recapitulate, for Kant the task was to combine and coordinate reason and experience. Reason gives form to the content of experience. Knowledge always requires both. This also means there is no knowledge where there is not some sensory experience. For Kant that meant that one cannot have scientific knowledge of soul, of God, or even of the world as a whole. He saved the validity of scientific knowledge, but at the cost of dissociating it from metaphysics. He got his metaphysics back by appealing to the moral dimension on practical grounds, even existential grounds, providing the basis for a metaphysical position that was based on the demands of practical reason. Some ambivalence remains in the Kantian scheme. The world of phenomena is the world of knowing. The world of noumena is the realm of the thing-in-itself. One has access to metaphysical reality through the will. One does not know oneself; one is oneself in one's willing. This comes very close to making the will so primary that it is very difficult to incorporate an intrinsic rationality into it.

Kant's famous statement near the end of the *Critique of Practical Reason* represents the issue. We must remember, however, that practical reason refers to the moral dimension. For Kant, practical reason, moral law, and will are all interchangeable terms. Reason in its practical use thus really means will and/or moral law.

> Two things fill the mind with ever new and increasing admiration and awe, the oftener and more steadily we reflect on them: the starry heavens above me and the moral law within me.[1]

Neither of these two dimensions has theoretical access to reality. Science

---

[1]Immanuel Kant, *Critique of Practical Reason,* trans. Lewis W. Beck (New York: Bobbs-Merrill, 1956) 166.

never gets an access to metaphysics; morality gets one only out of its practical need, not from theoretical justification. Though oversimplified, this is Kant's intellectual response to an incredible intellectual crisis in the life of Western human beings.

LOOKING AHEAD

Kant's emphasis was on these two perspectives, the world of phenomena scientifically understood and the world of noumena exhibited in the moral life, and on their separateness. The basic fallacy for Kant was the confusion of the phenomenal with the noumenal and of the noumenal with the phenomenal. He worked out what he thought was a viable balance of power between them. In this balance of power the emphasis is on the primacy of practical reason. The primacy of practical reason means that the moral life takes precedence over the scientific domain. The moral life provides the basis for the metaphysical concepts of God, freedom, and immortality. Determinism, which would follow if science had metaphysical import, is thus repudiated.

The impact of Kant's thought expressed itself in two divergent tendencies, though it cannot be said that this is what Kant intended. Stress on practical reason led to pragmatism and existentialism. Stress on theoretical reason led to positivism with its rejection of metaphysics. Thus the Kantian balance or coexistence tended to break down. Nothing is clearer on Kant's principles than this: if the criteria of knowledge are defined in terms of sense experience and science, then metaphysics is not possible, that is, metaphysics is not and cannot be knowledge. The sanction for metaphysical ideas (Kant's postulates of the practical reason) had to be noncognitive, thus subjective, existential, or even irrational. Hence, the polarity of facts and values, science and morality, reasserted itself in Western thought, in spite of Kant's valiant effort to maintain the balance of power.

HOW PERSONALISM IS INDEBTED TO KANT

It is time now to examine personalism's debt to Kant under three headings: the theory of knowledge, ethical theory, and the primacy of practical reason.

Theory of Knowledge

Personalism owes much to Kant's theory of knowledge. The central aspect of this theory is the activity of the mind. There is no knowledge that does not involve the mind's putting things together or, to use Kant's language, an a priori synthetic activity. "We can know *a priori* of things only what we ourselves put into them."[2] The mind is like the bee, in Francis Bacon's analogy, that gathers and digests and organizes and transforms the material on which it works. The mind is thus essentially a synthetic activity. Synthesis means putting things together according to rule. The mind is a sorting machine, and the sorting is its activity on the material that experience alone provides. For Kant, then, knowledge is constructing things according to a rule. Kant maintains that this synthetic activity characterizes knowledge anywhere and everywhere.

Personalists have emphasized the central place of the activity of the mind in knowing and being more than Kant and have fully acknowledged their Kantian source. Personalism has maintained with Kant that knowledge is an achievement, the product of the creative activity of the human being.

The second aspect of the theory of knowledge for which personalism is indebted to Kant is what is called epistemic dualism. It is my belief that the way most personalists interpret epistemic dualism is quite different from what it meant to Kant. The issues here are controversial and crucial.

Epistemic dualism means essentially that knowledge is always a matter of subject and object. To have knowledge there must be a knower (subject) and something else that is known (object). Kant believed that the distinction between subject and object was the most elemental rule of knowledge. There is no subject unless there is an object. There is no object unless there is a subject. For Kant, this distinction was a rule of the mind and does not presuppose that the object is the real thing itself. The object is the object as I construct it. I need to construct it out of my experience in order to gain coherence. That is, I don't know the "out there" as it really is. My "out there" (my object) is a construction, a projection that gives some intelligibility to the field of my sensory experience according to the rules that the mind itself supplies. My ready-made, built-in ways of organizing are the categories. The subject is the knowing apparatus that applies the categories to the raw material of sensation, which it then, by organizing, constitutes as an object for its knowing. For Kant these sub-

---

[2]Immanuel Kant, *Critique of Pure Reason,* trans. Norman Kemp Smith (New York: St. Martin's Press, 1973) 23 (B xviii).

jects and objects are merely presuppositions of possible, that is, intelligible, experience. I am sure he believed that it is the thing in itself that produces experience, but we do not know the thing in itself through experience. What we know is the way we put the experience together. My object never corresponds with what produced the experience in me because I construct the object according to the way my mind works (the categories). I just do not ever read off the character of reality itself. However universal scientific knowledge may be, and Kant believed that such knowledge was valid for all human beings, it is still knowledge of things only as they *appear to us*. We are confined to a human world of knowledge.

Most personalists reject the Kantian restriction of knowledge to phenomena. Although personalists agree with Kant that we do not have direct cognitive access to reality and that scientific knowledge is not metaphysical knowledge, personalists do not believe that metaphysical knowledge is thereby precluded. For personalists experience does provide clues to the way things are "out there." If the clues are interpreted coherently, one is entitled to speak of legitimate metaphysical knowledge. Personalists do not claim that such knowledge is certain; it is at best hypothetical. Kant would not have accepted such a conception of metaphysical knowledge because knowledge had to have the apodictic certainty of the kind represented in Newtonian physics. Once again we see that for Kant knowledge is identified with the paradigm of science.

In this connection, Borden Parker Bowne exhibited the personalistic stance vis-à-vis Kant. Peter Bertocci's section on Bowne's "Theory of Knowledge" (in his extensive essay "Borden Parker Bowne and His Personalistic Theistic Idealism"[3]) brings out clearly the difference between Bowne and Kant with regard to the problem of knowledge. Bertocci points out that Bowne's analysis of the categories "is essentially Kantian, but Bowne adds the category of purpose, not to be found in Kant's *Critique of Pure Reason*."[4] Purpose for Kant would fall squarely in the *Critique of Practical Reason* because it is a way of speaking of the will. Purpose also

---

[3]Peter A. Bertocci, "Borden Parker Bowne and His Personalistic Theistic Idealism," *Ultimate Reality and Meaning* 2, no. 3 (1979): 205-27. Reprinted in this volume by permission.

[4]Ibid., 210.

figures prominently in the *Critique of Judgment*. But in neither of the latter two critiques is purpose a category that belongs to knowledge. Thus Bowne's insistence that the category of purpose is relevant to knowledge is his way of avoiding the isolation of the moral and metaphysical realms from the field of knowledge. His reasoning comes out in *Theory of Thought and Knowledge*.

> The categories of being, space, time, causation, are necessary in order to have any articulate experience whatever. It is through them that we reach intelligible objects, or that world of facts which seems to be given to us ready-made in sense perception. But these categories alone would keep us among isolated things and events. Space and time separate rather than unite; and causality, at least in its mechanical form, provides for no system. For the further systematization and unification of our objects a higher category is needed; and this we find in purpose, or, rather, in the elevation of causality to intelligent and volitional causality, with its implication of plan and purpose.[5]

Bertocci concludes, rightly I think, that "Bowne's epistemic dualism, on the whole, follows a Kantian pattern, but his strong emphasis on the person as purposer and actor keeps him from the conclusion that we know nothing but the world as organized categorically."[6]

Ethical Theory

The next area in which personalism's debt to Kant must be considered is the area of ethics. We can deal with this topic more briefly, partly because the immense impact of Kant's ethics on personalistic ethical thinking is so clear and well known.

Kant, of course, deserves credit for his work in ethics independent of the personalist scenario. His insight into the concept of moral law or duty is a major aspect of his monumental achievement. Recognition that the moral will must operate according to rule, consistently, has never been put more powerfully. Another central aspect of Kant's ethics is the principle of autonomy. The only principles that are moral principles are principles

---

[5]Borden Parker Bowne, *Theory of Thought and Knowledge* (New York: Harper & Brothers Publishers, 1897) 104.

[6]Bertocci, "Borden Parker Bowne and His Personalistic Theistic Idealism," 210.

I impose on myself. As Brightman puts it in his Law of Autonomy, "All persons ought to choose in accordance with the ideals which they acknowledge. Or: Self-imposed ideals are imperative."[7] This is literally the Kantian principle of autonomy, as Brightman admitted. One other feature of Kant's ethics should be mentioned, namely, the principle of altruism. This is the relevant form of his famous categorical imperative: "Act so as to treat humanity, whether in your own person or in that of another, always as an end and never as a means only."[8] The centrality of the person is fundamental. Kant's pervasive emphasis on respect for human nature and on the importance of human rights is sometimes not adequately appreciated. Kant's ethics doubtless has some limitations, as we shall see, but any philosopher whose ethical theory has formulated the principles of moral law, autonomy, and altruism as powerfully as has Kant's will never be superseded in the field of ethical theory.

Brightman's *Moral Laws* is a permanent tribute to Kant's ethics. Nevertheless, Brightman also brings out their limitations. One of these is what Brightman calls the "defects of purely formal ethics."[9] Kant is clearly a formalist. That is, it is not a question of achieving worthy goals; it is a question of acting according to moral principles out of a sense of duty. Brightman also argued that, important as the formal laws of ethics are, Kant did not deal sufficiently with the area of values and the principle of personality. Brightman, therefore, supplemented his ethical system with axiological laws and personalistic laws. In my judgment, however, Brightman was more influenced by Kant's formalism than he realized. Brightman started with the formal laws and built the rest of his system from them. In another sense, paradoxically, Brightman's entire system of moral laws presupposes the principle of personality. That is, it does not arrive at but implicitly starts from the principle of personality. This is an issue that deserves more analysis than I can give it here. One final comment: there is

---

[7]Edgar S. Brightman, *Moral Laws* (New York: The Abingdon Press, 1933) 106.

[8]Immanuel Kant, *Foundations of the Metaphysics of Morals*, trans. Lewis W. Beck (New York: Bobbs-Merrill, 1959) 47.

[9]Brightman, *Moral Laws*, 121-24.

an individualistic tendency in Brightman's moral philosophy that to some extent has its roots in Kant. Muelder and Deats speak fully to this point.

The Primacy of the Practical Reason
and the Postulates of the Practical Reason

The last point I want to deal with in terms of the influence of Kant on personalism concerns the primacy of the practical reason and the related postulates of the practical reason. The primacy of the practical reason means that the affirmations of the moral life take precedence over scientific knowledge of phenomena. The postulates of the practical reason, which ground this precedence, are freedom, immortality, and God. The case for them is developed in the second part of the *Critique of Practical Reason*. Kant holds that, in order to have morality, there must be freedom. In order for virtuous people to be rewarded with happiness there must be immortality, since virtue is certainly not so rewarded in this life. And in order for there to be immortality there must be a God who so arranges things that virtue and happiness even up in the long run (that is, in immortal life).

All of these postulates are, in a sense, rationalizations of the moral life. According to Kant, they cannot be proved, nor can they be disproved. Will, he maintains, is the only access to the noumenal, that is, the metaphysically real. But this access is not cognitive, that is, not based on theoretical reason but on practical necessity.

The kind of stance Kant takes in regard to the practical justification of the basis of the moral life is vividly expressed in the following passage from his *Lectures on Philosophical Theology*.

> In the case of a creature who has conducted himself according to these eternal and immediate laws of nature, and who has thus become worthy of happiness, no state can be hoped for where he participates in this happiness; if no state of well-being follows his well-doing, then there would be a contradiction between morality and the course of nature. Yet experience and reason show us that in the present course of things the precise observation of all morally necessary duties is not always connected with well-being. Rather, the noblest honesty and righteousness is often misunderstood, despised, persecuted, and trodden under foot by vice. But then there must exist a being who rules the world according to reason and moral laws, and who has established, in the course of things to come, a state where the creature who has remained true to his nature and who has made himself worthy of happiness through morality will ac-

tually participate in this happiness. For otherwise all subjectively necessary duties which I as a rational being am responsible for performing
will lose their objective reality. Why should I make myself worthy of
happiness through morality if there is no being who can give me this
happiness? Hence without God I would have to be either a visionary or
a scoundrel. I would have to deny my own nature and its eternal moral
laws. I would have to cease being a rational man.[10]

I want to supplement this passage by citing an article of mine in which
I emphasize how important it was for Kant to save the "great thinkables,"
reason or no reason.[11] The great thinkables are God, soul, world, along
with the postulates. Kant never intended to jeopardize them by what he said
about scientific knowledge, but he knew he could not ground them by theoretical reason. What did he do? The opening sentence of his *Lectures on
Philosophical Theology* gives the clue: "Human reason has need of an idea
of perfection, to serve it as a standard according to which it can make de-
terminations."[12] Here he is stating the foundation of the ontological argument, which he has totally demolished as a rational argument.
Unfortunately, therefore, since Kant has made the terrible sacrifice of lim-
iting theoretical rational justification to knowledge of appearances, he could
only appeal to moral faith to ground his metaphysical beliefs. Although
this appeal is billed as the deliverance of pure and practical reason, the result comes out in the second *Critique* as follows:

> This command of [practical] reason . . . is, therefore, an abso-
> lutely necessary need and justifies its presupposition not merely as an
> allowable hypothesis, but as a practical postulate. Granted that the pure
> moral law inexorably binds every man as a command (not as a rule of
> prudence), the righteous man may say: I will that there be a God, and
> that my existence in this world be also an existence in a pure world of

---

[10]Immanuel Kant, *Lectures on Philosophical Theology,* trans. Allen W. Wood
and Gertrude M. Clark (Ithaca NY: Cornell University Press, 1978) 110. Brightman may have read these lectures in the original German.

[11]See John H. Lavely, "Comment" on John N. Findlay, "The Central Role
of the Thing-In-Itself in Kant," *The Philosophical Forum: Kant's Critique of Pure
Reason* 13, no. 1 (Fall 1981): 66-74, esp. 73.

[12]Kant, *Lectures on Philosophical Theology,* 21. See also Kant, *Critique of
Pure Reason,* 486 (A569/B597).

the understanding outside the system of natural connections, and finally that my duration be endless. I stand by this and will not give up this belief, for this is the only case where my interest inevitably determines my judgment because I will not yield anything of this interest; I do so without any attention to sophistries, however little I may be able to answer them or oppose them with others more plausible.[13]

Here he explicitly repudiates any rational justification and yet insists on saving the great thinkables, at all cost. The point is tellingly made in a poem by D. H. Monro.

> When Kant, aroused from his dogmatic dozes
> And conscious of the very little room
> For anti-scepticism left by Hume,
> Decided that the intellect discloses,
> Not what's out there, as everyone supposes,
> But only what it finds it can subsume
> Beneath the Categories (I assume
> That they're like spectacles upon our noses)
> He added that this blinkered human'll
> Catch still some glimpses of the Noumenal
> And that God, Freedom, Immortality
> Are hall-marked: Guaranteed Reality.
> This simply shows what tangled webs we weave
> When we are quite determined to believe.[14]

Kant says simply, "It is unavoidable for every rational being in the world to assume whatever is necessary to its [the moral law's] objective possibility."[15] This sounds strangely proto-existential. Without this (whatever the case may be) I cannot live. Imagine how many people would say what Kant says above, substituting something else for the moral law.

I have dwelt on this point at such length because of what I think is a remarkable connection with personalism. I vividly remember Brightman's frequent criticisms of Bowne for being lax in his standard of knowledge. I quote the famous statement from Bowne's *Theism* to which Brightman

---

[13]Kant, *Critique of Practical Reason*, 148-49.

[14]"The Sonneteer's History of Philosophy," no. 16: "Kant," *Philosophy* 55 (1980): 371.

[15]Kant, *Critique of Practical Reason*, 149 n. 6.

objected: "Life is richer and deeper than speculation, and contains implicitly the principles by which we live."[16] The law of the logician must yield, Bowne says, to "the law the mind actually follows . . . : Whatever the mind demands for the satisfaction of its subjective interests and tendencies may be assumed as real in default of positive disproof."[17] Brightman thought such a principle was much too loose. I think it sounds very much like the Kantian rationale for the practical postulates I have just examined.

In Bowne's essay "The Logic of Religious Belief," he says that "thought has the sole function of guiding life. . . . Belief is molded by practical aims and necessities rather than by the processes of logic."[18] This motif is reminiscent of Bowne's illustrious contemporary, William James. Albert C. Knudson picked up Bowne's theme and made it his position in *The Validity of Religious Experience.* Knudson quoted approvingly the passage from Bowne's *Theism* to which Brightman took exception (cited above) and then stated, "Life with us has the right of way, and whatever satisfies our deepest interests and needs commends itself to us as true."[19] Life is the determinative principle, but that is far too vague. It is a blanket that covers too much to provide a discriminating test of truth. However oblique or indirect Bowne's and Knudson's debt to Kant may be in this regard, it seriously weakens their standard of knowledge.

It would be ungenerous not to acknowledge the fundamentally positive feature of personalism's debt to Kant, as I think I have. I conclude, however, that for the reasons adduced in my analysis of the postulates of the practical reason, there is also a grave danger in being too indebted to Kant. It is for this reason, among others, that I admire Edgar Brightman. His passionate and persistent efforts to develop the principle of coherence as the broader logic of the total life are the best corrective to this danger.

---

[16]Borden Parker Bowne, *Theism* (New York: American Book Company, 1902) 18.

[17]Ibid.

[18]Borden Parker Bowne, "The Logic of Religious Belief," *Representative Essays of Borden Bowne,* ed. Warren E. Steinkraus (Utica NY: Meridian Publishing Company, 1980) 152.

[19]Albert C. Knudson, *The Validity of Religious Experience* (New York: The Abingdon Press, 1937) 176.

Personalism's Debt to Hegel

Walter G. Muelder

Each generation of the century-long tradition of Boston Personalists has had its distinctive relation to the idealist tradition, not least to Hegel. In one paper I can only trace the first two of five generations. Since that tradition goes back to Plato, Augustine, Berkeley, Leibniz, Kant, and Lotze, as well as to Hegel, personalists have been self-conscious about the great thinkers in the whole history of philosophy. And not only of philosophy but also of theology. In concentrating on Hegel, the portrait of his significance will become larger than life, because the host of other metaphysical giants in the idealist heritage can hardly be mentioned and so fade into the background of attention. I shall focus primarily on Bowne, Knudson, and Brightman.

Bowne seldom mentioned other thinkers in detail or in footnotes, except for Kant whom he appreciated and Spencer whom he despised because of his scientific superficiality, sensory epistemology, and uncritical use of the theory of natural selection. Yet Bowne was thoroughly grounded in historical and contemporary thought and spent formative years in Germany studying with Lotze. Knudson made a feature of relating the philosophy of personalism to its antecedents, its opponents, and its friendly critics. He did this on many issues and on movements as a whole. He also developed a personalistic "Hall of Fame" in which he summarized the distinctive elements in the philosophers under review. Hegel is there.

Brightman went even more thoroughly into the rival and concurring schools of thought in the whole history of philosophy. His historical seminars were major explorations into the depths of great thinkers. It was my privilege to do a year-long seminar on Hegel's *Encyclopedia of the Philosophical Sciences* at a time when the Hegel renaissance was taking place. Although the influence of Hegel on Brightman was significant, and distinguished him somewhat from Bowne and Knudson in method and style, scholars should examine his texts on ethics and metaphysics to note his appeal to and criticisms of numerous other philosophers as well. One important caveat, therefore, must be noted: while the classical idealist tradition after Hegel was *absolute idealism,* the direct line is not Hegel to Bowne to Knudson to Brightman. As students of Bowne in the era of neo-Kantianism and under the influence of Lotze, they were idealists of the personalist persuasion before they made their professional careers as authorities on Plato, Kant, Berkeley, Leibniz, and Hegel. Their allusions to Hegel are not primarily derivative, but concurring or rejecting. When Absolute Idealism threatened personality as the key to reality or the moral significance of the experience of the finite persons, they rejected the singularism of the Absolute. Moreover, the sense of philosophical security in the school of Boston Personalism is in large part due to the cumulative persuasiveness of the idealist truths in the tradition as a whole. Their concern was not so much for innovation in metaphysics, religion, and ethics as it was for coherent adequacy, taking consciousness as a whole.

Personalism, then, is not in the most direct line of Hegelian influence in American idealism. For this we must turn to the St. Louis Movement by way of Brokmeyer and Harris. They stressed the "practicality" of philosophy and found in Hegel's triadic dialectic (thesis, antithesis, synthesis) a ready-made formula for dealing with conflicting trends in American culture, including the Civil War.[1] They appealed to the dialectic as a corrective to special interests, with their one-sided distortions of truth, to the reconciliation of science and religion in a higher synthesis, to the reconstruction of the Union after the tragic "dialectic" of civil war, as a phi-

---

[1] See W. H. Werkmeister, *A History of Philosophical Ideas in America* (1949; rpt., New York: Ronald Press, 1981) 58-59, also 59n.

losophy of politics. Hegel had many applications. Moreover, when T. C. Harris became superintendent of schools in St. Louis, the whole system became imbued with the Hegelian spirit. He founded the first journal of philosophy in the English language, *The Journal of Speculative Philosophy,* and used it as an antidote to the philosophy of Herbert Spencer.

BOWNE AND HEGEL

Though Bowne had an appreciation for the stature of Hegel in the generation after Kant, he was generally opposed to his Absolute Idealism on both epistemological and metaphysical grounds. Bowne found both traditional realism and traditional idealism hasty and superficial. "No tenable idealism," he said, "can be founded on a theory of the knowing process alone," for all attempts must lapse into either solipsism or inconsistency and arbitrariness.[2] Idealistic metaphysics requires an analysis of the object known. Here Bowne was distinguishing his own epistemological dualism from that of both Hegel and Berkeley. Bowne regarded his own position as realistic in affirming an objective cosmic system independent of finite thinking.[3] The world of nature is known phenomenally. Two Hegelian elements are characteristic of Bowne's personalism: the generally superior emphasis on the spiritual side of experience and the incorporation of science into a fully religious world view.[4]

Bowne sought to distinguish his view from the school of philosophy at Cornell University known as Objective Idealism, which was positively influenced by the principle of Objective Mind that incorporates finite minds in the larger Mind of the cosmos. On this issue Bowne and later personalists are clearly pluralistic rather than monistic.

In interpreting Bowne's relation to Hegel, Bishop Francis J. McConnell compared them as follows:

Hegel took his start from Kant's thing-in-itself and showed that things must come within thought or go out of existence. If they cannot in any degree be compassed within thought-terms, we can affirm nothing of

---

[2]B. P. Bowne, *Theory of Thought and Knowledge* (New York: American Book Co., 1897) 326-27.

[3]Ibid., 342-43.

[4]Werkmeister, *History of Philosophical Ideas,* 318.

them whatsoever. If we cannot know anything about them, we cannot know that they exist. This was indeed a fine start on Hegel's part, but he forthwith proceeded to a theory which put thought before thinkers. He spelled Thought with a capital "T," and ended in impersonal idealism. Nevertheless, Bowne always extolled Hegel as having immortal merit. The Hegelian doctrine of thesis, antithesis, and synthesis—Bowne used to tell his classes—was a genuine evolution, as compared with the tawdry cheapness of Spencerianism, with its homogeneities, its heterogeneities and differentiations and integrators and its concomitant dissipations of energy, and all the rest of it.[5]

The principal criticism here is Bowne's stress on the fallacy of abstraction. Later writers also call it the fallacy of misplaced concreteness. Bowne is often quoted as saying that "the fallacy of the universal is the universal fallacy." This fallacy leads to that of impersonalism.

One of the most famous chapters in Bowne's work *Personalism* (1908) is entitled "The Failure of Impersonalism," in which he attacked naturalism and idealistic impersonalism, both arising from the fallacy of the abstract.[6]

Uncritical minds always attempt to explain the explanation, thus unwittingly committing themselves to the infinite regress. Accordingly when they come to living intelligence as the explanation of the world, they fancy they must go behind even this. We have the categories of being, cause, identity, change, the absolute, and the like; and intelligence at best is only a specification or particular case of these more general principles. These principles, then, lie behind all personal or other existence, as its presupposition and source, and constitute a set of true first principles, from which all definite and concrete reality is derived by some sort of logical process or implication. This is a species of idealistic impersonalism. In its origin it is antipodal to naturalism, but in the outcome the two often coincide. Strauss said of the Hegelian idealism that the difference between it and materialism was only one of words; and this was certainly true of Hegelianism of the left wing.[7]

---

[5]F. J. McConnell, *Borden Parker Bowne* (New York: Abingdon, 1929) 114.

[6]Bowne, *Personalism* (Boston: Houghton Mifflin, 1908) ch. 5.

[7]Bowne, *Personalism,* 218f.

Bowne thus established the priority of the person. All abstract ideas, including the categories of knowing and metaphysical existence, are "owned or belong to some one, and mean nothing as floating free."[8] They get their "real significance only in the concrete and self-conscious life of the living mind."[9] "When we ask what we mean by any of these categories, it turns out . . . that we mean the significance we find them to have for our self-conscious life. . . . If we suppose them to precede personality, we must ask where they exist. The only intelligent answer that can be given would be that they exist either in space and time, or in consciousness."[10] Therefore, when we conceive the intellect as merely a set of logical relations, as is the tendency in Absolute Idealism, we err, for such an intellect is totally incapable of explaining the order of experience, logic being itself non-temporal.[11] "A purely logical and contemplative intellect that merely gazed upon the relation of ideas, without choice and initiative and active self-direction, would be absolutely useless in explaining the order of life."[12] Life, Bowne often said, is deeper than logic. To be is to act, and to act is to will.

The above attack is not specifically against Hegel, but Bowne had Hegelians like Bradley clearly in mind. Students of Bowne had to do a careful critique of F. H. Bradley's *Appearance and Reality*. The contradictions of impersonal idealism are not resolved by referring them to the Absolute. Unless the Absolute is personally conceived, argued Bowne, the fallacies of self-contradiction pursue Mr. Bradley in his doctrine of the Absolute.[13]

KNUDSON AND HEGEL

Knudson was a faithful disciple of Bowne, and a number of the criticisms and appreciations of Hegel are repeated by him, as I shall note. In

---

[8]Ibid., 253.

[9]Ibid., 254.

[10]Ibid., 255.

[11]Ibid., 256.

[12]Ibid., 257.

[13]Ibid., 260.

the concluding chapter of his systematic exposition of personalism, Knudson listed the personalistic Hall of Fame in chronological order. The number ten was assigned to Hegel.

> Whether Hegel may with propriety be classed as a personalist or not, is a question. But in any case he made one very significant contribution to the personalistic philosophy. He established the rationality of the real. In this truth is to be found the ultimate basis of the immaterialism of Leibniz and Berkeley, and of idealists in general. The material or space-time world cannot meet the test of rationality. It is shot through and through with inconsistencies and contradictions, and hence must be condemned to phenomenality.[14]

Thus, Knudson followed Bowne in conceding certain ''immortal merits'' to Hegel:

> It was he who gave to the problem of knowledge perhaps its clearest and sharpest formulation. It was he who established once and for all the doctrine that the real is necessarily rational. Whatever is irrational is unreal and impossible. Only as being is shaped by the categories of thought can it be given an intelligent content. It is, therefore, according to Hegel, futile to try to conceive of reality apart from reason. This profound insight constitutes, in spite of all their differences, a permanent bond of union between personalism and Hegelianism. . . . If the real must be rational, then it must also be nonmaterial or ideal in nature. . . . But the tendency in Hegelian absolutism is to restrict the ideal and the rational to thought or to ideas in their logical relation to each other.[15]

The real, according to Knudson, must include the will and the self's experience as a whole.

On the other hand, there are four principal objections to Absolute Idealism in its impersonal Hegelian form, that is, a rationalism that is simply a dialectical unfolding of thought.[16] The first is as a necessitarian system. Though it differs from materialism in being a logical rather than a causal necessitarian system, Absolute Idealism has speculative consequences

---

[14]A. C. Knudson, *Philosophy of Personalism* (New York: Abingdon, 1927) 432.

[15]Ibid., 384.

[16]Ibid., 378-83.

similar to materialism. In both real progress is impossible. There is no real development where consequences are already implicit in the premises. There is no place for time in logical implication; hence, the universe is eternal and static. We have already met this objection in Bowne's critique. Moreover, in such a system error is as necessary as truth, and there is no criterion or way to use a standard to choose between truth and error. Choice presupposes freedom. Human error as well as truth must, in Absolute Idealism, be referred to the absolute reason, and thus the system contradicts itself. Genuine metaphysical freedom is a prerequisite for both religion and ethics.

A second difficulty in Absolute Idealism is that it is as helpless to account for concrete reality as materialism is to account for mental existence. It gives us thought without a thinker. Here Knudson developed an objection that I have also noted in Bowne. Among the personalists who have emphasized the realistic element in the cosmos is Ralph Tyler Flewelling, the distinguished founder of *The Personalist* at the University of Southern California. Reality, said Knudson, is always concrete. It is an agent or system of agents. Without an agent there can be no activity, either mental or physical. Hegel never solved the problem of the transition from universality to individuality. Knudson recognized three orders of generality: categories, laws, and facts. But these orders, he said, cannot be bridged by logic alone.

Related to this difficulty of Absolute Idealism in relation to concrete fact is its doctrine of epistemological dualism. The identification of thought and thing fails to give adequate recognition to the "given" element in experience. Things are not simply our thought. Solipsism is absurd. Monism makes error impossible; hence, the theory founders not only on logical necessitarianism, as noted earlier, but on the fact of error.

A fourth difficulty is that Absolute Idealism leads to pantheism and tends to undermine religious faith. From the standpoint of philosophy of religion, this is a serious difficulty. Though Hegel tried to work out a final synthesis of philosophy and Christianity, his method and logic eventually proved to be adverse to religion by making the Absolute impersonal. Knudson's criticism of pantheism in its Hegelian form seeks to conserve what is most characteristic of religion. "What religion is primarily concerned about is not the metaphysical union of the human with the divine, but a relation of mutual understanding between them, a relation that expresses itself on our part in worship and in an attitude of love and obedience. Such a relation, however, is possible only between persons and between persons that retain their own distinct individuality."[17]

At the cost of some repetition, I must here retrace my steps somewhat and relate Hegel to eighteenth-century rationalism and his efforts to develop a synthesis of science, philosophy, and religion as a dialectical whole. I must also discuss his efforts to go beyond the dualisms left unresolved by Kant between the theoretical reason and the practical reason, between phenomena and things-in-themselves, and between morality and religion.

Knudson acknowledged Hegel's criticism of traditional rationalism, since Hegel found it superficial both intellectually and religiously. Moreover, Hegel rejected rationalism's opposition to reason and history and also its opposition to characteristic Christian doctrines like the Trinity and the Incarnation. In *Present Tendencies in Religious Thought* Knudson noted that eighteenth-century rationalism sought a synthesis between religion and culture by surrendering the distinctive elements in Christianity, and he concurs with Hegel that at the root of the surrender was a wrong method.[18] Instead of sacrificing Christianity to culture, Hegel sought to raise modern thought to the level of Christianity through a higher synthesis. This attempt rendered a great historical service to Christian faith in that era. Knudson quoted Werner Elert with approval: "Hegel's apology for Christianity is the most brilliant but also the last synthesis in heroic style that has been attempted between Christianity and science."[19]

However, Knudson faulted Hegel for introducing a new form of rationalism that could be fatal to historic Christianity. On the positive side, Hegel saw in history the unfolding of divine reason, and he saw in Christianity the absolute religion. Accordingly, the doctrines of the Trinity and Incarnation are embodiments of the highest philosophic truth. Hegel gave to the Absolute a trinitarian form, and he reestablished unity in the life and spirit, both through the synthesis of nature and spirit and through the goal

---

[17]Ibid., 383.

[18]Knudson, *Present Tendencies in Religious Thought* (New York: Abingdon, 1924) 214.

[19]Werner Elert, *Der Kampf um das Christentum* (Munich: Oscar Beck, 1921) 35.

of the perfect union of finite and infinite being as exemplified in the Incarnation.

Thus, Hegel exalted Christianity but exalted reason and philosophy even more. Like the earlier rationalists Hegel held onto an intellectualistic conception of religion. Both forms of rationalism emphasized the rational content of religion rather than its experiential and vital side. This method implied a subordination of faith to reason. "For Hegel," said Knudson, "faith was not self-verifying; it found its justification in philosophy." The form that truth takes in philosophy *(Begriff)* Hegel held to be superior to that which it takes in religion *(Vorstellung)*. That is to say, concept, or notion, is superior to imaginative representation. By taking this line it is philosophy, not religion, that represents the ultimate form of truth. The same, argued Knudson, is the consequence for the content of philosophy and religion, respectively.[20] In other words, Hegel places speculative thought on a higher plane than revelation, as the source and the test of truth. This result is in sharp contrast to the method and criterion of empirical coherence in personalism.

BRIGHTMAN AND HEGEL

Of all the Boston Personalists, the one who studied Hegel most closely and stood closest to him in interpretation was Edgar S. Brightman. He viewed reason as empirical coherence and used the term "concrete" in its Hegelian sense, not simply in its realistic, particularistic sense. Both thinkers viewed metaphysics as the "Holy of Holies" of any civilization.[21] To be concrete in the Hegel/Brightman sense "is to think interconnectedly and 'holistically'; it is to see the parts as related to the whole to which they belong, and to create a way of thinking in which no aspect of experience is neglected and all aspects are seen in their relation to each other."[22] Brightman was a metaphysician for whom metaphysics is "the

---

[20]Knudson, *Present Tendencies in Religious Thought,* 216.

[21]E. S. Brightman, *Person and Reality* (New York: Ronald Press, 1958) 13, 14. See G. W. F. Hegel, *Science of Logic,* trans. Johnson and Struthers (New York: Macmillan, 1929) 1:34.

[22]Brightman, *Person and Reality,* 14. See Brightman, *Introduction to Philosophy* (New York: Henry Holt and Co., 1951) ch. 2, 27f.

mind's effort to view experience as a living whole'' and thus is close to Hegel's basic intent, though he drew divergent conclusions from that effort. He went beyond Hume and Kant, and even Hegel, in that his grasp of experience was broader than the first two and in method went beyond Hegel's rules of logic. ''Metaphysics is critical understanding of all human experience in a coherent perspective.'' Hence, with respect to religion ''it [metaphysics] cannot be identified with any religion, nor can it be a rejection of the fact of religion.''[23] Philosophically speaking, Christianity cannot be exalted as the absolute religion as Hegel tried to do.

The chief factors in empirical coherence as goal and method are consistency, system, inclusiveness, synoptic hypotheses, verification, and the dialectic. The dialectical factor is more than the Hegelian system of thesis, antithesis, and synthesis. The metaphysician must observe the principle of development at work in an inclusive grappling with experience whether in reason, personal growth, art, religion, ethics, social growth, or philosophy. In dealing with any datum (or specious present) he must seek the ''other,'' the ''negative,'' the beyond, the more.[24] In all this the spirit of Hegel is clearly acknowledged. The dialectical acknowledges the dynamic element in experience and orders it in coherent meaning.

Thought begins, of course, in the immediate present, what Brightman called the ''shining present.'' Like Hegel, however, Brightman taught that there is no immediate experience that does not have an element of meditation. It has a relational and, therefore, a rational purposive ingredient rooted in the experient, the subject. In the *Phanomenologie des Geistes* Hegel argued that ''nothing is known which is not in experience.''[25] This means at least that knowledge is based on the evidence of experience and points beyond itself to other experience. Present experience not only points beyond itself horizontally as to something external, but also vertically, for it has levels of understanding and discloses norms of interpretation. Brightman would agree with Hegel that pure ''being'' is empty abstrac-

---

[23]Brightman, *Person and Reality,* 21.

[24]Ibid., 28-32.

[25]Hegel, *Phanomenologie des Geistes* (Leipzig: Philosophische Bibliotek, 1928) 258.

tion—nothing at all.[26] We turn, therefore, to the stages, levels, or realms of being as they may be called. The two philosophers were akin in dealing with what Hegel called the stages of *Sein, Wesen,* and *Begriff,* Brightman preferring the use of the German terms to their misleading translations "Being," "Essence," and "Notion."

The realm of *Sein* is that of immediacy, the "point of view" of the shining present. Here Hegel restricts it to sensory experience, while Brightman is more inclusive. Thought reaches out beyond the immediate to an "other" and thus to the realm of *Wesen,* the realm of external relations. In this activity analytic and causal science finds its place. But thought goes farther to *Begriff,* the realm of synoptic method and wholeness—the realm of spirit or personality. In moving from realm to realm Brightman seeks to avoid the rigidities sometimes ascribed to the Hegelian logic. He says that *Begriff* (Notion) almost means personality for Hegel.[27]

Having identified the realms of being, one turns to the categories of being, or experience. Brightman reminds the reader that Hegel's logic is not an a priori construction, but it is based on the survey of experience, as in the *Phenomenology of Mind.*[28] For Brightman a category "is a principle the denial of which would make the entire universe of discourse to which it applies either impossible or fundamentally incoherent."[29] Since both thinkers hold that the true is the whole, "a category is what is essential to an empirical whole." On this issue Brightman was clearly more Hegelian than Bowne, who like Lotze was more Kantian in his treatment. Yet Bowne distinguished, as Kant did not, the categories of knowledge from the metaphysical categories.

When one considers a basic category like time, one must note that time is intimately involved in the experience of purpose, and purpose is close to the very essence of selfhood. What must explain the immediately present involves process, or becoming. Here Hegel and Brightman concurred once again. This process of going beyond the "shining present" is called the "illuminating absent" and must include, said Brightman, all selves or

---

[26]Brightman, *Person and Reality,* 76

[27]Ibid., 83-84.

[28]Ibid., 95n.

[29]Ibid., 98.

shining presents that are not "mine."[30] All being is temporal; therefore, all being is personal.[31] This hypothesis means that the universe "is a society of persons, derived from the unity of an ever-enduring source of all other duration (beyond my own experience), the unbegun and unending person called God."[32]

Moving from the category of time to that of substance, with its dilemmas of continuity and discontinuity, the quest of metaphysics is for generic empirical structures rather than for abstract necessities. On this category both Kant and Hegel are noted as erring because of their emphasis on the factor of "necessity" in the concept of substance. Neither absolute metaphysical pluralism nor absolute singularism adequately explains the empirical data involved in continuity and discontinuity. The Absolutist errs in reducing everything to or including everything in the continuous present.[33] Brightman argued for an organic interactive pluralism in which continuity and discontinuity are related after the model of actual conscious experience. "Selfhood thus becomes the key to all substance."[34]

Though dissenting from Hegel on the issue of abstract necessity in the theory of substance, Brightman was a protagonist for him in holding that substance is person, as efficient final cause, in a complex unity of active consciousness. He translated from the *Encyclopädie der philosophischen Wissenschaften* (par. 50) the thesis that "the Essence of the World-Substance—the universal power and purpose—has its being only for thought." In the *Encyclopädie, Begriff* is equated with "I," "free spirit," "love," and "bliss."[35] Here Brightman brought Hegel into the personalist camp. He added that Hegel's personalism was developed more from a study of history than from a study of nature; by contrast Bowne's personalism was inspired by modern physics.[36]

---

[30]Ibid., 127.

[31]Ibid., 135.

[32]Ibid., 136.

[33]Ibid., 184.

[34]Ibid.

[35]Ibid., 199.

[36]Ibid., 206.

A word more about Nature is required here. Nature for both Bowne and Hegel was quasi-phenomenal. The term "quasi" was employed by Brightman because neither held that phenomenal knowledge is all that we know, or that sensory facts exhaust experience.[37] The essential definition of Nature is organization of sense data by categories of order. Bowne liked the term "activity" in dealing with Nature and matter, and in this he was followed by Brightman. "Energy" is also a term with which "matter is convertible."[38] There are, of course, materialistic theories of energism, and the difference between them and personalism is whether "energy" is defined in terms of "an unverified nonmental power or is interpreted empirically in terms of conscious will."[39]

Having said that Nature is the experience of an ordering, creative Mind rather than any human mind, Brightman added that it is only one realm of experience within that Mind.[40] Nature fails to account for the whole evidence that appears in the human experience, affording no theory of value or the goal of evolution, particularly of human life. Persons are thus more than Nature, and they are not literally parts of the eternal Person. Therefore, Brightman used the term "create" in a qualified sense regarding both Nature and finite human beings. He noted that the personalistic view was clearly summarized by Hegel in his "Proofs of the Existence of God," when he held that "Nature is sustained in the Spirit, created by it . . . and it is in itself only something posited, created, and ideal in the spirit."[41]

Thus Nature is obviously not all of the metaphysical story. Brightman did much of his greatest work on problems in the realm of value, as in religion and ethics. And here, again, he concurred with Hegel that there is a

---

[37]Ibid., 242n.

[38]Ibid., 245.

[39]Ibid.

[40]Ibid., 248.

[41]Brightman's translation of von Georg Lasson, ed., *Hegel's "Werke"* (Leipzig: F. Meiner, 1930) 14:64. See English edition, *Lectures on the Philosophy of Religion,* ed. and trans. from 2nd German ed. by E. B. Spiers and Y. Burdon Sanderson (New York: Humanities Press, 1962) 3:210.

realm of true value, that is, of goods that ought to be.[42] But here also are some of the sharpest differences, as Brightman made plain in *Nature and Values* (1945) and in *Person and Reality,* edited and summarized in part from the former work by Bertocci and Newhall. There is a marked contrast between absolutistic and personalistic idealism with respect to value-theory.

In pinpointing this contrast, it is clarifying to quote Brightman's summary view of the relation of subjective value as experienced and the objectivity of the norms of value.

> It probably is true that values are subjective. My experience of justice or of love can exist nowhere save in me. But the doctrine of the subjectivity of values is matched by the doctrine of the objectivity of norms. Norms are not confined to the person who acknowledges them or who applies them. They are rational, universal, true for all. Indeed, there are signs that valid norms are definitions of the objective teleological structure of the universe. They seem to be the controlling goals of all evolutionary struggle. We may think of them as purposes of the Divine Mind, if not of an absolutely omnipotent and all-creating Deity. Whatever their relation to Deity or to any other possible metaphysical reality, norms are imperatives of reason, and their home is wherever reason dwells, and their work is wherever persons exist.[43]

The contrast lies in the constitutive difference between Absolute Idealism and relative pluralistic idealism, or organic personalistic pluralism. "Idealistic absolutism is the doctrine that the entire universe is one perfect and all-inclusive mind (or at least mind-like unity); everything that is, whether in nature or in human individuals and societies, is a phase, an aspect, a stage—that is, in the broad sense, a part—of the one absolute Mind. This view is essentially pantheistic, although its exponents, Hegel, for example, do not care to be called pantheists."[44] We have already met this criticism in Knudson. Though Brightman raised no serious objection to the Absolutist's view of Nature, a totally different picture is disclosed on finite personality and value. Error, imperfection, and moral evil or sin are un-

---

[42]Brightman, *Person and Reality,* 280.

[43]Ibid., 294.

[44]Ibid., 297f.

deniable facts of human experience. A personalist says to the Absolutist, "If error and evil are wholly overcome in the Absolute, then they do not exist in the Absolute as they do in me, the human person. In me, error is really taken to be the truth, and evil is really chosen instead of good. What there is in me cannot possibly be in the Absolute as I experience it. My ignorance cannot mean that the Absolute is ignorant. And since all of my life is to some extent imperfect, none of my personality can be in God as part of him."[45] Hence, there is "an ineradicable logical contradiction in saying that man the imperfect is a part of God the perfect."[46]

At stake here is not only a matter of the status of error and value, but the metaphysical status of persons. Also, religious absolutism is defective. Though absolutism seems to be harmonious with the mystical sense of unity with God *(unio mystica),* it imperils other aspects of religion. "If the soul is literally one with God in its very being, then man's responsibility and his moral life as a person are at an end."[47] But even the mystical sense of unity becomes meaningless unless at least two persons are communing or cooperating—God and finite human beings. "Personalism, however, with its fundamentally social philosophy, retains the separateness and the dignity of all personalities, while finding profound meaning in oneness of purpose, worshipful communion, and loving cooperation between God and man."[48]

Hegelian singularism thus stands finally opposed to personalistic theism. The problem of good and evil makes this point clear. The absolutistic solution views evil as included and transcended in the Whole. Brightman's hypothesis was finitistic personalism, in which the divine Experient is conceived as including within that self's own consciousness both a creative will for value and also an experience of limits (a Given), both rational and nonrational in kind.[49] Thus Brightman's view is more empirical, temporalist, and inherently historical than Hegel's, and thus it vin-

---

[45]Ibid., 298.

[46]Ibid., 298f.

[47]Ibid., 299.

[48]Ibid.

[49]Ibid., 320.

dicates the personalistic break with much nineteenth-century idealism, for all its merits. Brightman followed Hegel in devotion to the Whole, in synoptic vision, and in dialectical process, but the personalistic stress on organic pluralism kept Brightman closer to empirical reality, and conversely.

Hegel's lack of adequate regard for the finite person had implications for moral theory and violated what Brightman was to call the moral Law of Individualism: "Each person ought to realize in his own experience the maximum value of which he is capable in harmony with moral law."[50] Hegel put the moral value of human life in social relations and social loyalties. He is devoted to social institutions, particularly the state, putting it at the pinnacle of ethical ideals. His interest in society led him to neglect the individual person.[51] His organic ethics almost caused individual responsibility to vanish.[52]

This brings to a conclusion my summary of Bowne, Knudson, and Brightman with respect to their debts to Hegel. I shall have more to say later on Brightman's use of Hegel in social philosophy and ethics. It is worth noting at the end as at the beginning that Brightman was a confirmed follower of Bowne's personalism before the Hegelian renaissance took place and that Hegel research became an important part of Brightman's career. Personalism is not a heretical derivative from Absolute Idealism. Hegel is often cited, as are many other thinkers, more in appreciative concurrence than in dependence. Brightman saw personalism as a dialectical cumulative coherent synthesis, not as an eclectic summary, of the truth that the history of philosophy and his own devotion to experience as a whole had produced. In this the personalistic deviations from Hegel are as significant as the agreements.

---

[50]Brightman, *Moral Laws* (New York: Abingdon, 1933) 205.

[51]Ibid., 212.

[52]Ibid., 236.

Borden Parker Bowne and His Personalistic Theistic Idealism*

Peter A. Bertocci

Personalists differ among themselves as to their thoughts about the nature of the finite and infinite person, the relation of mind to body, and the relation of cosmic Mind to Nature and to persons. But—and the roots of this view extend back to Anaximander in Western philosophy—personalists find the key to ultimate value and reality in the dynamics of personal being. In common they defend the intrinsic unity of mind (soul, self, psyche, person, spirit), and they resist reduction of the person to, or his or her absorption in, any environment.

Personalists have conceived of the cosmic Person by cautious analogy with finite persons; usually they have identified the cosmic Person with God, especially on the evidence of the religious consciousness. The dominant trend in personalism is theistic, not pantheistic or monistic.

------

*Reprinted, with some alterations, from *Ultimate Reality and Meaning* 2, no. 3 (1979): 205-27, with the permission of the editor. The journal holds the copyright.

It is to Borden Parker Bowne (1847-1910) that we must look for the most systematic development of the personalistic theistic idealism that characterizes the dominant personalistic trend. Much influenced by his teacher, H. Lotze, he sought in his metaphysics, epistemology, ethics, and philosophy of religion to weave into a new system insights, as he saw them, especially of Berkeley, Leibniz, and Kant. He could say, "I am a Personalist, the first of the clan in any thoroughgoing sense."[1]

Bowne's ancestors William and Anne Bowne, English Puritans, came in 1631 to Salem, Massachusetts. When later they moved to New Jersey, they became involved in fair dealing with the Indians as that state was settled. Bowne, born in 1847, one of six children, was the son of a morally direct and straightforward (abolitionist) justice of the peace; his mother's more mystic vein did not keep her from meticulous attention to the farmhouse not far from the sea. The impact of both parents, in this natural setting, left Bowne with a sense of moral tidiness, an enjoyment of nature, and a feeling for religious transcendence that was no flight from orderly thought, nor from firm moral practice, as he searched for the essential in his Christian tradition and in the Methodism of the late-nineteenth-century ferment in America.

One notable instance of this constant search for fundamentals was his willingness in his later years to set aside metaphysical-moral "reflection" and come to the defense of the freedom of speech of a colleague in the department of Old Testament in Boston University School of Theology whose affirmation of the scientific findings about evolution, coupled with the higher biblical criticism, had aroused serious objection to his continuance as professor. Such activity was to involve Bowne in defense of himself in 1904 in a heresy trial. He was acquitted unanimously once he could show that free speech was not a privilege but the moral-spiritual thrust of any attempt to discover the meaning of issues essential to religious integrity, rather than to embalm them in the literalism of a creedal faith.

Bowne's thinking and life were part of a growing urban university, whose theological school was a dominant force in America's theological climate and in a large American denomination that was battling the tension between "faith" and "reason" on more than one front. Bowne's meta-

---

[1]Francis J. McConnell, *Borden Parker Bowne: His Life and Philosophy* (New York: Abingdon, 1929) 280.

physics, epistemology, and ethics were not intended to support a given version, if any, of *the* faith or of a particular denominational creedal outlook.

A graduate of New York University (A.M. and M.A.), Bowne studied in Paris, Halle, and Gottingen (1873) and began his work at Boston University, where he spent the rest of his days (1876-1910) teaching in the College of Liberal Arts, the School of Theology, and in the Graduate School (of which he was the first dean). In his book *Personalism* (1908), Bowne summarized ideas that are most adequately argued in *Metaphysics* (1882, revised 1898), *The Theory of Thought and Knowledge* (1897), and *Theism* (1902). Among his seventeen books and numerous essays, his *Principles of Ethics* (1892), *The Immanence of God* (1905), *Studies in Christianity* (1909), and *The Essence of Religion* (1910) express Bowne's unflinching effort, on the one hand, to unmask the pontifical claims made in his day in the name of Christian supernaturalism, and, on the other, to show that a personalistic-theistic idealism is the more reasonable support for the ideals of the scientific, ethical, and religious life.

CENTRALITY OF THE PERSON

The conviction underlying all of Bowne's philosophical and theological work is that only those hypotheses can be considered true that, more than any other, render coherent the varied data manifest in human experience. Reason, for Bowne, is neither to dictate to life, nor to flout logical law, but to relate every dimension of human experience into as systematic a whole as possible. Bowne required that the deductive method of ''rigor and vigor'' be seen for what it is, a part of experience that has no data of its own. Accordingly, it is to guide the person in making decisions that will encourage making the most of life as a whole. The philosopher can never neglect the fact that persons live with each other in an orderly world. The ultimate nature of that orderly world and the ultimate nature of persons can be discovered only by understanding the relation of each to the other.

I now come, then, to Bowne's fundamental thesis with regard to the person. The person, who acts in and makes cognitive claims about the world that his or her acting and knowing do not create, is an indivisible unity. Even the simplest logical judgment and the simplest factual judgment involve successive experiences. But there can be no succession of experience unless there is an experience of succession. Some cognitive unity, aware of succession, must persist through change if change is to be known as successive. But change in awareness presupposes an abiding ontic unity also. Therefore, to be a person is to be an indivisible, self-conscious unity that itself exists through, and knows, succession. To deny such personal existence is to deny both the possibility of any knowledge and of any meaningful action. If the knower and actor, and if what is known, were only changing, or were a sheer collective plurality, we could not account for the order presupposed by our knowing and acting.

Focusing on the nature of this personal unity, Bowne argues (on the whole, for he sometimes wavers) that there is no changeless "soul" independent of consciousness but known only in and through its conscious activities. "Each new experience leaves the soul other than it was; but, as it advances from stage to stage it is able to gather up its past and carry it with it, so that, at any point, it possesses all that it had been. It is this fact only which constitutes the permanence and identity of the self."[2] It is this kind of being, a complex, abiding unity of conscious experience, without which neither states of consciousness could become consciousness of states, nor memory and knowledge of change could exist, that constitutes the finite person. "The self itself" is "the surest item of knowledge we possess."[3] It is this quality of unitary being that will serve as the best analogue for the cosmic Unity and Continuity.

THEORY OF KNOWLEDGE

Granted the centrality of the person, Bowne's epistemic dualism has far-reaching effects on his theory of nature, of value, and of God. In knowing, a person refers what is experienced to what is not that experience—that is, to some being or event, past, present, and future—presumptively not "created" by the act of knowing. However, from this experience of objective reference, it does not follow, as realists and materialists seem to assume, that what is referred to as beyond oneself is nonmental. In trying to decide what the nature of the object is, the knower must keep in mind the possibility of error. Hence, Bowne argued, no matter how convinced

---

[2]Borden Parker Bowne, *Metaphysics,* rev. ed. (New York: Harper and Brothers, 1898) 63; and *Introduction to Psychological Theory* (New York: Harper and Brothers, 1896) 28.

[3]Bowne, *Personalism* (Boston: Houghton Mifflin Co., 1908) 88.

the knower is of direct knowledge of the object—finite or divine—the occurrence of error should keep one from holding that the mind and the object known are cognitively one, or ontically identical in any way. Thus, epistemic monism—realistic, idealistic, or rationalistic—must give way to epistemic dualism. What is known must remain open to reasonable interpretation. Indeed, since error cannot occur in what is known, error means that the mind in knowing is no passive recipient.

The person, then, as knower and actor, may be assumed to be in interaction with a world neither merely made nor merely received. Nowhere is this more apparent than in the sensory experiences that hold us to some order we do not ourselves create. Yet, sense experience as such does not yield knowledge; it must be interpreted. The mind is now thrown back upon its own capacities for organizing what is given in sense. The knower does not "embrace" the object, but thinks it in accordance with principles immanent in cognitive activity.

At the same time, from the fact that the knower does construct a known order that enables acting with reasonable confidence in a realm one does not create, it follows that the mind in knowing is not alien to the ultimate nature of the world. There is indeed no way of comparing one's experience with "the thing itself," but this does not mean that we know nothing at all about the nature of what is not ourselves, of the world with which we interact. Nor does it necessarily follow that since all objects are objects of thought, the order inferred must be of the nature of thought.

Bowne, then, was not a victim of what R. B. Perry was to call "the egocentric predicament." Bowne, arguing his particular idealistic conclusions, contended that an idealistic view of reality renders what we know more intelligible than other views. Notable about his argument is the fact that the categories that he expounds in the *Theory of Thought and Knowledge* (1897) as immanent principles of the phenomenal world, he also shows by independent investigation to be most reasonably understood as forms of the cosmic Mind's activity.[4]

The very fact that the object of knowledge must be thought means that the mind, in knowing, organizes the relative flux of sensory impressions given to it, in accordance both with logical principles and with categories actively immanent in the knowing process. Thus "the color sensation must

---

[4]Bowne, *Metaphysics* (1898).

become a sensation of color."[5] Furthermore, "the sensation as occurring has no unity and no identity. As temporal, its successive stages are mutually internal and mutually other, or different. Like an exploding catherine wheel, the occurring impression sputters all around the circle; and when we attempt to grasp it only a mental blur results, unless the mind fixes the dissolving impression into a single and abiding meaning. Only thus can a sensation become an object for thought." The categories in turn "are the organic principles by which experience is built up." Interestingly enough, Bowne thought that the simplest relations possible among objects, likeness and unlikeness, even though they are foundational to all other relations, are not themselves categories. "The essential power of the mind is the power of perceiving likeness and difference."

The categories of time and space are a priori intuitions. Bowne's analysis of the other categories—number, space, motion, quantity, being, quality, identity, causality, necessity, and possibility—is essentially Kantian, but Bowne added the category of purpose not to be found in Kant's *Critique of Pure Reason*.

> The categories of being, space, time, causation, are necessary in order to have any articulate experience whatever. It is through them that we reach intelligible objects, or that world of facts which seems to be given to us ready-made in sense perception. But these categories alone would keep us among isolated things and events. Space and time separate rather than unite; and causality, at least in its mechanical form, provides for no system. For the further systemization and unification of our objects a higher category is needed; and this we find in purpose, or, rather, in the elevation of causality to intelligent and volitional causality, with its implication of plan and purpose.

Bowne's epistemic dualism, on the whole, followed a Kantian pattern, but his strong emphasis on the person as purposer and actor kept him from the conclusion that we know nothing but the world as organized categorically.

Does epistemic dualism apply to self-knowledge? Yes and no. Knowledge claims about oneself (other than "a thinking being exists") can be mistaken, especially since the person is more than "a thinker" alone. All truth claims are therefore subject to further scrutiny. Even with regard

---

[5]Bowne, *Theory of Thought and Knowledge* (New York: Harper and Brothers, 1897) 38, 39, 61, 65, 104.

to specific knowledge about oneself, then, the criterion of truth must remain the person's own appeal to coherence, itself a formulation of the person's experienced reason. If reason is wrong, only a reasoning person can make this judgment. Skepticism and solipsism can never be finally refuted, but if they are defended by reason, a reasoning person does so. Hence, while the decision to trust reason remains an act of faith, it is no blind faith; and insofar as reason is a dimension of self-experience, and appeals to what is experienced, there is no better method or criterion of truth.

THE DOCTRINE OF FREE PERSONAL WILL

There is a third thesis without which Bowne's personalism would become even for him a hollow shell: the doctrine of free personal will. For Bowne, and for theistic personalists generally, there is no meaning to truth and falsity (let alone to moral good and evil) if persons are not free to choose. To say that the human person can arrive at truth, Bowne argued, makes no sense at all if truth is only the outcome of the strongest stream of events in one's experience. The knowing person must hold to the norm of truth in collecting the data that become the evidence for a reasoned conclusion. As Bowne never tired of reminding us, if mechanical causation is the last word about life and existence, then that "last word" about mechanical causation cannot be trusted, for it would itself be the outcome of events and no truer than any other "last word" that is the outcome of mental events. There would be no freedom, no reason, no reasonable conclusion, and no meaning to truth as coherent judgment about the world. In Bowne, then, faith in truth (let alone the possibility of duty) stemmed from a Kantian conviction in the primacy of the practical reason that involves free will. But, enlarging Kantian conviction, Bowne added that will and reason are both partners in the discovery of truth in every dimension of human experience and in human experience as a whole.

In order to dispel the skeptical doubt suggested by his own Kantian epistemology Bowne advanced one basic thesis. If the phenomenal world is the joint product of the knower-actor's interaction with a realm beyond self, how dependable can that appearance be? Or, again, if thought and thing are not identical, if the person's freedom forbids any view of unity with Being, why trust the phenomenal world? Bowne replied: the ventures of the person, active in organizing the phenomenal world, could not succeed as well as they do were the person's nature alien to reality. The conclusion that the phenomenal world must mask the real order of things is incoherent with the fact that intelligent and responsible persons do find support for their thought and action in the ontic structure of things. It is this working harmony between the disciplined cognitive-active efforts of person and reality that prompts the hypothesis that persons are interacting not with a mindless realm but with a supportive cosmic Intelligence. In sum, Bowne argued that if we are to understand why persons can count on their reasonable knowledge and action in the world in which, after all, their efforts are achieved, there is no better postulate than an intelligent Ground as the ultimate source of both the knower-actors and of the ontic realm with which they interact.

THE CONCEPT OF REALITY

General epistemic considerations, then, point to the likelihood that finite, personal intelligence has a counterpart and source in a cosmic Person. However, can this view of the phenomenal world, as the cooperative byproduct of active, finite persons and of an active, cosmic Person, be confirmed by examining the nature of the space, time, and causality, for example, that characterizes our phenomenal world? The answer to this question is part of Bowne's answer to the larger question as to whether there are adequate grounds for supposing that there is a nonmental order (whether dependent on God or not). Bowne's argument at this point sustains a broader conviction that even though the existence of God does not finally depend on any specific view of the natural world, the realistic belief in a nonmental world, independent of a finite and infinite Mind, opens the way for materialist and naturalist claims that finite minds are products of nonmental events, and that the hypothesis of a cosmic Mind is, to say the least, superfluous. Throughout Bowne's metaphysical idealism there runs the theme that no realm of being can be reasonably understood as ultimately autonomous of the cosmic Person, if entities, like space and time and matter, are reified and held to be understandable apart from the activity and purpose of the cosmic Person.

These basic tenets in Bowne's personalistic idealism are grounded ultimately on his contention that to be is to act and to be acted upon. To know a being is to know also the difference it makes. Thus, "thinghood" cannot be inactive substance: the "unities" we find in our world must be causal if they are to be real. But since "causes" do not look but act, the real is not picturable. Our formulations of the real forever remain our convenient generalizations about an unpicturable causal realm.[6] To conceive the underlying, unpicturable, causal realm we find the best experiential clue in the nature of persons.

With this central thesis in mind, we can see why, for Bowne, time and space, the organizing principles of our inner and outer experience, respectively, cannot be held to be real independent of the beings they supposedly relate. Granting that independent space and time create more problems than they solve, they are not intelligible solely as products of human intelligence. After all, spatial and temporal phenomena appear as they do, where and when they do. They must then be related to the nonphenomenal realm. Bowne concludes that the totality of things we know as our phenomenal world is grounded in the unpicturable spaceless and timeless "infinite consciousness and will." Neither space nor time is something that mind is "in." They are forms of organizing our limited experience, by way of which nonspatial volitional Activity expresses itself in an all-embracing, nonsuccessive present. The Ground is no "statically immovable and intellectually monotonous being." It is active nonspatially in the world we best understand as spatial and temporal.

Accordingly, "Nature" cannot be understood as a bulky "substantial" order independent of all minds; yet, its continuity is not a human product. The causal order, known to us phenomenally, is our response to the dynamic, active Person who enables us to experience the order of change that underlies the interplay of events as we know it. Were Nature only a sequential order, with no productive causality supporting it, there would be no reason to trust the world in which we act. "God's cosmic activity is not confined to producing presentations in us, but is rather directed to producing the great cosmic order itself, which thus has existence for him apart from its relation to us."

While Bowne would not consider that he had "proved" this view of Nature as expressing God's idea and deed, he contended that such fixed order, as is assumed in inductive causality, remains opaque if the orderly succession of events is not conceived as the manifestation of one unified, purposeful Creator. Nature, in short, is the activity of the Creator on a

---

[6]Bowne, *Personalism*, 96, 123, 142-51, 160.

cosmic level; the real world is the Creator's thought acted out. The Creator remains immanent in nature but is not exhausted in the system that, like our phenomenal world, is the joint product of finite minds and the Creator's volitional activity.

This "Kantianized Berkeleian" conception of reality was developed as Bowne examined the presuppositions of a philosophy that was advanced as if it were the requirement for scientific progress, namely mechanistic materialism. The mechanist sees Nature as a nonmental realm, composed of matter, motion, force, space, and time, whose laws are "self-executing necessities."[7] But if we ask what the connective principle among these ultimate components of Nature is, we realize that no one of them, nor any collection of them, can justify either the claim to necessary causality or the actual order of the world as we know it in its particular organization. By themselves these elements would never compose the Nature we know. In order for them to become a machinelike Nature, what needs to be added is the very mechanical order that presumably was to explain the regular order of events. At best, then, space, time, matter, motion, and force might be considered components of Nature, just as letters of the alphabet make up literature. But literature, like Nature, is more than letters that in themselves have no meaning.

The illustration is apt, especially if we try to understand the relation of the "physical" world to the lawful realms of life, mind, and society. Bowne reasoned that the continuities and discontinuities observable between the physical, organic, and mental realms are best understood as the working of a self-conscious, creative Person. The materialistic mechanist succeeds only by hypostatizing laws that at best we might find in the phenomenal world, but he fails to explain why these inductive laws and not others are valid.

Again, Nature, Bowne reminded us, is no closed system from which particular events can be deduced. It is a system of law that would indeed be a miracle if there were no abiding purpose uniting the many existents in different ways so that they do form a dynamic universe. Into this system of lawful events, human freedom and intelligence come not as violent eruptions or intruding interventions. Both express the aims of an imma-

---

[7]Bowne, *Metaphysics* (1898), 273.

nent Agent who is not the victim of the world that ultimately expresses the Agent's manifold deed and purpose.

If, then, we stay close to the observed facts and refrain from dogmatizing either in the name of "what science requires" or "what religion demands," we shall take biological evolution as a description of organic changes and not as an extension of "natural causation" or of supernatural intervention. To hypothesize a finite teleological system in which the physical, the organic, and the mental, each with its own kind of order, are related, is only to reject that idol of the speculative den, necessary causation, and to pave the way for a more coherent view of the continuity of law and the concrete system with which we are involved. As Bowne put his view,

> There is no substantial nature, but only natural events; and a natural event is one which occurs in an order of law, or one which we connect with other events according to rule. But this order has no causality in it. In the causal sense it explains nothing. It is only a rule according to which some power beyond it proceeds. Its value for us is practical rather than speculative. But the cause lies beyond the law; this is the supernatural. But this cause is essentially personal and purposive; and the system of law represents only the general form of its free causality. The supernatural, then, is nothing foreign to nature and making occasional raids into nature, but so far as nature as a whole is concerned, the supernatural is the ever-present ground and administrator of the natural. . . . Hence events in general must be said to be at once natural in the mode of their occurrence, and supernatural in their causation.[8]

In such a teleological system, a miracle is not some arbitrary event but one "arriving apart from the accustomed order and defying reduction to rule." At the same time, Bowne thought that it is theoretically and practically foolhardy to appeal to what is "antecedently incredible" to explain any set of events—unless we can specify an ethical goal that will also be consistent with our need to be instructed by the consequences of our actions.

Bowne, then, has found epistemic and metaphysical grounds for postulating a living Will at work in Nature and evolution. It is surprising, but not in fact inconsistent with his methodological caution, to find him re-

---

[8]Ibid., 288-89, 292, 295-96.

luctant to accept the teleological argument for God. For such data as we have does not provide adequate evidence for any specific ethical goal. "Viewed as a whole, the great cosmic drift does not seem to set very decidedly in any direction, and the mass of results seem more like products than purposes." Indeed, belief in a specific cosmic purpose has its special embarrassments. "In particular, it precipitates upon us the great mass of failure, insignificance, and mischief which forms so large a part of visible nature, and demands an interpretation." So Bowne concluded, "The problem of evil . . . admits of no speculative solution at present. We cannot give up our affirmation of purpose, but we must admit that the purposes of the system are mostly inscrutable."

THE INDIVIDUAL PERSON
AND THAT PERSON'S BODY

The body, like any other part of the phenomenal system, is ultimately part of the "deed," of the "silent factor in all finite ongoing."[9] This means that the mind, not caused by the body, is "posited" by God in relation to its organism. In this view, both the unity and the autonomy of the finite mind are recognized, without denying the concomitance observed in the relation of mind and body. Indeed, in holding that "the soul is that with reference to which the organism has its existence," Bowne was also saying that the soul, in interacting with its body, is in fact interacting with the cosmic Person in accordance with the provisions of the orderly system of things, persons, and organic beings.

One might wish for unwavering clarity as Bowne sought to protect the individuality and irreducible quality of the finite person and yet relate the person to the organic body within the order of Nature as instituted by the Person. Bowne was not concerned with laying a foundation for belief in immortality that governs his thought, since it was his view that no metaphysical doctrine could by itself justify belief in the immortality of the soul. His conception was governed by his view of what the data reasonably allow.

More crucial to Bowne's thinking than is often realized was his almost passing comment that "A thing must always be allowed to be what it seems unless reasons can be given for going behind the appearance."

---

[9]Ibid., 369, 332.

This principle that dominated his interpretation of free will, as we have seen, dominates his approach to the truth about mind. It is this view of an indubitably known self-conscious unity that lay behind Bowne's refusal, already noted, to think of mind either as "a bare substance or as blank subject," or as a "stream of consciousness," in order to account for the identity of the successive states.

In defending this intrinsic unity against the contention that self-identity consists in successive states of consciousness, Bowne tended to speak soul-substance language, and in this he was encouraged by his view of the phenomenal character of time. Still, his stress was unmistakable; a stream of thought cannot itself account for identity since successive states are after all mutually external to each other. "[T]he consciousness in which identity resides is not the particular states nor the flowing stream, but something continuous and active. It must comprise the states in its own unity; it must distinguish itself from them as their abiding subject, and must work them over into the forms of intelligence."[10]

Something like this view guided Bowne as he boldly faced a problem that is difficult for any philosophy that does not allow words or labels to substitute for ideas, namely, that of explaining how the mind can be defined as a self-identifying consciousness in view of intervening periods of unconsciousness. As Bowne said, a "completely satisfactory answer is hard to find." Since the mind's body is phenomenal, Bowne could not say that during intermittence the mind is the body. Furthermore, since he could not accept any "backlying substance" or any "changeless cores and abstract identities," he now clearly fell back upon his earlier metaphysical contention. Minds are different from things, whose identity is ultimately the idea of the Mind that expresses itself in them. Minds have existence for themselves; therefore, what happens to them during periods of unconsciousness? For an explanation Bowne could turn nowhere other than to the Person who is responsible for the mind to begin with, and who can now be said to reconstitute it under conditions that accord with the system of natural order. The activity of the organism cannot account for the self-identifying unity of the mind to begin with, let alone during intermittence. The actual facts as Bowne saw them are these: (1) The finite mind needs its body as "the fixed system for receiving and giving impulses." (2) The actual mind

---

[10]Ibid., 332, 340-41, 346.

and body are conditioned by each other ''in the sense of mutual concomitance in their respective changes.'' (3) The relation of mind and body is contingent, that is, neither is dependent on the other for its existence, and there is no reason for supposing that the service performed by the body now could not be performed ''in other and better ways.''

Bowne, once more, would not, in the face of serious difficulty, allow himself to resort to ontic additions that were more picturable than enlightening. He preferred to accept the mystery of intermittence as existence in a cosmic Mind (that is, capable of positing finite minds to begin with) than to suppose that the organism can account for it at all. He has already rejected the reduction of mental being and activities to the bodily, even though reduction seems easier. But reduction obscures the real mystery.

We must realize that, in this or any view, interaction is mysterious. Whether interaction be between like or unlike existents, mystery resides in how beings can be themselves as they affect and are affected. Bowne held that it is a gratuitous mystery to postulate a sheer plurality of independent beings that are presumably without a system and then add that ''by interaction'' they produce the bodies and minds we know. Beings that are in no way responsible for each other's existence, and yet are related to each other in dependable ways, must not be endowed surreptitiously with powers they do not have. The system in which they participate must be unified by some being related to each and with other attributes that render the systematic order intelligible. This consideration counts when the unity of personal experience is being considered in view of its possible relations to the body and to whatever is involved in periods of intermittence.

The basic problem of continuing unity and interaction cannot be resolved by appeal to the kind of organization that animal existence may be presumed to have, for the same problems reoccur there. In Bowne's rather sketchy view, the behavior of animal bodies bespeaks an inner life of feeling and emotion comparable to human ones. Animals are not automatons. Thus, Bowne seems to grant animals a unity of mental being that is concomitant with their bodies.

In other words, the unity and continuity of subpersonal or personal minds, let alone the organization of their bodies, are not explicable by any aggregate of elements, be they molecular or psychic. So Bowne turned to the cosmic Intelligence as the source of mental unities wherever and under whatever conditions we observe them to occur. In the expanded earlier edition of *Metaphysics* there might seem to be some hint of autonomy for the body in some passages: "God, who is the omnipresent factor in all on-going, posits with the growing organism a new being, which develops along with it as the subject of the apparent thought and sensibility. . . . We hold, then, that the creative action of God is not confined to the production of the physical elements . . . but that it includes also the production of animal and human minds according to that order which he has adopted as the norm of his action."[11] In the end, however, Bowne persisted in the phenomenalistic view. In the revised edition, speaking of the human mind and its interaction with the body, he concluded,

> In this view the soul is posited by the infinite, and the body is simply an order or system of phenomena connected with the soul which reproduces to some extent features of the general phenomenal order, and which also expresses an order of concomitance with the mental life. Thus it becomes a visible expression of personality, a means of personal communion, and also a means for controlling to some extent the inner life. The concomitance is the only interaction there is; and its determining ground must be sought in the plan and agency of the infinite. . . . Each [soul and body] is adjusted to the other in accordance with the plan of the whole; . . . and any dynamic relation which we may affirm must be seen to be only a form of speech.[12]

What then does Bowne's view of the mind's interaction with the body come to? *The soul is "posited," but the body must be seen as the phenomenal expression of the Person's nature as a whole,* and with allowance for the scope of personal freedom. This, I take it, means that the Infinite makes those changes in the body willed by the Infinite Mind in accordance with the laws that express the total Infinite Will at this point. If this unpicturable view seems strange to "common sense," since it withdraws the possibility of each body's being either an independent system of living "selves" or of molecules, we should recall that in any view the existence of the body depends upon its interaction with Nature. If we imbue Nature with special powers to regulate interaction, we are in fact granting it the powers and plan that Bowne granted only to Mind as it expresses its will in the complex orders we know as the realm of Nature. To say that we interact with

---

[11]Bowne, *Metaphysics: A Study of First Principles* (New York: Harper and Brothers, 1882) 341.

[12]Bowne, *Metaphysics* (1898), 343, 368.

our bodies and with each other and things "according to natural law" may be to describe the facts in an impersonal way, but it should not hide from us the more intelligible dynamics of thought and deed of the Infinite Will at work as Nature.

We may now review, in this larger metaphysical setting, Bowne's view of the nature of the self-identifying person and of the continuity of its being insofar as it is related to its body and the world. The origin and destiny of each mind, Bowne maintained, remains with God, whatever its "physical" and "biological" parentage. "Parents are not creators. They and their deeds are only the occasions on which the world-ground produces effects and introduces new factors into the system." What we do know about the mind in this life takes us no further than the observable relations between the mental, the physiological, and the physical. Nothing about these relations shows that destruction of the body implies the destruction of the mind. Yet in the idealistic universe Bowne had in mind, it is not unreasonable to say, "The soul, when the body fails, has not to go wandering through space to find another home: it is continuously comprised in the thought and activity of the infinite. God gave it life, and if he wills he will maintain it." No metaphysical argument demonstrates that the mind is immortal.[13]

THE DOCTRINE OF GOD, THE ULTIMATE

It is here that we make, with Bowne, the transition to his philosophy of religion, including the Christian faith. With his epistemic and metaphysical analyses in mind he said, "Speculation makes room for belief, but for positive faith we must fall back on the demands of our moral and religious nature or on some word of revelation, or on both together."[14] In *Theism* (1902), which is the revision of *Philosophy of Theism* (1887), we see the cosmic Intelligence of Bowne's philosophical investigations become the person-al God whose nature grounds the whole of the human quest for goodness, truth, beauty, and for religious satisfaction. Far from "engaging in a polemic against logic and metaphysics," Bowne was nevertheless convinced that philosophical reason at critical points presupposes

---

[13]Ibid., 375, 279.

[14]Ibid., 379.

"the practical certainties" of daily life, certainties that express the whole nature of humans' affective tendencies, moral life, and yearning for perfection, as well as cognitive needs. For Bowne, in short, the justification of basic theistic tenets was not a philosophical stepsister. Bowne sometimes seemed to be scornful of the sense-bound materialism that claims to be the proper undergirding of science, and of the rationalism that demands deductive demonstration of truth claims. Such scorn was probably his response to what he took to be their overweening arrogance and their failure to realize that they too rest on postulates. "In every department our knowledge is patchwork, and rests on assumption." "If theism is an hypothesis, atheism is no less so." Believer and unbeliever must realize that critical reflection comes onto the scene of human development after a great deal of living has already gone on.[15]

It follows that, be it in religion or in science, immature beginnings must be evaluated in light of more mature development in the total life of persons. The religious life in particular, however, must be seen as "a function of the entire man" and not be viewed as independent of the developing emotional, aesthetic, and ethical demands of human beings. At the same time, only shallow conceptions suppose that the task of philosophy is to discourage beliefs that cannot be demonstrated. In the last analysis, the philosophical aim is to satisfy especially those interests and satisfactions that—like the catholic beliefs in humanity—encourage us to live most fully "in default of positive disproof."[16]

It is these methodological tenets, so similar to much in William James's "Will to Believe" and "The Sentiment of Rationality," that Bowne kept in mind as he considered the "arguments" for God that do not depend upon more subtle epistemic and metaphysical considerations. With Everyman, then, we may assume that things affect each other and are interrelated parts of a comprehensive, causal system. "Everyman lives on the assumption that what takes place occurs uniformly and not at random. The problem is to understand what is buried in this conviction that all things interact as parts of a dependable causal system. Observation, after all, does not show that events imply each other. Yet, if we assert that 'in the beginning' the many simply existed in mutual indifference, how can we explain

---

[15]Bowne, *Theism* (New York: The American Book Co., 1902) 33-34, 42.

[16]Ibid., 9, 18.

the interacting order in which nothing can 'be all that it is apart from all the others.' "[17] Indeed, what reasonable grounds can keep us from hypothesizing that individuals are related to each other *because* each of them is dependent on a common Ground that, however distinct from them, mediates their mutual relationships?

Once we realize that the One, in order to be an adequate source of order, must not be under restrictions imposed upon it from without, we can affirm that the One is absolute and infinite. The attributes of absoluteness and infinity are ways of accounting for relations and facts about the world and humans—for example, their existence in an interactive, uniformly dependable system. The existence of God can be reached not deductively but cumulatively. One conclusion cannot be derived from another without pointing also to the data it illuminates better than any alternative.

If indeed Nature is an orderly system, is it reasonable to consider Nature the work of mindless existents without guiding Intelligence? If human mathematical intelligence can help us understand entities in space, what good reason do we have for saying that in themselves these entities, part of no intelligent whole, are ultimately a collocation of aimless beings? Materialism, Bowne persisted, seems plausible only because powers not observed, laws not there, are bootlegged into the "System." We must remember that our point of departure is neither mechanism nor purpose, but change according to rule. But once we realize that intelligence purposely works toward ends in as orderly and dependable a way as possible, while nonintelligence never explains purpose except by verbal magic, we can more reasonably refer to cosmic Intelligence as both the interrelation of the orders of Nature and the intelligence that explores and counts on the regularity they exhibit.

Bowne emphasized that the teleological argument he defended was not one built upon outstanding or fascinating instances of contrivance in the physical, biological, and psychological world. Indeed, all such "evidences" of cosmic design would never support the God of theism. But the case is weaker if we fail to realize that the Designer remains constantly involved in the order of achievement.

But how shall we deal with the Humean objection that since we ourselves do not observe alternative worlds being made, we cannot know

---

[17]Ibid., 57.

whether the hypothesis of a purposive Cosmos-Maker explains the world we are in better than the hypothesis of mechanical causation? The skeptic claims that analogical thinking from human intelligence to an intelligent Purposer must break under the burden of moving from a known to an unknown that is simply not open to our gaze.

Bowne granted that we do not behold different universes being made. But he insisted that our task remains one of choosing between hypotheses regarding this universe. No hypothesis has more than the interrelated realms of the inorganic, the organic, and human intelligence to go on. Any thesis assumes universal validity for itself at this point. The central question is whether cosmic mechanism enables us to explain the interrelated realms more reasonably than a cosmic Intelligence that is working its will in and through these interrelated orders of beings. If a personalistic theism does furnish greater basis for our confidence in the order of Nature and the mandates of person-al experience, why withdraw the hypothesis, especially since the opposing hypothesis makes its own truth an unnecessary mystery? On his own grounds, why should the skeptic's hypothesis be more worthy of truth than the believer's?

Granted an intelligent Designer at work in the total evolutionary process, does the "observed" in biological evolution rule out the notion of special creation? Not at all, if we think concretely. The composer of the later parts of a symphony that are continuous with earlier parts is still creating new musical components consistent with the whole being produced. Whether we speak of the successive interactions within the organic world, or the successive "ascending" orders in the biological evolutionary scale, the existence of new beings, however "continuous" with the old, needs to be explained. "Free intelligence is the condition of any real progress; and progress itself, if it be anything more than a meaningless stir of world-substance, cannot be defined without reference to teleology."[18]

But how far can we press the analogy from finite to infinite intelligence? Bowne had no delusions as to the limits of our knowledge of the ultimate—and in particular of the how of the relations that we depend on. All the more scrupulously, then, must we relate analogical reasoning to the supporting data. Failure to do so results, for example, in substituting an "inscrutable transcendental" Being for Person, and, in so doing, mouth-

---

[18]Ibid., 109.

ing a phrase without experiential referent. Bowne would, of course, grant that the infinite Person may have characteristics that have little or no analogy in the finite. We cannot assume, for example, that cosmic reason must be confined to the discursive reasoning of finite persons. But if "inscrutable transcendental" is to suggest some superpersonal quality, we should be told what it is, and in what direction to look for its meaning.

It is this demand—that attributes be related to evidence—that lies behind Bowne's unwillingness to move from cosmic Intelligence to a good God on the basis of the evidence for teleology in the world. Interestingly enough, Bowne claims that "experience shows that we are largely unable to trace the purpose in cosmic arrangements and events."[19] At the same time, he warns us that we should not allow natural evils, which indeed must not be minimized, to be used as counterevidence against either God's goodness or his omnipotence.

Bowne, despite his doubts about the adequacy of the evidence in nature, despite his affirmation that God's attributes should be adequately confirmed in the observed and experienced realms, at this point affirmed, "Its [God's] unchanging fullness yet without monotony, the structure of the absolute reason also which determines the eternal contents of the divine thought, the timeless and absolute self-possession—how mysterious all this is, how impenetrable to our profoundest reflection." And, he added, "Here we reach a point where the speculation of philosophy must give place to the worship and adoration of religion."[20]

Is there then, in the last analysis, only a juxtaposition of the philosophical and the ethico-religious quests? While Bowne at critical points does allow ethico-religious demands to settle a question that might not yield readily to his solution, his procedure generally is (a) to lay epistemic and metaphysical groundwork for our thought about the nature of God and God's relation to the world and persons and (b) to rely upon ethical and religious insights to help in the further definition of divine aims. This procedure underlies Bowne's examination of the meaning of attributes that are common to the cosmic Person and to the God of religion.

(a) The *unity* of God and the unity of the personal World-Ground are identical. For there is no unity more real than that exemplified in the per-

---

[19]Ibid., 170.

[20]Ibid., 171.

son; indeed, any other model for unity is only makeshift until we can make our way to the unity exemplified in persons. An ultimate plurality leaves such organization as we observe in the world, and which we presuppose in thought and action, an arbitrary mystery. The unity of a personal God, free to posit and relate to creation, justifies the faith underlying our thought, our action, and our religious experience.

(b) Bowne's view of the *unchangeability* of God reveals the recurring ambivalence in his thinking about time. Clearly untenable is an "absolutely rigid substance," some sheer identity that "would contain no explanation of the advancing cosmic movement, and would admit of no change in action and knowledge." Indeed, "the changelessness we need is not the rigidity of a logical category but the self-identity and self-equality of intelligence." So Bowne rests with "the constancy and continuity of the divine nature which exists through all the divine acts as their law and source."

(c) The *omnipresence* of God cannot be adequately defined without reference to a metaphysics of Nature. Since Bowne held that space is phenomenal, omnipresence means not that God is extended everywhere in space, but that God's active being is present immediately and completely in the world.

(d) If the thrust of omnipresence is to reject limitations in the *here* and *there* of spatiality, the thrust of *eternity* is to deny the *now but not then* suggested by time. The concept of eternity focuses on the fact that the Ground of all being must be unbegun and unending, must changelessly know change, and never be its victim.

Bowne saw nothing but darkness if anything were to undermine the crucial epistemic and metaphysical thesis that change and temporal relations can have meaning only for something not-changing. So he finally points to "life," to "the living experience of intelligence," to suggest the way out of his theoretical quandary.

(e) The *omniscience* of God cannot be understood by "etymologizing." God, no more than finite persons, can think contradiction. God knows all that is expressed in the order of Nature; God can know all the choices open to free, finite persons; but God cannot foresee the specific acts a free person will make.

Interestingly enough, at this point, Bowne raised a question not usually raised: Does God know the specific knowledge of a finite mind *as* that finite mind is experiencing it, in view of the fact that "the thing itself is realized only in immediate experience"? How can an infinite being know what a finite being knows? Bowne realized that "to press this difficulty would make an impassable gulf between the finite and Infinite." So, Bowne concluded, we must attribute to an infinite and all-knowing God modes of knowing that we cannot comprehend. God must comprehend finite experience even if God does not participate therein.

(f) Finally, to attribute *omnipotence* to God is to say that God is not restricted by anything either beyond or in his nature. Accordingly, God is not constrained "by" truth, nor does he make it up arbitrarily; neither truth nor rational principles are to be viewed in abstraction. Furthermore, in willing free, finite persons into existence, God is not constrained by anything beyond God's self, whose willing is limited only in accordance with the goodness and rationality intrinsic to God's nature. God's willing does not create either God's goodness or the validity of the principles of reason.[21]

The meaning of God, the Person, is Bowne's determination to avoid faulty abstractions and any view of the attributes as independent of each other, or, finally, in abstraction from the drift of one's epistemology and metaphysics. That is, what it means to be God is thought and deed. In this context, Bowne stressed that the world is neither "a part of God," nor "an emanation," nor something that God creates "out of" nothing.

Consequently, it is a groundless interpretation of Bowne's personalistic idealism to suppose either that the world we know is God or that the world we know is no more than an intersubjective human product. For both personalistic realist and personalistic idealist the world cannot be understood apart from God's activity. But Bowne was convinced that by viewing the realm of Nature as a system that has some existence independent of God, rather than *being* God's activity, the realist opens the way to simplistic conceptions of God—for example, that God and the world can be understood apart from each other.

---

[21]Ibid., 178-79, 181, 184-86, 188, 202-204.

(g) At the same time, still attacking abstract thinking about God's relation to the world, and to persons, Bowne asked us to conceive of God's *creation* of free persons not as a creation of something from nothing. No being can take a "mass of nothing" and make persons (or the world) out of it. Nature is God's deed, but God is not defined by that system alone. The world and persons are not simply "parts" or "modes" of the God who transcends them. For God delegates to persons an autonomy that Nature does not have. Consequently, while the perfect Person is always actively at work in Nature, and responsive to the finite persons in relation to the system of Nature, God does not arbitrarily invade the scope of persons' freedom.

Can God be God without a world? The God that Bowne envisaged is "not a God who blocks existence by absorbing all things into himself, but the living and immanent God in whom we live and move and have our being, and whose tender mercies are over all his works; a God also in whom revelation and mystery mingle, who comes near enough for love, and rises high enough for awe and voiceless adoration." For God to be is to be active in the realm that expresses God's thought and deed and that finite persons depend upon for the realization of their created self-identity.[22]

(h) Yet, granted that there is relative human autonomy in an orderly world, on what grounds may God be said to be *good,* especially if we do examine the world order and human history? As we have already noted, for Bowne, a teleological interpretation of history rests on data so fragmentary that no clear direction is discernible. He observed that the mix of good and evil simply will not justify the goodness of God. Thus, on purely "inductive" grounds, the "meaningless aspects of existence, the cosmic labor which seems to end in nothing," suggests "a being either morally indifferent, or morally imperfect, or morally good but limited by some insuperable necessity which forbids anything better than our rather shabby universe." Yet, Bowne added, "But the mind is not satisfied to take this road."[23]

It is at such points in the argument that Bowne asked us to consider what the task of philosophizing is and to stand back and see what the al-

---

[22]Ibid., 218.

[23]Ibid., 258.

ternatives are, without assuming that the burden of proof must fall on the theist—as if some other alternative is already better established.

> In the physical realm disorder and unintelligibility dispute the reign of law and intelligence. In the moral order also, we find clouds and darkness as well as the throne of justice and judgment. But in both realms conviction of the universality of the intellectual and the moral order grows with the deepening life of the race . . . the deepest things are not reached by formal syllogizing but by the experiences of life itself. . . . And in all reasoning upon reality the same thing is true. There is an element of immediacy back of all inferential conviction which logic only very imperfectly reproduces. . . . Here the whole man enters into the argument.

This, however, does not mean that the concrete incidence of evil in an individual life will not often be such as to create doubt about God's goodness. Hence Bowne concluded that in the end the question is "not whether experience proves the goodness and righteousness of God, but whether it is compatible with faith therein."[24]

The remainder of Bowne's argument for the goodness as well as the other attributes of God presupposed this theoretical and practical posture. With his interpretation of the good for humans (elaborated in his *Principles of Ethics,* 1892) in mind, Bowne asked whether what we do know about the world supports persistent and underlying faith in God's goodness. Assuming what is there argued, that the essential good in human life consists not of the experience of passive pleasure but of "conscious self-development, growing self-possession, conquest, the successful putting forth of energy and the resulting sense of larger life," the case is far from hopeless. Again, "if the aim of the human world is a moral development for which men themselves are to be largely responsible, working out of their salvation," then the organization of Nature may be viewed not as "finished perfection" but as "furnishing the conditions of a true human development," as well as providing the "possibility of being made indefinitely better."

The dysteleology and the mix of good and evil in world-history kept Bowne from affirming God's goodness, if those grounds are considered in abstraction from the requirements of moral (and religious) ideals. But "So

---

[24]Ibid., 259, 263.

long as man is as he is, none of the general conditions of existence could be changed without disaster. The dark things also have their uses in the moral order.'' On the whole, Bowne's absolutistic theism rested on his morally justified conviction that, even given the cataclysms and eruptions to which humans are subject, Nature is not so hostile that free persons are not sustained as they develop a mutually supportive moral order in loyalty to each other and their God.[25]

CONCLUSION

Bowne's work as a whole was inspired by a relentless meliorism. Rooted in the ''inextinguishable hopefulness of humanity,'' such meliorism is no steady growth in scientist, prophet, saint, or philosopher. In the last analysis, it needs the nurturing and encouragement of the faith ''that we are in our Father's hands, and that, having brought us thus far on our Godward way, he may well be trusted to finish the work he has begun.'' No product of deductive reason, like the ideals of the human rational venture, meliorism springs from nonrational human nature, even as it inspires the human concern to avoid self-contradiction and dogmatism. Bowne's own strong character and his dominant concern as a philosopher were informed by his conviction that the total human venture should be allowed to remain a venture in soul-making. Bowne's underlying crusade against atheism was against what he considered its unjustified and overconfident denials. ''Atheism is quite successful in making grimaces at theism; but it limps terribly in its own account of things.'' ''Atheism must justify itself on its own premises and on its own principles, if it is to be a rational theory of life.'' But, as his own struggle in behalf of academic and scholarly freedom against ecclesiastical dogmatism showed, he insisted that faith live in constant interaction with the changing horizons of culture.[26]

It should be noted that for this theistic idealist, human obligations, such as justice, truth, benevolence, and gratitude do not depend for their validity and abiding quality upon the existence of God. ''There are absolute moral intuitions. If no one regarded them, they would still be valid. Certainly, if they depend at all on theism, it must be indirectly.'' This means

---

[25]Ibid., 275, 278, 281.

[26]Ibid., 283-84, 293, 297; See also McConnell, *Bowne*.

that the autonomy of the moral life does not warrant our conceiving of the ethical venture in abstraction from the general conception of the human place in the nature of things. Each dimension of human existence must be confronted by the convictions and ''conclusions'' of other dimensions before it can be a guide of life. A general theory of reality should not be developed without considering intellectual and moral parasitism.[27]

Bowne's personalistic idealism and theism were products, then, of an experientialism in which reason, as a concern for the whole, operates. Bowne's idealism was his own synthesis of trends that were expressed particularly in the empiricism of Berkeley, in the Kantian synthesis of the pure and practical reason, and in the fundamental Platonic conviction that in the end the human mind finds in the good the source of both being and being known. A rationalism that results in a unified system of reality at the expense of personal individuality and freedom, a mysticism that conceives of the highest moment of being as a loss of personal unity, an empiricism that confines truth to the restrictive demands of the possibilities of sensory experience, an ecclesiasticism that ultimately protects itself in the supposed sanctuaries of faith—all these, Bowne was convinced, must be saved from their own tendencies to minimize the insurgent demands of the creative human person. Whatever the disagreements among Bowne's followers, they never lose sight of this central conviction of Bowne.

---

[27]Bowne, *Theism,* 296.

Albert Cornelius Knudson:
Person and Theologian

S. Paul Schilling

The life and work of Albert Cornelius Knudson spanned eight decades, from his birth on 23 January 1873 to his death on 28 August 1953. I knew him over a period of twenty-seven years as teacher, dean, correspondent, and friend.

ALBERT C. KNUDSON: THE PERSON

The son of Asle and Susan Knudson, and the fourth of nine children, Albert was born in Grandmeadow, Minnesota, where his father was pastor of the Methodist Episcopal church. He earned the A.B. degree at the University of Minnesota in 1893 at the age of twenty, and his S.T.B. at Boston University in 1896. As Jacob Sleeper Fellow of the School of Theology he continued graduate study at Boston University for one year, concentrating on philosophical studies with Borden Parker Bowne. In 1897-1898 he pursued studies in New Testament, church history, and systematic theology at the universities of Jena and Berlin, Germany.

Knudson began his teaching career at Iliff School of Theology in Denver in 1898, with church history as his chief field. In June 1900 he received his Ph.D. from Boston University in philosophy, and on 7 July 1900 he married Mathilde Johnson, daughter of John H. Johnson, a Norwegian-born minister, and his wife. Then followed teaching assignments in philosophy and English Bible at Baker University (1900-1902) and Allegheny College (1902-1906).

In 1906 Knudson became professor of Hebrew and Old Testament exegesis at Boston University, succeeding his former teacher Hinckley G. Mitchell. In 1910 he was granted leave to pursue special Old Testament studies at the University of Berlin. Borden Parker Bowne died in 1910, and in 1911 Knudson was invited to succeed him as professor of philosophy. However, the time and energy he had already invested in the Old Testament field led him to feel that a shift to philosophy would be unwise. Nevertheless, an understanding was reached that on the retirement of Henry C. Sheldon from the chair of systematic theology Knudson would succeed him. This new phase of his career began in 1921. In the meantime he had written three books on the Old Testament and made other important scholarly contributions to the field.

In 1926 Knudson was invited to become dean of the School of Theology. He hesitated, fearing serious interference with his scholarly writing, but accepted when assured of substantial administrative assistance. The soundness of this decision is confirmed by the fact that during his tenure as dean, which continued until 1938, he produced four works in philosophical and systematic theology to add to *Present Tendencies in Religious Thought* (1924). These were *The Philosophy of Personalism* (1927), *The Doctrine of God* (1930), *The Doctrine of Redemption* (1933), and *The Validity of Religious Experience.* (1937).

In 1936 the Century of Service campaign of the School of Theology was launched, designed to reach its climax in the centennial year 1939. Due to impaired health and increased administrative burdens, Knudson asked to retire as dean in 1938, when he was sixty-five. However, he continued his full-time teaching responsibilities until 1943, and his scholarly writing until very near the end of his earthly life. Three books appeared during this period: *The Principles of Christian Ethics* (1943), *The Philosophy of War and Peace* (1947), and *Basic Issues in Christian Thought* (1950).

In December 1948 Albert Knudson was deeply saddened by the death of his wife, who had been an invalid for many years. Mrs. Stella Peterson, a widowed sister, who had come to live with the Knudsons when Mrs. Knudson was in the hospital, stayed on thereafter, and Albert continued to reside in his Cambridge apartment until his death in August 1953.

I now turn to examine somewhat more carefully several aspects of Knudson's life and character, thinking of him as teacher, scholar, churchman, administrator, and warm-hearted person.

Teacher

Knudson was completely at home in the classroom, where he could share the insights gained from years of painstaking study and reflection. He used the lecture method primarily, but he was always ready to discuss informally questions raised by his students. His presentations, based on careful preparation, were systematic and lucid, moving logically from point to point and from premises to conclusions. Convinced of the truth of the positions he championed, he could be scathingly critical of alternatives. For example, he often took pains to expose what he termed the "amazing superficiality" of the "Chicago school" of humanistic naturalism. However, he was equally ready to state why he regarded such views as wanting and to offer rational support for his own. Serious students who sat under his teaching were made aware of the important theological issues and challenged to think their way through to defensible conclusions.

Scholar

Throughout his life Knudson was a diligent, disciplined scholar. Possessed of great native ability, his well-stored mind persisted in raising and seeking answers to difficult questions, and he steadfastly resisted the appeal of competing interests. Fortunately, during his deanship he had the support of an exceptionally qualified assistant, Miss Helen Dame, who bore competently many administrative responsibilities. Often he was able to leave the office at noon and spend the rest of the day researching and writing.

This determination remained evident during his retirement. In a letter written in 1948 he said, "I keep as busy as ever, at least so it seems, with lecturing and book writing, and the continued activity apparently agrees with me." In 1952 he was working on a new problem. Responding to a letter of mine seeking counsel on a vocational decision, he wrote in April of that year, only sixteen months before his death, "I am plugging away on 'The Political-religious Problem in America,' but am finding it a slow and difficult task." He was never able to complete this project. Significantly, much of his scholarly work during his last decade dealt with ethical issues—a new emphasis, though a natural outgrowth of his earlier work.

Churchman

The child of dedicated Methodist parents, and raised in a parsonage, Albert Knudson was a man of deep and genuine religious experience. Midway in his college years he decided to become a minister, and the religious conviction that led to this decision was central throughout his life. Elmer A. Leslie, who knew him over many years as his student, pastor, and colleague, testifies to Knudson's regularity in worship at Harvard-Epworth Methodist Church in Cambridge, and to his positive Christian witness in the weekly prayer meeting.[1] I recall that when Knudson led worship at the School of Theology the pews were filled with students who had learned that they could confidently expect to be led by him into the renewing presence of God.

Knudson also served the wider church in important ways. The New England Southern Conference of the Methodist Episcopal Church elected him to membership in two General Conferences and to the Uniting Conference of 1939, which merged three long-divided Methodist bodies. Many articles from his pen appeared in the *Methodist Review, Religion in Life, Zion's Herald,* and other religious journals. He was also one of a number of theological seminary professors who conducted units in the so-called Conference Course of Study required for many years of ministerial candidates who lacked seminary training. He was an official Methodist delegate at the Edinburgh Conference on Faith and Order in 1937.

Administrator

Administration was never first in either his interests or his abilities. Nevertheless, his selfless willingness to serve where he was needed led him to devote more than twelve years to the deanship. Elmer Leslie testifies that Knudson brought to this task "mature wisdom, good common sense, and long experience in theological teaching."[2] He so identified himself with the school he loved that during his administration it gained considerable

---

[1]Elmer A. Leslie, "Albert Cornelius Knudson, the Man," *Personalism in Theology,* ed. Edgar S. Brightman (Boston: Boston University Press, 1943) 19. I am indebted to this article for much of the information contained in the first part of this essay.

[2]Ibid., 17.

financial support for both current expenses and the Century of Service campaign inaugurated in 1936. Through his academic leadership he won the wholehearted support of students, professors, and the general church. His leadership contributed significantly to the achievement of higher educational standards and performance.

Warm-hearted Person

Knudson embodied his personalistic world view in his own personality, as well as in his interpersonal relationships. His life was a multifaceted pursuit and realization of the whole range of human values. He was not content only to challenge the minds of his students; he cared about them as persons. Knowing him as their friend, they could refer to him affectionately as "Knudie." I distinctly remember one sentence from a chapel talk of his on the task of the Christian ministry. "The minister's passion," he said with deep emotion, "is compassion"—a conviction abundantly illustrated in his life.

The feeling aspect of Knudson's character appears vividly in a letter he wrote to me in January 1949, responding to a letter of mine occasioned by the death of his wife Mathilde. Referring to the pain of parting after forty-nine and a half years of marriage, he said, "The past five weeks have been the saddest of my entire life. . . . I am not infrequently weighed down with a sad and heavy heart." Yet, he added, "the sympathy of friends and our common faith have done much to ease the burden of grief." It is worth recalling also that in 1933 he dedicated his *Doctrine of Redemption* to Mathilde, referring to her sympathetic cooperation during many years of illness. Knudson was much more than an intellectual champion of Christian faith. His life was a persuasive manifestation of its meaning and truth.

ALBERT C. KNUDSON: PHILOSOPHICAL THEOLOGIAN

Personalism

Although in 1911 Knudson had declined an invitation to succeed Bowne as professor of philosophy, when in 1921 he shifted his teaching field from Old Testament to systematic theology, he quickly began to devote his major attention to philosophical research. A result was the publication in 1927 of *The Philosophy of Personalism,* which manifested the concern that was to dominate the remainder of his career. Henceforth, he would seek to expound personal idealism as the philosophy best qualified to provide an intellectual foundation for Christian theology. Here he defined personalism as

> that form of idealism which gives equal recognition to both the pluralistic and monistic aspects of experience and which finds in the conscious unity, identity, and free activity of personality the key to the nature of reality and the solution of the ultimate problems of philosophy.[3]

Already during his college years Knudson had rejected as untenable common sense realism as well as naturalism in both its materialist and positivist forms. Neo-Hegelian idealism he found impressive but vague, abstract, and confusing.[4] The end of his college studies left him "in a fog" regarding his worldview, and his seminary studies brought only partial clarification. But his year of graduate study with Bowne changed everything. Here he found a keen and profound mind and a system of thought that matched his own needs. He discovered "the conditions of a sound metaphysic" that guided him in all his subsequent thinking. He describes the year as "a veritable *Aufklärung*," bringing "a mental relief and an intellectual illumination . . . akin to a redemptive experience."[5]

According to Knudson, if we take personality as the key to reality, we gain our soundest understanding of the ultimate problems of both epistemology and metaphysics. With respect to the former, the best explanation of the trustworthiness of our knowledge of the external world is that the creative activity that grounds the world is personal and intelligent, "casting the world in the mold of thought." More broadly, belief in the intelligibility of the universe implies an intelligent Author; our knowledge of nature is possible because mind is active at both ends. Rooted in thought,

---

[3]*The Philosophy of Personalism*, 87. This and all other books by Knudson were published by Abingdon or Abingdon-Cokesbury. The dates appear in the body of the text of this essay. A reprint of *The Philosophy of Personalism* was published by Boston University Press in 1949.

[4]Knudson, "A Personalistic Approach to Theology," *Contemporary American Theology*, ed. Vergilius Ferm (New York: Round Table Press, 1932) 221-22.

[5]Ibid., 223. See also *Present Tendencies in Religious Thought*, 227; *Basic Issues in Christian Thought*, 45.

nature conveys meanings, and the thought of finite minds enables them to receive and understand those meanings.

In metaphysics, Knudson believed that personalism meets better than any competitor the mind's demand for a causal ground that is distinct from the world yet maintains its own identity through change. An impersonal cause would disappear in its effect, leaving reality without a sustaining cause. Only a personal being can persist through change and still remain itself. The abiding cause of the cosmic process is thus best conceived as the energizing of the divine will. Without the continuous activity of God, the material world would have no existence.

A related question concerns the essential structure of ultimate reality. Here we are confronted by seeming contradictions (Kantian antinomies) like those between unity and plurality and identity and change. Seen as abstract, impersonal principles, such opposites are mutually exclusive. But if we conceive of ultimate reality in personal terms the problem is solved. A person experiences itself as one, yet it does many things without losing its unity. It is also conscious of its own identity over time, while also aware that it is constantly changing. Personality thus has the unique capacity to combine in its own experience identity with change and unity with plurality. How this is possible we do not know, but it is a given fact. Hence, if we conceive of ultimate reality in personal terms we find the best—Knudson says the only—solution of this age-old problem. With Bowne, Knudson affirmed that the categories of thought do not explain intelligence but are explained by it.[6]

Personalism and Christian Theology

Since Knudson was known primarily not as a philosopher but as a Christian theologian, the question naturally arises as to the relation between his personalist philosophy and his theology. Some critics have held that his personalism controlled his interpretation of Christian faith; others have believed that it was basically the tool of his religious belief. Did his philosophical stance dominate his theology, so that the latter became simply the development of a metaphysical system using the language of Chris-

---

[6]*Basic Issues in Christian Thought*, 68-75. See also *The Doctrine of God*, 139-45; "A Personalistic Approach to Theology," 235; *The Philosophy of Personalism*, 77.

tian doctrine? Or was his worldview imported from secular thought to support and validate Christian teaching previously accepted?

Neither judgment would be correct. In 1943 Knudson wrote that his teaching and writing had sought to solve the problems of theology "in the light of a thoroughgoing and consistent personalism."[7] But "in the light of" does not mean "dominated by." On the other side, he found in personalist metaphysics "a powerful bulwark of the Christian faith."[8] But this is not equivalent to making it the handmaid of preconceived beliefs. Knudson was strongly influenced by both religious commitment and a philosophical quest for truth, and he found that the two creatively enriched and complemented each other. They were so harmoniously related that together they provided a unified, consistent, and satisfying answer to his quest for both truth and salvation.

Theological Method

For Knudson theology was "the systematic exposition and rational justification of the intellectual content of religion."[9] In its exposition of the Christian faith its method is that of the normative sciences, involving an impartial study of the relevant data of Christian experience and history. In its attempt to reach a defensible interpretation of faith it avoids reliance on any external, definitive authority and follows instead a critical method that "takes serious account of the subjective conditions of knowledge and belief."[10]

Both tasks require the unfettered use of human reason. Theology is the product of hard thinking and cannot be content with declaring a miraculously revealed truth. Faith as well as Scripture must be open to "critical

---

[7]*The Principles of Christian Ethics,* 7. See also "A Personalistic Approach to Theology," 225.

[8]*Basic Issues in Christian Thought,* 45. See also *Present Tendencies in Religious Thought,* 226.

[9]*The Doctrine of God,* 19.

[10]Ibid., 189-90; cf., 188-98.

inquiry and reasoned judgment.''[11] Our basic source of theological authority is ''the human mind quickened by the divine Spirit.''[12]

Knudson was a strong defender of natural theology—knowledge of God attainable by human reason unaided by special divine revelation. Hence he opposed both the antimetaphysical positivism of humanistic naturalism and Karl Barth's insistence that revelation is self-authenticating. Both of these positions represented to him an irrationalism that religion needs to fear more than the rationalism they decry, and neither points the way toward true understanding.[13] ''A theology that feeds on philosophical skepticism will perish thereby.''[14] Only a theistic metaphysics can meet the demands of faith today.

However, it is important to recognize that reason, for Knudson as for Immanuel Kant, is practical as well as theoretical. The term may be used to cover all of ''the structural interests of the human mind,'' the subjective conditions of our total experience:[15] theoretical or cognitive, moral, aesthetic, and religious. Each of these ways in which the mind operates presupposes a distinctive capacity, though all belong to a unitary self. Each capacity is in the Kantian sense a rational a priori: it is a structural condition of some aspect of our experience. Each of these interests has its own rationality, its independent grounding in human reason.[16] Thus Knudson, following Friedrich Schleiermacher and Rudolf Otto, affirmed the reality of a religious a priori that is as constitutive of our humanity as the other three a prioris. Religion represents an original, unique, and independent

---

[11]*Basic Issues in Christian Thought,* 40. See also *Present Tendencies in Religious Thought,* 113; ''A Personalistic Approach to Theology,'' 231.

[12]*Basic Issues in Christian Thought,* 40, 41.

[13]Ibid., 7.

[14]Ibid., 39.

[15]*Present Tendencies in Religious Thought,* 249; *The Validity of Religious Experience,* 145.

[16]*Basic Issues in Christian Thought,* 43, 45-46; *Present Tendencies in Religious Thought,* 249.

capacity of the human spirit. Like our other fundamental interests, it has autonomous validity. "It stands on its own feet. It verifies itself."[17]

Knudson made no claim that the religious a priori provides proof of the reality of the object of religious belief. It depends for its validity on faith. However, the same is true of the other a prioris. All are based on trust in the reliability of the activities structural to the human mind, and their implications for knowledge may be accepted if they involve no rational contradiction. Thus, science assumes that the world is intelligible and that we are able to understand it, but it cannot demonstrate the truth of this assumption. Our intellectual interest in and need for truth lead us to trust our thought processes. Knudson accepted Bowne's pragmatic principle: "Whatever the mind demands for the satisfaction of its subjective interests and tendencies may be assumed as real in default of positive disproof."[18]

Representative Christian Beliefs

In interpreting basic Christian beliefs Knudson typically began with biblical teaching, moved through historical developments, and then, after critical examination of alternative views, stated his own conclusions. Evident at every point is the close relation between his doctrinal positions and the implications of his philosophical standpoint. I summarize his teachings in five important areas.

God. Knudson formulated and evaluated with great care what he regarded as the chief arguments for the existence of God: the religious argument from the religious a priori; the moral argument from the practical reason or the moral nature, centering in the implications of conscience; and the theoretical or rational arguments: causal (both cosmological and teleological), conceptual or ontological, and epistemological. All of these fall short of demonstration, but they strengthen the spiritual interpretation of

---

[17]*The Validity of Religious Experience,* 161-67, 186, 232-33. See also "A Personalistic Approach to Theology," 234-35; *The Philosophy of Personalism,* 251-52.

[18]*Basic Issues in Christian Thought,* 46, 66; *The Doctrine of Redemption,* 235; *The Validity of Religious Experience,* 175-76; Borden Parker Bowne, *Theism* (New York: American Book Co., 1902) 18.

the universe. Theism is "the line of least resistance" for the intellect as well as for the moral and religious nature.[19]

In his thought of God Knudson rejected the notion of substance as completely as do the process theologians of today. God is more truly conceived in terms of energy, will, and purpose, and especially after the analogy of the dynamic activity of personality. Personhood is essentially "selfhood, the power to know, the power of contrary choice, and the capacity and desire for fellowship with other persons."[20] These qualities offer our best clue to the nature of God. In us, however, they are far from perfect. Perfect personality is found only in the Supreme Person.[21]

Knudson's conception is definitely trinitarian, but in the form of a modified modalism that affirms the differentiated personhood of God, not persons *in* God. The richness of the divine life is suggested when we think of three main manifestations, forms of activity, or modes of expression within the abiding unity of God, who is the creative source and sustainer of the world; redemptive, reconciling love; and indwelling spiritual presence constantly seeking fulfillment of the divine purposes.[22]

Knudson had no qualms about speaking of God as the Absolute, in the sense that God is the creator of the universe and its independent and self-existent ground.[23] God knows no limitation except self-limitation— that involved in the fact of God's own concrete and definite nature and the freedom granted to finite persons. Here Knudson differed sharply with his colleague Edgar S. Brightman, who postulated a "Given" within God that limits the divine power.[24]

Humanity. In Knudson's view the fundamental and distinctive feature of the Christian view of humanity was its emphasis on "the supreme value of the soul, the sacredness of personality." This high estimate is expressed ethically in the conviction that the human individual is intrinsi-

---

[19]*The Doctrine of God*, 241.

[20]*Basic Issues in Christian Thought*, 56.

[21]*The Doctrine of God*, 241.

[22]*Basic Issues in Christian Thought*, 86.

[23]*The Doctrine of God*, 263.

[24]"A Personalistic Approach to Theology," 237.

cally valuable, an end in itself; and religiously in the belief that the human person is akin to God and capable of eternal fellowship with God.[25] These two affirmations of faith support each other. Our kinship with God is expressed in two biblical metaphors: the image of God and divine sonship. To be created in the divine image means to be endowed with the capacity for knowledge, morality, and religious faith—potentialities that must be actualized by our own free choice and action. Likewise, our capacity for sonship, according to the New Testament, is a spiritual attainment, realized only as we become new creatures. "We are not born sons of God, we are reborn such" according to the new type of humanity introduced by Christ and realized through him. The true nature of humanity is therefore found in the second Adam rather than the first, not in what human beings originally were but in what they are destined to become.[26]

In Knudson's stress on human freedom he disclosed his close ties with both James Arminius and John Wesley. Philosophically, he supported his position by reference to "the overwhelming testimony of common sense," the impossibility of truly moral conduct without the possibility of choice between alternatives, and the comparable fact that the pursuit of knowledge requires the capacity to weigh ideas and form judgments between the true and the false.[27] However, Knudson fully realized that our freedom is limited and subject to radical abuse. Not only do we need in exercising it the strengthening power of God, but freedom itself is a gift of divine grace. The Christian life is not the work of either God or the human agent alone. It is to be seen synergistically, as "the result of the combined activity of the human and the divine."[28]

Sin. Knudson's stress on freedom as the power of contrary choice provides the best clue to his understanding of sin, which for him is essentially our misuse of this power.[29] Sin is "a defective attitude toward God,

---

[25]*The Doctrine of Redemption,* 78.

[26]Ibid., 86-89.

[27]*Basic Issues in Christian Thought,* 77-80; *The Doctrine of Redemption,* 158-60, 164.

[28]*Basic Issues in Christian Thought,* 164-65; *The Doctrine of Redemption,* 165.

[29]*Basic Issues in Christian Thought,* 113.

toward other people, and toward our true selves, for which we are accountable in God's sight.''[30] Accountability is important if merit or guilt is to be assigned. But this requires greater than human knowledge. The moral law violated when we sin is not a static, abstract principle that applies equally to all persons, but the law as it is perceived to be binding by individuals of various ages, abilities, insights, educational opportunities, and environments. It is the law that they *ought* to acknowledge as binding. Hence Knudson joined F. R. Tennant in asserting that sin is ''moral imperfection, for which an agent is, *in God's sight,* accountable.''[31]

Whence, then, is sin? Knudson rejected the traditional notions of the Fall, original sin, and human depravity. These doctrines are intelligible when seen in the light of the vast gulf between what we are and what we ought to be, and of the distance by which we fall short of the divine perfection. But when we move from the language of religious feeling to that of theology we must go beyond nonvolitional, necessitarian explanations. We are not inherently sinful. We have not inherited a corrupt nature. In varying degrees we recognize the good and our responsibility to attain it. We are gifted with the power of choice. Why, then, is sin the universal plight of human beings?

Knudson distinguished between sin and the materials of sin. All of us are endowed with appetites, impulses, and instincts that are neither good nor bad, but nonmoral. However, they are necessary to human life, and we must moralize and guide their expression in accord with ethical ideals that emerge later on the scene, and that often run counter to the powerful example and influence of parents and others whose attitudes and practices easily become normative. The result is the enormous difficulty of full obedience to the moral law and the practical impossibility of avoiding any lapse in our effort to fulfill the divine will.[32]

Knudson maintained nevertheless that human misuse of freedom has resulted in far more than even the difficulties in the path of complete righ-

---

[30]*The Doctrine of Redemption,* 226.

[31]Ibid., 247; *Basic Issues in Christian Thought,* 119; F. R. Tennant, *The Concept of Sin,* (Cambridge, England: Cambridge University Press, 1912) 45.

[32]*Basic Issues in Christian Thought,* 115-17; *The Doctrine of Redemption,* 265-67, 274.

teousness would account for. Indeed, his estimate of the human condition was at heart not utterly different from that of the traditional Calvinists he criticized. "The human world," he wrote, "must be regarded as morally in a fallen state. It has fallen far from the divine intention."[33] In the same context he declared that actions and conditions for which individuals are not responsible must be regarded either as part of the neutral material of sin or as a pathological state. Unfortunately, to my knowledge, he nowhere explained just what he meant by *pathological,* though he obviously did not regard the suggestion as violating his freedomistic view of sin.

Christology. However sin is defined, human beings need to be saved from its devastating power. Therefore, Knudson devoted major attention to the person and work of Jesus Christ, who for Christian faith is the center of the redemptive activity of God. The influence of Knudson's personalism is clearly apparent in his Christology.

Behind the two-nature doctrine of the person of Christ, formulated at Chalcedon in 451, lay two Platonic conceptions that Knudson regarded as erroneous: the notion of reality as substance and as a universal form of being. In opposition to these views, personalism regards reality as active or dynamic and as individual or concrete. Chalcedon was right in affirming both divine and human action in the unified personality of Jesus Christ, but it was misleading in its substantialist view of their relationship. "Neither human nor divine nature has any existence apart from personality."[34] Hence, Knudson substituted for a metaphysical union of Jesus and God an interaction in which the divine Spirit, active in Jesus to an unparalleled degree, wins the trusting, obedient response that enables Jesus to become the definitive disclosure of God in human life.

> We are to think of Christ as a man in whom God was present in a unique manner and to a unique degree. This presence consisted in a unique metaphysical dependence on God and in a unique reciprocal interaction with the divine Spirit. As a result of this twofold relation to God there emerged in Christ a unique and potent God-consciousness in which God was both causally and consciously present and which expressed itself in

---

[33]*The Doctrine of Redemption,* 270.

[34]*Basic Issues in Christian Thought,* 137.

qualities of mind and heart that have made him in the faith of the church the ideal man and perfect organ of divine revelation.[35]

Knudson examined carefully three widely held theories that regard the Atonement as an objective transaction, since they locate the chief obstacle to human redemption in the nature of God. These are the satisfaction theory of Anselm and Aquinas, the governmental conception of Hugo Grotius, and the penal substitutionary view of the Protestant reformers. Understood metaphorically, these theories conserve the profound truth that sin is so serious a matter that it cannot be lightly forgiven; certain moral conditions must be fulfilled. They also assume that ultimately the work of Christ that changes our human status is an expression of divine love. Taken literally, however, they are fictitious.[36]

The primary defect in all of the objective theories is the abstract, impersonal way in which they construe the relation between God and sinners. One person may pay a financial debt incurred by someone else, but not a debt involving guilt and punishment. "Merit and guilt are inalienable from personality. They cannot be detached from one person and transferred to another. Nor can one person morally be punished in place of another."[37] These theories also entail for Knudson a sub-Christian view of God, representing the divine as a feudal overlord, a stern judge, or a political governor rather than the Father disclosed in Jesus Christ.[38]

In Knudson's view the decisive barrier to human redemption is not in God, but in the sinner. The obstacle can be removed only by spiritual means, through a change in the attitude of those who need forgiveness and reconciliation. How can their wayward wills be transformed? The answer is to be found in the moral or personal theory implicit in the Fourth Gospel and first clearly formulated by Abelard. Here the life and death of Jesus Christ are our fullest revelation of the sacrificial love of God, moving human beings to respond in gratitude, repentance, and loving devotion to the divine will. This conception, of course, has its roots in the Pauline faith

---

[35]Ibid., 148; see also 136-42. *The Doctrine of Redemption,* 302, 315-25.

[36]*Basic Issues in Christian Thought,* 142-46; *The Doctrine of Redemption,* 353-68.

[37]*Basic Issues in Christian Thought,* 144.

[38]Ibid., 144-45; *The Doctrine of Redemption,* 366-68.

that God was in Christ reconciling the world to God, so that Jesus' supreme act of self-sacrifice is seen as a mirror of the heart of God. The result is the moral and spiritual transformation of sinners, who thus enter a new personal relation with God.[39]

Natural Evil. Fullness of life is obstructed not only by the moral evil of sin, but by evil inflicted by natural events in which human agency is minimal or nonexistent. Believers in the goodness of God face the agonizing problem of accounting for the presence in God's good creation of so much suffering that seems to undermine the divine intention.

Knudson rejected the pessimism of naturalistic determinism, as well as the Buddhist and Stoic understandings of natural evil. He also dismissed after careful evaluation the theories advanced by some biblical and Christian writers who treat natural evil as punishment for sin, the theodicies of Leibniz and the Hegelians, and various finitistic theories that attribute the evils of nature to God's lack of power to prevent them.[40]

Knudson's own view, following Kant, shifted from the theoretical to the practical arena. Experience shows that injurious events may have meaning and value as they contribute to the growth of human character. Hence, the world in spite of and even partly because of its hurtful features may be a training school for humankind. Religious people after all earnestly seek victory over evil rather than a full explanation of it. God alone knows the explanation, and we can leave it to him trusting that our destiny lies within his chastening and sacrificial love. Within the divine providence, hardship and suffering often strengthen, purify, and ennoble human souls and lead them into closer communion with God.[41]

Pertinent here was Knudson's critical response to Brightman's hypothesis of a finite God. Impressed by the extent and power of evil and the inadequacy of traditional absolutistic views of God to account for it, Brightman posited within the divine nature a recalcitrant element, the

---

[39]*Basic Issues in Christian Thought,* 146-48; *The Doctrine of Redemption,* 371, 377-78.

[40]*Basic Issues in Christian Thought,* 90-104; *The Doctrine of Redemption,* 169-96.

[41]*Basic Issues in Christian Thought,* 104-107; *The Doctrine of Redemption,* 196-200, 215-21.

Given, that resists and sometimes thwarts the fulfillment of God's wholly good will, and hence constitutes a problem for God as well as for us.

Knudson found this theory interesting, stimulating, original, and even attractive. However, he offered eight criticisms that led him to reject it. I cite only four of them. (1) Brightman's conception compromises the divine unity, thus failing to satisfy reason's demand for an ultimate monism. Its separation of the divine will from the divine nature is an illicit abstraction, resulting in effect in a dualism that fails to account for the oneness of reality.

(2) The hypothesis compromises God's goodness, thus failing to support the demands of religious faith. The worshiper trusts a goodness that not only means well and intends the good, but is so linked with power that it can accomplish the ends willed. If it is impossible for God to prevent the ills of life, there is no basis for belief that God can overcome them.

(3) In freely creating the world, God presumably had adequate knowledge to foresee the evils that would inevitably result from the hampering influence of the Given. God might have avoided those evils by refraining from creating. The fact that God nevertheless created indicates divine approval of the expected outcome as justified for both God and the creatures. Therefore, God is at least indirectly responsible for the resulting suffering—a conclusion not essentially different from traditional Christian teaching.[42]

(4) Brightman's theory assumes that much evil is not and cannot be a means to an ultimate attainment of good, hence cannot be ethically justified. But our knowledge is too limited to warrant this judgment. "If we knew all, as God does, the unideal aspects of the world would not seem so entirely out of harmony with an absolute and holy love as they now do."[43] It is wiser to confess our own ignorance than to surmise God's impotence.[44] The extent and intensity of suffering may baffle us if we affirm divine omnipotence, but faith is essentially trust in both the goodness and

---

[42]*The Doctrine of God*, 258, 272-75; *The Doctrine of Redemption*, 204-208; *Basic Issues in Christian Thought*, 104.

[43]*The Doctrine of God*, 366.

[44]*The Doctrine of God*, 258-59; *The Doctrine of Redemption*, 208-209, 219-20; *Basic Issues in Christian Thought*, 104.

power of God in spite of appearances. "Better a baffled faith than no faith at all."[45]

Christian Ethics

Though a strong ethical concern was evident throughout Knudson's career, it was not until the last decade of his life that he devoted major attention to scholarly work in Christian ethics. Two of his last three volumes deal centrally with ethical issues. In *The Principles of Christian Ethics* Knudson examined the history of Christian ethics, its validity, its presuppositions, and its practical application to major areas of human life. His last book concentrated entirely on issues of war and peace. We shall sample his ethical thought under three headings.

The Validity and Distinctiveness of the Christian Ethic. For Knudson there was no sharp division between Christian and natural ethics. The former presupposes the latter. Innate in all human beings is a common moral capacity that constitutes the true unity of the human race. In this is to be found the validity of the ethical imperative. Knudson appealed to a moral a priori comparable to the cognitive, aesthetic, and religious a prioris discussed earlier in this presentation. "There is in the human spirit a native and distinctive capacity for moral experience." Original, underivable, and constituent in human nature "it is autonomous and exists in its own right."[46] It enables us to distinguish between right and wrong, to form ideals, and to guide our actions in accord with them. The validity of this understanding of the ethical life cannot be intellectually demonstrated, but it is based on our "ineradicable faith in the reality of the rational and the ideal," a faith that is "one of the chief cornerstones of the personalistic theory of knowledge."[47]

Though Knudson insisted that Christian ethics presupposes philosophical ethics, he also affirmed its distinctive character. He noted four fundamental features that are united by "their basic moral personalism": the centrality of the principle of love as *agape;* the basic importance of moral perfection or inward purity; the grounding of ethics in living faith in

---

[45]*The Doctrine of God,* 259.

[46]*Basic Issues in Christian Thought,* 183. See also ibid., 178-82, 214; *The Principles of Christian Ethics,* 33-34, 281-83.

[47]*Basic Issues in Christian Thought,* 214.

God as disclosed in Jesus Christ; and emphasis on the example of Christ and personal loyalty to him.[48]

Christian Love. Representative of Knudson's conception of the Christian ethical life is his interpretation of Christian love, which appears most clearly in his discussion of the relation between craving and giving love. The classic view, formulated by Augustine, holds that love includes both elements, but fundamentally the former. In contrast to Augustine, Anders Nygren follows Luther in asserting that *agape* in the New Testament sense is exclusively a giving love that takes no account of merit in the beloved and is not motivated by desire for its object.

Knudson rejected Nygren's theory as contradictory to the command to love one's neighbor as oneself and to other teachings of the New Testament, such as its plea for moral purity and its conception of eternal life. The true Christian ideal is not self-sacrifice alone, but self-realization through self-sacrifice. It involves self-love as well as love for others. Moreover, other-love is not unmotivated, but conditioned by the moral worth of the other. "It is the sacredness of personality that makes love morally obligatory. In our interpersonal world self-love cannot be separated from love for others; both are moral obligations, and both are grounded in our love for God and God's love for us."[49]

War and Peace. In applying Christian ethical principles to concrete moral problems, Knudson considered both the duties and rights of the individual and the social issues relating to five main "orders of creation" or fundamental areas in the structure of society: the family, the state, the church, the culture, and the economic order. We consider here only his discussion of the international relations of the state, to which he devoted an entire book, *The Philosophy of War and Peace.* He explored various political bases for the achievement of world peace, including historic efforts to distinguish between just and unjust wars. He examined the chief causes of modern wars and evaluated critically eight main methods of attaining peace that have been tried or proposed: a universal state, the balance of power, mediation and arbitration, disarmament, the outlawry of

---

[48]Ibid., 181; *The Principles of Christian Ethics,* 162.

[49]*Basic Issues in Christian Thought,* 190-92. See also *The Principles of Christian Ethics,* 119-33.

war, absolute pacifism, a world federation, and the spirit of international cooperation.

Typical of his middle-of-the-road position[50] is his discussion of the relation of imperialism to war. In Knudson's view an exclusively derogatory use of the term *imperialism* is unjustified. The word may be used to denote two very different systems, with both good and evil impacts on subject peoples. Imperialism may be coercive, expansionist, selfish, and aggressive, exhibiting a tyrannical exercise of power; or it may be more cooperative, manifesting a genuine desire to aid colonial populations by promoting their material welfare and preserving law and order. Writing in 1947, Knudson believed that the better side of imperialism was "on the whole growing stronger under the influence of public criticism and changing world sentiment."[51] He clearly recognized the oppressive aspects of political and economic domination of a people by a foreign power, and likewise the part played by struggle for markets and raw materials in causing wars. Nevertheless, he believed that many subject peoples "are not ready for self-government" and "still need a long period of tutelage." The Western powers still have "a civilizing mission" in Africa and elsewhere.[52] Christian belief in the sacredness of personality and the right to freedom demands that subjugation be brought to an end. Progress in this direction should be sought through moral trusteeship and the gradual establishment of self-government.[53] In 1947 Knudson could not have foreseen the collapse of empires and the formation of scores of independent states that would occur within the next several decades, rendering irrelevant his hope for a gradual transfer of sovereignty.

With regard to the threat of widespread war, however, Knudson betrayed a real sense of urgency. He declared that wars are becoming so destructive that humanity must act in self-defense to abolish them. He quoted with approval the declaration of King George V on 14 August 1945 that

---

[50]*The Philosophy of War and Peace,* 7.

[51]Ibid., 72.

[52]Ibid., 90.

[53]Ibid., 91-92.

the devastating power of the atom bomb made plain that the nations "must abolish recourse to war or perish by mutual destruction."[54]

What, then, is the way to peace? Though Knudson found positive values in mediation and arbitration, a world organization like the United Nations, and the spirit of voluntary cooperation, his greatest hope lay in the growth of moral responsibility, the will to peace, and the cooperative spirit, since without these no external arrangements can succeed. In this respect Knudson has been strongly influenced by Kant's basic philosophy of peace, especially by two elements in it: its affirmation that the ideal of perpetual peace is inherent in the precepts of right and duty, an ideal that *can* be achieved because it *ought* to be achieved; and its insistence that something in nature, the moral structure of the universe, or, speaking religiously, Providence, demands the struggle for better human relations, so that it must lead eventually to the attainment of both political unity and diversity and the abolition of war.[55]

The primary appeal of the peace movement must be to "reason, conscience, and faith."[56] This appeal assumes that men and women are sufficiently free and responsible to control the forces that produce international strife. As a personalist, Knudson opposed both naturalistic determinism and the subvolitional view of original sin that tends to paralyze moral endeavor.[57]

Arms cannot now be dispensed with, but they cannot themselves secure lasting peace. Nations must learn to live together by sympathetic adjustment of their economic, political, and racial differences. Such actions must in turn be grounded not only in aversion to the suffering caused by war, but in firm belief in the sanctity and dignity of all human life, in the spiritual destiny of humanity, and in a universal human brotherhood.[58] Underlying all else we need profound faith that world peace is "the divinely appointed good of human history."[59]

---

[54]Ibid., 199.

[55]Ibid., 143-45, 147-49.

[56]Ibid., 201.

[57]Ibid., 101.

[58]Ibid., 202-203.

[59]Ibid., 208.

Some Critical Questions

A complete account of Knudson's thought would honor him by comprehensive evaluation of his major ideas. I can only indicate several areas in which questions arise.

(1) The validation of religion in terms of the religious a priori, while supporting the objective reference of religious faith in general, offers no guidance for discrimination among the truth-claims of particular religions. Does every kind of religion "stand in its own right"? Deep religious devotion can lead to mass suicide in Jonestown, the execution of scores of Bahais in Iran, or bloody Christian-Druze conflict in Lebanon.

(2) Closely related to Knudson's belief in the self-verification of religion is his agreement with Bowne that whatever is demanded by the mind's subjective interests may be accepted as true "in default of positive disproof." Minds differ as to what their interests require. Further, awareness of the self-centered bias of our subjective tendencies makes plain the need for rigorous evaluation of the beliefs that accompany uncriticized religious experience. The absence of positive disproof is a flimsy foundation for faith. To this must be added affirmative support that meets the test of comprehensive coherence.

(3) Knudson's view of human personality rightly emphasizes its creation in the image of God but tends to give inadequate recognition to the power of the passions and appetites that distort the divine image and alienate us from God. In view of these, can we soundly limit sin to freely chosen departures from the divine will? In any event, we need to be saved from the wrongs we do not will as well as from those we choose.

(4) As pointed out by another personalist, Paul E. Johnson, stress on the self as rational self-consciousness largely overlooks the influence on the conscious ego of the dynamic motivations of the nonrational unconscious. But these are "essential and integral" to the wholeness of personality.[60]

(5) There are some regrettable gaps in Knudson's treatment of Christian social ethics. He is quite realistic in listing attitudes of racial superiority among the major causes of war, but he makes no mention of racial

---

[60]Paul E. Johnson, "The Trend toward Dynamic Interpersonalism," *Religion in Life* 35 (1966): 752.

segregation and other forms of injustice to minorities within nations like the United States. Likewise, his condemnation of Hitler and Nazism omits any reference to the anti-Semitism of the Nazis or their murder of six million Jews.

Edgar S. Brightman: Person and Moral Philosopher

Walter G. Muelder

SKETCH OF BRIGHTMAN'S LIFE[1]

Edgar Sheffield Brightman was born in Holbrook, Massachusetts, on 20 September 1884 to George Edgar and Mary Sheffield Brightman. He studied at Brown University (A.B., 1906; A.M., 1908). During the next two years he completed both S.T.B. and preliminary doctoral programs at Boston University (1910), the latter under Borden Parker Bowne, who died in that year. As Jacob Sleeper Fellow he studied in Berlin and Marburg, Germany (1910-1911), receiving his Ph.D. degree from Boston University in 1912.

While in Germany he met Charlotte Hulsen, and they were married in 1912. She died in 1915. In 1918 he married Irma Fall. There were three children: Howard Hulsen and two from the union with Irma Fall Brightman, Miriam Fall and Robert Sheffield, the latter now a Methodist minister in Connecticut.

---

[1]Jannette E. Newhall, *Art,* vol. 1 of *Encyclopedia of World Methodism,* ed. Nolan B. Harmon (Nashville: The United Methodist Publishing House, 1974).

Brightman was ordained as a deacon on 3 April 1910, in Attleboro, New England Southern Conference. After 1915 he belonged to the New England Conference, taking an active part in local and Conference committees, especially those dealing with social concerns. He taught frequently in pastors' schools across the country.

From 1912 he taught psychology, philosophy, and Bible at Nebraska Wesleyan University. Then at Wesleyan University, Middletown, Connecticut, he was professor of Ethics and Religion. In 1919 he became the Borden Parker Bowne Professor of Philosophy in the Graduate School of Boston University and served there until his death. His teaching influenced many students over his forty-year career. An exponent of Bowne's personalism, he developed more fully its historical and contemporary connections, making a major contribution to the metaphysical theory of personality. In philosophy of religion he stressed the problem of good-and-evil in relation to God. He wrote fourteen books and several hundred articles and reviews. He died 25 February 1953 and was interred in Elmwood Cemetery, Mystic, Connecticut.

CHURCHMAN AND SEEKER

Edgar Brightman attended the Newton Centre Methodist Church regularly on Sunday mornings and for midweek prayer meetings. He usually followed the New Testament lesson with his Greek New Testament. He took the Methodist emphasis on experience seriously, making it the primary datum for his reflection. In his latter years he was a close friend of Swami Akhilananda and followed many of his suggested spiritual practices. He read the great classics of mysticism, East and West. In 1928 he offered a course in this field for which the students studied numerous classics ranging from Lao-tze and Isaiah to William Law and John Woolman. Students were asked to read these texts with four questions in mind: (1) What was the preparation for the experience? (2) How was the experience described? (3) How did the mystic interpret the experience? (4) What were the fruits of the experience? These questions are a clue to Brightman's holistic concerns. He was so radical a religious seeker and thinker that his concern for the problem of good-and-evil led him to develop the hypothesis of a "finite" God, a venture that created controversy and even doubts about him. So misunderstood was his theory that as late as the winter of

1983-1984, a classmate of mine asked me during the intermission at the symphony whether Brightman believed in God.

OTHER ASPECTS OF HIS PERSON

Edgar was so overpoweringly brilliant that some people never came to know him personally. He was the most organized and disciplined individual I have ever known in my relationships as student, colleague, and neighbor. He was so intellectually intense that many people failed to recognize his openness and humility. He kept his promises and commitments, sometimes at cost to his family, accomplishing in productivity what others might achieve in three career-lives. His little black appointment book was both famous and notorious, depending on one's encounter with it. As a committee person and teacher, he planned months in advance, causing others to complain that meeting schedules tended to revolve around his prior commitments. He, in turn, would get upset if the university, for example, changed its schedule after having once officially announced it. This was not arrogance on his part but an extension of an oft-repeated comment: say what you mean and mean what you say.

Brightman had a bad case of the Protestant Ethic in its John Wesley style: "Be diligent. Never be unemployed. Never be triflingly employed. Never trifle away time; neither spend any more time at any one place than is strictly necessary." Of course, he played, but with a purpose. On a typical day, Brightman got up early and picked up the mail at the Newton Centre, P. O. Box 35, by 7:35 A.M. (He could do this quickly because he lived on Braeland Avenue, only three minutes away from the post office and only a minute from the platform of the Boston and Albany Railway Station.) On Tuesdays and Thursdays he took a train before or about 8 A.M. and read en route to Trinity Place, Boston (this might include Li'l Abner and Uncle Dudley in the *Boston Globe*). He walked to the College of Liberal Arts at 688 Boylston Street and began office hours of 15 minutes each at 9 A.M. (People were expected to get to the point at once. However, if he knew that a student or colleague had a serious personal problem, Edgar could find time to follow through as fully as possible.) After the CLA classes, he walked from Back Bay to 72 Mt. Vernon Street for his 3:40 P.M. class, which lasted until 5 P.M. From class, he walked to South Station with any student who wished to follow up on a problem, and then he read the evening edition on the train home. After supper he washed the dishes, spent a brief time with the family, and retired to his study.

Wednesday mornings Brightman walked the seven miles into Boston via Beacon Street and Commonwealth Avenue to the University Club, took a swim, had breakfast, and walked to CLA. On Wednesday afternoons he had his major seminar from 4 P.M. to 6 P.M. Thereafter, students were invited to join him at a Chinese restaurant. As a graduate student I often met him at Cleveland Circle for the walk into town to discuss some metaphysical issue.

Later, when I was his colleague and dean, I frequently walked from my home in Newton Centre to his, met Dr. Newhall there, and drove into Boston with them both, discoursing on personnel, policy, and philosophy. This was particularly the case after the present facilities were constructed. I found him always candid and supportive.

He carried on an enormous worldwide correspondence. He was the master of several languages: Hebrew, Greek, Latin, German, French, and Spanish. His Old Testament teaching is demonstrated in *The Sources of the Hexateuch* (1918). His editorial expertise is shown not only in that volume but also in his being selected to edit the *Proceedings of the Sixth International Congress of Philosophy* held at Harvard in 1926. Papers were read and published in Italian, Spanish, French, and German as well as in English. Special interest in Spanish and Latin American thought developed later in his career, since he was also a member of the Catholic Philosophical Association, as well as serving a term as president of the American Philosophical Association. He was once invited to go to Buenos Aires to receive an honorary degree, but would not accept because of the domination of fascism in Argentina at the time.

BRIGHTMAN AS TEACHER

As a student I could never, contrary to the present mode, call Brightman, even behind his back, Edgar. Later, even as dean and colleague, I often lapsed into Dr. Brightman. He was both courtly and awesome. I first met him at the annual formal faculty reception for students in 1927 at 72 Mt. Vernon Street. When I came to his place in the receiving line and was presented, he said with obvious surprise, ''Not Epke's son?'' Epke was an *Ostfriesen* name. The two had sat side by side in Bowne's classes, and Edgar was so proud when my father complimented him on getting Bowne's

German quotations down correctly. Bowne frequently quoted German philosophers in the original. Happy the student who kept up with him.

From the first seminary semester I started taking as many of Brightman's courses as possible. This required walking to CLA several times a week. He kept his eye on me, on Nels Ferre and Peter Bertocci—occasionally in the same foundation courses. I owe more to this amazing teacher than to anyone else in higher academe. A complete syllabus was handed out at the beginning of the semester, complete with assignments and basic bibliography. His use of 3 x 5 cards was a badge of the Brightman style. Students were encouraged to write out questions during their preparations and to leave them, signed, as they came into the classroom. Students could take any seat in the room, but were expected to keep the same ones for the term. Attendance was taken from a chart. Edgar would sort the submitted questions and then go to work on the first order of the day. After that he would lecture informally on the syllabus.

He usually answered questions at the logical level, sometimes failing to see the question behind the question. This was a weakness in a brilliant mind that wanted everyone to say what he meant and to mean what he said. As Brightman's dean in theology, I ventured to suggest late in his career that he try to be more psychologically interpersonal in his approach, and he replied, quite correctly for him, that he was too old to change.

Occasionally, there was a snap quiz to keep us students on our toes. There were also hour quizzes, term papers, and book reports. The latter deserve a special comment. The instructions in my era were to read fifty pages of collateral material, summarize it in fifty words on a 3 x 5 card, then write three or four critical comments, one each on a 3 x 5 card. The discipline of writing concise summaries and criticisms was one of my best learning achievements, since it made for incisive thinking. However, I have found that it also makes for overcondensed habits of writing.

Brightman liked students to challenge his ideas, but most were too timid to venture much. They feared his rebuttals, for he did not hesitate to deal with their comments as if they were from professional colleagues. Dialogue with him took courage, but it contributed to respect and intellectual friendship.

I would like to illustrate his openness to and appreciation for his graduate students by citing an event in Berlin in 1931 while he was writing *The Finding of God,* a sequel to *The Problem of God.* Jannette Newhall, the Ewart Turners, the Paul Schillings, and I were in Berlin at the time. Every week, for a period of six weeks, we gathered to hear Brightman read a new chapter. Then we were expected to pitch in with all the criticisms we could muster, or to raise questions about anything obscure, just as if he were a doctoral candidate writing or defending a dissertation. In this encounter we came to appreciate his ability to accept student criticism.

Edgar's love of dialogue is finally reflected in the group of about fifteen seminary theologians and philosophers from Greater Boston that he and Dr. Newhall organized in 1946 and called Philosophers Anonymous. The group met monthly during a dozen academic years for exactly 100 sessions, continuing for several years after Brightman's death. There were people like Amos Wilder, Henry Cadbury, Nels Ferre, Peter Bertocci, Paul Tillich, Paul Minear, Roger Hazelton, Harold DeWolf, and, of course, Brightman, Newhall, and myself. The rules were that the leader for the evening chose the topic, opened with a ten minute presentation (unwritten), and then each person made at least one comment. The host kept the minutes, which were restricted to one page in a small notebook. Those evenings spent in various homes in Newton and Cambridge were exciting interdisciplinary occasions. No one attended more regularly than Brightman or entered more vigorously into a debate.

BRIGHTMAN AS A MORAL PHILOSOPHER

Since I have already written a synoptic account of Brightman's social philosophy in the *Philosophical Forum* in 1950, I will take a somewhat different approach here. One of his great contributions was a radical metaphysical formulation of personality, which shaped his moral and social thought.

My first impression was that personalism had a predominantly individualistic ethic, that Bowne had optimistically appropriated the virtues of capitalism, and that he was interested only in such "radical" issues as temperance and, later in life, was an earnest advocate of women's suffrage. As a student I was brash enough to ask Brightman whether personalism had a social ethic. He replied that he knew what sociology was and what ethics was, but turned to me and asked what social ethics was. Still more brashly, I replied that John Dewey knew. Why, with such a magnificent view of God as person, did personalists not have a social ethic as pragmatists did? He said there was Bishop Francis J. McConnell who was deeply involved in social issues, but that McConnell was more of a Social Gospeler than a social ethicist.

I was then already a member of the Socialist Party and deeply concerned about personalism's significance for it. At that time Brightman still thought of Marx as a social hedonist. When he took his sabbatical year in Germany in 1930 he became profoundly moved by the plight of the German people, by the movements of fascism, communism, socialism, and rising National Socialism under Hitler. In 1932 as I was completing formal doctoral studies in a directed study on teaching philosophy, he assigned me to outline a course in social ethics. The next year he offered his first course in social philosophy. Thereafter, I saw his library in that field grow from a few volumes in 1932-1933 to a whole wall of works dealing with philosophical and descriptive social problems. He became a staunch defender of social democracy and interpreted Hegel's dialectic in favor of socialism, opting in the Great Depression for the democratic socialism of Norman Thomas. When World War II came, he was a staunch advocate of civil liberties and academic freedom, and supported conscientious objection.

Edgar was always true to the principle of organic pluralism and the method of beginning moral enquiry with the significance of the moral subject, in other words, with personality as the metaphysical principle. The ethical life has to do with persons, and all value is of, by, and for persons, human and divine. During World War II he wrote the essay ''Personality as a Metaphysical Principle'' for the *Festschrift* in honor of Knudson, *Personalism in Theology* (1943).[2] The attributes of a person defined metaphysically are all relevant for various principles in ethics and social philosophy, and each finds its place in his theory.

PERSONALITY AS A METAPHYSICAL PRINCIPLE

Personality is an empirical, complex whole, both active and interactive, a unitary agent, free to choose among given possibilities. It is purposive, rational, and social.[3] Each of these traits is significant in ethics.

---

[2]E. S. Brightman, ed., *Personalism in Theology. Essays in Honor of Albert C. Knudson* (Boston: Boston University Press, 1943).

[3]Ibid., 56-60.

Experience is complex and holistic and thus demands synoptic as well as analytic method. It is active, hence a subject that is involved within itself, with its body, with nature, and with beings (in other words, it is interactive). The conscious subject is a unitary agency despite the complexity of multisided experience; hence, it requires attention not only to individual values but also to itself as an integer. Its freedom is that of conscious and self-conscious choice as an agent, not that of will as a separate faculty. The experient entertains a range of possible futures that must be evaluated; being temporal it is purposive, hence inclined to seek ends and to relate means to ends. Finally, personal experience is rational, therefore critical, relational, and systematic so as to deal with its wholeness; and it is social. Various moral laws are normative specifications of these attributes of metaphysical personhood.

To say that personality is social does not mean that "some magic power known as a social mind can swallow up individuals and turn them into some depersonalized, or de-individualized monsters." In such a statement Brightman shows his antipathy to certain traits in Hegel and to the age of totalitarian collectivism in which he was writing during World War II. To say that persons are social "means only that persons communicate with each other. . . . True communication . . . is a sharing of thought and purpose and feeling between persons." Sharing, again, is not to be taken literally. It does not mean that one personal consciousness can merge into the consciousness of another person. "It does mean," he says, "that one can be aware of what another means, what he purposes, what he feels, and commit himself to like meaning, purposes and feelings. Social communication, personalists believe, is the ultimate key to all interaction, all 'prehension,' all organization among the parts of the cosmos."[4]

In this statement Brightman is accenting organic pluralism in contrast to Hegel's organic or absolute monism. One can identify parallel and distinguishing characteristics growing out of his metaphysics of the person when compared with Hegel. First, both philosophers accept *perfectionism* of a broadly Aristotelian type in that both embrace a teleology that moves from more instrumental to more intrinsic values and points to ultimate Good.[5] Second, both develop thought from the more abstract to the more

---

[4]Ibid., 60.

[5]Brightman, *Moral Laws* (New York: Abingdon Press, 1933) 17.

concrete. For example, sciences tend to be abstract, while philosophy is concrete; the latter relates what the special sciences have artificially separated.[6] Ethics, too, while more concrete than social science, points beyond itself without denying its own realm of autonomy. Third, ethics must be systematic because personality is rational and holistic. The moral laws comprise a regulatory system, and Hegel contributed greatly to their development.[7] Each law must be finally considered in conjunction with all the others. The more inclusive or concrete laws presuppose the more formal or abstract ones. Fourth, Brightman accepted the Hegelian dialectic in his treatment of the Axiological Laws.[8] After affirming the synoptic law of values, he proceeds to deal with the theses and the limits of principles like consequences, specification, the best possible, the most inclusive end, and the law of ideal control of values.

Fifth, as in Hegel, so in Brightman, the moral life is a special instance of the relation of the universal to the particular. The Law of Specification is a case in point.[9] Just as in the Personalistic Laws there is a Law of Individualism, so in the Axiological Laws there is a principle for the particular situation. "It points out," he says, "that we always deal with a concrete, empirical situation of a particular kind, with its own specific experience of value."[10] The ideal of the rational whole ought never violate the pluralistic reality of the person as a true subject or of the plural values experienced. Sixth, in dialectical tension with the principle of specification is the Law of the Most Inclusive End. Reason dictates not only individual development, but also social development and the extension of life by participation in the values of social institutions, as Hegel insisted.[11] Here, however, Hegel went too far in his view of the state; therefore, Brightman stressed the pluralistic element in organic idealism. Hegel opened the door to totalitarianism, to exaggerated national sovereignty, to fascism—while

---

[6]Ibid., 25.

[7]Ibid., 88.

[8]Ibid., 129.

[9]Ibid., 171.

[10]Ibid., 172.

[11]Ibid., 187.

Brightman on both metaphysical and moral grounds stressed democracy, the rights of persons. This was very important to Brightman, for Hegel "makes the Absolute a spiritual personality" and "does not entertain much respect for the individual human personality."[12] Seventh, for these reasons the Law of Altruism gets a different treatment by the two moralists. All persons must be treated as ends in themselves. For Hegel, individuals seem to count only as they live in and for institutions as a whole. Humanity as a whole is not for Brightman the subject of the moral life[13]

Brightman's organic pluralism and his reaction to totalitarianism caused him to neglect an empirical study of historical wholes. The empirical evidence of persons-in-community led DeWolf to formulate and me to adopt and develop additional moral laws, the Communitarian Laws, which presuppose dialectically the foregoing system of moral laws.

PERSONALITY AND MORAL LAW

At the risk of some repetition I shall now comment on personality in relation to moral law, drawing on Brightman's participation in several conferences. Moral law requires loyalty to reason and such loyalty is humble, generous, and social.[14] When Brightman uses the term *reason* he recognizes both *abstract* reason as in formal logic and mathematics and *concrete* reason, which is "the consistent, systematic, inclusive, and experimental judgment on experience."[15] Such large relational activity is rough and "toughminded," since it is by its nature an appeal to all the facts and specifically to "larger purpose" so far as that can be discerned. And it is admittedly incomplete in its demonstration. It must take into account the "irrationals" of sin, ignorance, and free decision, including the non-

---

[12]Ibid., 212.

[13]Ibid., 236.

[14]Lyman Bryson, Louis Finkelstein, and Robert M. MacIver, eds., *Learning and World Peace* (New York: Harper and Row for the Eighth Symposium of the Conference on Science, Philosophy, and Religion, 1948) 508.

[15]Ibid., 509.

rational element of the Given in God. He favored the teaching of Hegelian logic to undergraduates because it taught dynamic relatedness.[16]

As we have seen, the system of moral laws has a Hegelian structure in that it moves from the most formal or abstract level of ethics, that of bare consistency and categorical autonomy, to empirical reason embracing values and theory of values, to the even more concrete self-and-other relatedness of persons as subjects of the formal and axiological choices, to the ideal of personality itself, and finally to the cosmic ground of the whole moral order in God.

Where do these moral laws come from? They are embedded in all human consciousness inasmuch as personal experience includes principles as well as particular facts.[17] These laws are not present in a ready-to-use form but require the use of ethics as a rational normative science to bring them coherently to light. For this reason total moral experience must be analyzed systematically. Such principles are universal and rational. They are not specific cultural prescriptions that apply to the particular experiences of only one society. They are principles of rational development that ought to control in a regulative way the choices of all persons. The laws postulate "that there are many selves who have moral experience in interaction with each other and with a common environment."[18]

In such a regulative system the logical order is to begin with formal principles of *ought*, like consistency and autonomy, and then to examine the value content of consciousness. Since such laws and the content of value experience arise out of, and are present in, personal consciousness, the system of laws must be directed also to the free subjects, or persons themselves. These laws are the personalistic laws, for all values are *of, by, in,* and *for* persons. They do not float free. When expounding these levels of laws Brightman not only moved from the most formal to the most holistic personal level of fulfillment, but also illustrated them in the heritage of

---

[16]Bryson, Finkelstein, and MacIver, eds., *Approaches to National Unity* (New York: Harper and Row for the Fifth Symposium of the Conference on Science, Philosophy, and Religion, 1945) 690.

[17]*Moral Laws,* 81.

[18]Ibid., 97.

ethical theory and the debate regarding them in the history of ethics. Hence, a mastery of the moral laws entails an understanding of the coherence of ethical theory with respect to the principles involved and some appreciation of the appeals to them that have been made explicitly or implicitly in the Western moral tradition.

THE AUTONOMY OF MORAL LAW

The issue of the autonomy of the moral laws is sufficiently complex that Brightman devoted a whole chapter to the subject. There is, first of all, the question of the nonreducibility of moral *ought* or conscience. Then, there is the question of personal responsibility, the obligatory character of self-imposed standards or ideals. Third, there is an issue arising from the fact that some ethical systems and moral demands are heteronomous, that is, the commands on behavior are externally imposed. There is also the question of ethics as a whole in relation to such disciplines as logic, aesthetics, social science, religion, cosmology, and metaphysics. Finally, there is the question of autonomy in relation to theonomy, God as ground of the moral order. These are all relevant problems because all facets of experience tend to influence one another and values interpenetrate. When a philosopher emphasizes the dialectic of the whole, and says that the true is the whole, the kind of autonomy intended about a particular choice or about the system taken together is important to identify.

Three statements, briefly, are in order in relation to these questions. The Law of Autonomy as a *formal* principle presupposes the logical law of consistency and metaphysical freedom and then states that self-imposed ideals are imperative, that is, obligatory. Heteronomy may be a social fact, but a self-imposed ideal is not necessarily a self-manufactured one. Autonomy in this sense appeals to the freedom of the rational self as a real moral agent and subject. Persons ought to accept responsibility for their freely chosen acts. At the axiological level, values interpenetrate and the dialectic of the laws of value shows that regulatory principles, such as taking foreseeable consequences into account and choosing the best possible, ought to be rationally chosen. Rational freedom is thus the basic mode of autonomy of a person.

With respect to ethics as a whole, Brightman recognized that there are many ethical systems, atheistic and religious, but ethical obligation is logically prior to religion, as formal autonomy is prior to valuational reflection and choice. Religion, of course, influences the actual content of choice. Some religious systems are predominantly heteronomous. Metaphysics, for its part, must take ethics into account in developing a theory of reality, for moral experience ought not to be ignored. What, then, is the relation of autonomy to theonomy? The view that the moral life has been given by God and that God's own moral law is written in the self is a theological or metaphysical statement, not an ethical one. The validity of the moral laws as a system does not depend on the general dependence of human persons on the divine person. The content of the good life is influenced by religion, but the rational volitional integrity of ethics, as formulated by Brightman, stands. The moral laws of the Best Possible, of Ideal Control, and of the Ideal of Personality point beyond themselves as merely regulative principles, but their authority is autonomous.

APPLYING THE PERSONALITY PRINCIPLE

The democratic way of life was in jeopardy during World War II and led a considerable number of scholars to participate for about a decade in what was called the Conference on Science, Philosophy, and Religion in Their Relation to the Democratic Way of Life. Brightman not only contributed papers of his own but commented vigorously and frequently on many other papers. His comments reveal a profound social understanding. The papers and comments were edited in annual symposia by Lyman Bryson, Louis Finkelstein, and Robert M. MacIver. In what follows I shall draw freely on Brightman's application of the personality principle.

He criticized Shridharani, for example, for wanting anthropology to "convey a sense of the equality of man, based on the equality of cultures, in spite of valuational differences."[19] Brightman responded that Nazi culture, Slavic culture, Aztec culture, and Chinese culture are all human, but surely not equally valuable, and if they were, such equality would not be established by anthropology, but only by ethics and religion.

He contributed an essay called "Philosophical Ideas and Enduring Peace" in which he laid down certain axiomatic principles that by now will have a familiar ring. First, *"Personality is the seat of value. There is no*

---

[19]Bryson, Finkelstein, and MacIver, eds., *Approaches to World Peace* (New York: Harper and Row for the Fourth Symposium of the Conference on Science, Philosophy, and Religion, 1944) 170-71.

intrinsic value in territory, *Lebensraum,* armaments, gold, or any form of
wealth. Value as T. H. Green has so well said, is always 'for, of, or in a
person.' "[20] Therefore, "peace is not merely the absence of war; it is the
presence of respect for humanity, and so for opportunity for all men. The
very structure of value experience thus points to something like democracy
as the basic condition for any enduring peace."[21]

Second, *"Personality Idealizes."* Brightman's commentary on this
principle demonstrated his social consciousness. "Peace can never be permanently established on a purely realistic basis. . . . There should be respect for the idealization which, however mingled with evil, animates even
our enemies in this war."[22] Then he referred specifically to the Nazis, the
Japanese, and the Italians. Group tensions, he noted, root in a sense of social, economic, and political injustice more than in group pride. Negro-
white, Indian-British, Korean-Japanese, Jewish-Nazi, Latin-Anglo/Saxon
tensions, while exhibiting wounded pride, are a product of unjust treatment. "In all normal persons, idealizing points to its highest form in the
ideal of reason, which has been expressed historically in the very important principle of Natural Right. A study of Grotius would help us today."[23]

Third, *"Personality is free."* This principle involves both an ideal and
a fact. "To be a person is to choose, and to choose or to select is to exercise
freedom."[24] "Freedom is the principle of individualism."[25] But freedom
is not restricted to the fact of choice; it involves the effectiveness of the
choice. It "depends for its full reality on the plasticity and responsiveness
of both the subjective and the objective orders." Freedom also involves
responsibility. "A free person is not only an agent; he is a responsible
agent." Here Brightman commented on the contemporary tragedy of freedom, apart from the ever-present tragedy of sin. The latter can never be
banished from the soul. The tragedy of freedom is "the frustration of the

---

[20]Ibid., 544.

[21]Ibid.

[22]Ibid., 546.

[23]Ibid.

[24]Ibid.

[25]Ibid., 547.

potentialities of freedom—in that countless souls, born to be free, have no choice open to them save that of a greater or less degree of heroism in facing death by famine, by torture, or by bombs, or a life of degrading slavery. . . . Freedom requires a free community.''[26]

Fourth, *"Personality is social."* In his commentary on this axiom he disclosed how far he had developed since the early 1930s. ''Personality is no self-sufficient atom. It is organic to a social order, and its social causes and effects may extend as far as society extends.'' The social principle requires reconciliation. ''Reconciliation does not mean blind and sentimental forgetfulness of evil and weak confidence in the good intentions of evil men. It means the much more difficult task of convincing all men of their universal social nature, of men's need of each other, of the interdependence of nations and cultures.''[27]

Fifth, *"Personality is growth through dialectical tensions."* Here the complexity of persons as a metaphysical principle comes into play. ''The human personality is not a homogeneous substance, but an arena of oppositions, which have well been called tensions.''[28] For example, there is the tension between mind and body arising from their interdependence. As long as a person lives, he or she is a citizen of two worlds—the personal and the physical. There is also the tension between the conscious and the unconscious. ''The wise peacemaker will . . . not expect too much from the surface of men's minds and will patiently work at psychotherapy until the wounds of the subconscious are healed and more productive tensions between conscious and unconscious can ensue.''[29] Third, there is the tension between means and ends. Critical knowledge of each is necessary, but even that is futile until means and ends are correlated. Fourth, there is tension between freedom and necessity. Anarchy and determinism are social extremes to be rejected. Finally, there is the tension between the universal and the particular. Here Brightman cited Hegel's dialectical tension between subjective morality (*Moralität*) and objective social and institu-

---

[26]Ibid., 548.

[27]Ibid., 549.

[28]Ibid., 550.

[29]Ibid., 552.

tional order (*Sittlichkeit*). He also cites provincialism against humanity and world government.

Finally, *"Religious personality is rational love."*[30] "A religious state," he argues, "is committed to the principle of rational love, which is peace. Rational love is close to the core of all religion at its best." "In the interrelations between love and reason we have the loftiest form of dialectical tension experienced by the human mind." Reason here means adequate and complete coherence of all experience, and love means cooperative commitment of persons of good will to mutual respect and the creation of shared values. These are really different aspects of the same ideal of personality. Peace is possible without any avowal of religion but it is not possible without the coherence of reason and love. Irrationalism and hatred are demonic forces that guarantee permanent warfare.

In the formulation of these six axiomatic statements of the personality principle in ethics and in his commentary on them we have a typical presentation of the Brightmanian method of working on applied moral philosophy. On the occasion of his memorial service I selected these sentences from his essay "The Best Possible World":

> What the sinful and war-mad world proves is not that love is impossible or, much less, that love is evil. What it proves, positively, is that love is more difficult than we knew—more difficult than war and more difficult than any "peace" we have had. Just as reason is rigorous discipline and never happens of itself, but only by great effort, so love, as an effective will for cooperation, requires knowledge, sympathy, . . . and unspeakable patience. This is what the cross of Christ means, that love is costly. . . . We shall have the best possible world, the world of reasonable love, as soon as we are willing to pay the price of justice, sacrifice, and cooperation.[31]

---

[30]Ibid., 553.

[31]"The Best Possible World," 1943, 15f., quoted in "Edgar Sheffield Brightman's Message in the Hour of Bereavement," *In Memoriam,* an Interpretation by Walter G. Muelder, February 1953, and printed by Brightman's family.

Edgar Sheffield Brightman: Good-and-Evil and the Finite-Infinite God

John H. Lavely

INTRODUCTION

More than half a century ago, Edgar Sheffield Brightman first propounded his radical and original conception of a Finite God. In two books, *The Problem of God* (1930) and *The Finding of God* (1931), Brightman carved out, with evident intellectual pain and passion, the main features of a position that has come to be known, for better or for worse, as theistic finitism. In the first of these books, the index lists several references to "The Given." In *The Finding of God*, there are not only more references to "The Given" but, in addition, eleven references to "Finite God" appear in the index. Both of these terms will require careful analysis.

In later work Brightman articulated and refined the position first put forth in these two early books, but he never, I think, modified its fundamental features. In his presidential address to the American Philosophical Association (Eastern Division) in December 1936, he formulated and defended the hypothesis he believed most adequately grounded the new conception of God. This address, "An Empirical Approach to God," has been incorporated into the posthumously published *Person and Reality* as section 5 of chapter 16.[1]

In 1940 came Brightman's comprehensive work *A Philosophy of Religion,* in which his theory of God as "Finite-Infinite Controller of the Given,"[2] as he now called it, occupies a central and culminating place in his systematic analysis and interpretation of religion. I have already mentioned *Person and Reality* (1958), edited skillfully by Peter Bertocci with the assistance of Jannette Newhall and Robert Brightman. In *Person and Reality* theistic finitism is woven integrally into a book subtitled *An Introduction to Metaphysics.* Although there are other relevant treatments (particularly those dealing with his temporalist view of God), the works we have mentioned provide more than enough resources for the topic before us.

In his study *Recent American Philosophy,* Andrew Reck gives the following assessment: "Brightman's role has been that of the creative thinker who has imparted to personalism systematic coherence, empirical inclusiveness, and conceptual originality of the first order."[3] I think it is fair to say that the intense grappling with the problem of evil and the conception of God that emerged from this grappling are major reasons for the distinctiveness of Brightman's philosophy. Although there have been adumbrations of a theistic finitism all the way from Plato to John Stuart Mill, William James, and A. N. Whitehead, to mention only a few, Brightman developed an explicit, original, and fully worked out finitism. What is more, his conception grew consciously out of the religious consciousness and in the conviction that his view gave to the religious dimension its most adequate interpretation. It was not, therefore, a product of mere abstract speculation. As a result, Brightman's finitism received a considerable amount of recognition. For some, like myself, it opened an avenue for faith

---

[1]Edgar S. Brightman, *Person and Reality: An Introduction to Metaphysics,* ed. Peter A. Bertocci, Jannette E. Newhall, and Robert S. Brightman (New York: Ronald Press Company, 1958) 309-20.

[2]Edgar S. Brightman, *A Philosophy of Religion* (New York: Prentice-Hall, 1940) 336.

[3]Andrew J. Reck, *Recent American Philosophy* (New York: Pantheon Books, 1964) 312.

when other paths were leading into blind alleys. For others, he became notorious; to some, his shocking departures from orthodoxy verged on heresy. A relatively mild castigation contained in a sermon preached at the Old South Church in Boston, 28 March 1943, illustrates this reaction. The minister spoke in part as follows: "Two American theologians of the left wing have been engaging lately in a literary debate as to whether God is good or powerful. Both are agreed that in a world like this He cannot possibly be both. There is the strangest intellectual pride in that allegation."[4] The sermon goes on, in words that I will not take time to quote, to attack this theological position in rather intemperate and inaccurate ways. I hope you will be able to see before very long the ways in which this quotation misrepresents Brightman's position.

It is ironic that these words came from the pulpit occupied earlier (from 1884 to 1929) by George A. Gordon, one of the great pioneers of theological liberalism in New England. It is also informative that some forty years after the sermon I have quoted, a book like Rabbi Harold S. Kushner's *When Bad Things Happen to Good People* has had such wide popularity. Perhaps the agonies of this century have made us more receptive to rethinking our understanding of God's relation to evil and suffering. Another indication of Brightman's place in the present theological climate is David R. Griffin's recent book *God, Power, and Evil: A Process Theodicy.* Griffin devotes a substantial chapter (sixteen) to evaluating Brightman's theodicy before opting for a process nontraditional theodicy. Be that as it may, Brightman's finitism was indeed provocative and controversial, and remains so today.

Now we are ready to examine how this product of "a conservative Methodist parsonage" (to use Bertocci's phrase) became an advocate of and perhaps, during the last twenty years of his life, the leading spokesman for a radical theistic finitism. Brightman would have had to make two fundamental moves in order to reach this position. First was the shift from the traditional theological position, which I will refer to as orthodox supernaturalism, to personalistic idealism. Brightman had already, under the influences of his philosophical training at Brown University and under Bowne

---

[4]From a printed sermon, "Sorry Surprise," by Russell Henry Stafford, 28 March 1943, 7. I do not know who the other theologian was, but one of them was Brightman.

at Boston University, made the move to personalism before he came on the philosophical stage at Boston University. I remind you that for Brightman this move was in no sense a repudiation of his Christian faith. His personalism was rather an authentic expression of his faith and a more adequate grounding of it than traditional supernaturalism. A graduate of the School of Theology, he was an ordained Methodist minister and all his life a devout and active churchman.

The guiding principle of Brightman's personalism is that the term *person* refers to the ultimate and irreducible unit of reality. There are no realities other than persons. "Everything that exists (or subsists)," he wrote, "is in, of, or for a mind [person] on some level."[5] This personalism was, first, theistic: the ultimate and uncreated Person is God, the ground of all being, the creator of human persons, and the source and sustainer of values. This personalism is, second, pluralistic: since God creates human persons, they are genuine centers of being; that is, they are free. Reality is, therefore, a society or community of persons, sustained by the power and nurtured by the creative concern of the Supreme Person. This personalism, is, third, idealistic, in the metaphysical sense. That is, the natural world is not created *ex nihilo* by God as a separate order of being and existing external to the divine being. The physical world is not an independent substantial reality. Nature exists as a partial manifestation, an epiphany, if you will, of the divine Person. Nature is thus the form in which God's activity is accessible to us in sense experience. It is at this point that Brightman's personalism departs most sharply from the traditional theological dualism of the supernatural and the natural, for reasons I will note.

The second move Brightman made did not take him out of the personalistic camp. It did, however, involve a major modification of the personalism Bowne espoused. It was this move that eventuated in the conception of the Finite-Infinite God (theistic finitism). And it is this conception and the rationale for it that I will spend the rest of my time elucidating.

I want to emphasize that personalism is not equivalent to finitism. Some personalists (Bertocci, Muelder, Schilling, and Lavely) follow Brightman in holding to the finitist conception of God, though not without variation. Some personalists (Knudson and DeWolf) essentially follow

---

[5]*Person and Reality,* 135.

Bowne. And perhaps some follow neither. Furthermore, some nonpersonalists are finitists. I think it is fair to say that Brightman's departures from Bowne's personalism, as well as his departures from supernaturalism, are the result of his effort to take personality seriously as the basic explanatory model. Thus he viewed theistic finitism as the outcome of a resolute and consistent personalism.

Incidentally, my object is not primarily to provide an *apologia* for Brightman's theistic finitism. I view my task as an exercise in sympathetic internal criticism. That is, I want to try to make clear what made his position credible, cogent, convincing, to him. Thus, I will be engaging in what I consider appropriate argument *ad hominem.* I may put some issues and arguments in my own way, but I will attempt to represent Brightman's evidence and logic fairly. I will, of course, refer to objections to finitism (by Knudson and DeWolf, for example), but I will reserve my own major criticisms and/or modifications for a later chapter.

THE ISSUES

Let us turn to the issues out of which Brightman's position comes. What raises the problem for us? Why is the problem of evil particularly related to religion? I will approach this by noting several provocative references.

Hegel once said, "There are evils over which one should not be consoled."[6] Conrad Aiken's poem "Sound of Breaking" contains these lines:

> *It is a sound*
> *Of everlasting grief, the sound of weeping,*
> *The sound of disaster and misery, the sound*
> *Of passionate heartbreak at the centre of the world.*[7]

In his posthumously published essay "Nature," John Stuart Mill has a vivid statement of the problem of evil. It concludes, "Everything, in short, which

---

[6]Quoted in Gustav Mueller, *Dialectic* (New York: Bookman Associates, 1953) 169.

[7]Conrad Aiken, "The Sound of Breaking," in *Collected Poems* (New York: Oxford University Press, 1953) 461-62.

the worst men commit either against life or property is perpetrated on a larger scale by natural agents [forces]."[8]

We could multiply such allusions to the harsh reality of evil many times. The factual here-and-nowness of evil is what raises the problem: suffering, pain, frustration, disease, death, ignorance, sin, despair, dread, guilt, not to mention specifically moral categories. Brightman says, "No objection to religious faith compares in seriousness with that arising from the fact of evil."[9] Indeed, I have a colleague who has argued powerfully in several articles that evil is decisive evidence against the existence of God.

Another approach to the issues will help us formulate the problem more precisely. George Santayana was teaching philosophy at Harvard with William James and Josiah Royce, while Bowne was teaching at Boston University. Santayana made a bitter criticism of "Royce's Theodicy [as a] justification for the existence of evil."[10] He argued that Royce's theodicy "leads to praising evil." In contrast, Santayana approved of Spinoza: "I gathered at once from him a doctrine which has remained axiomatic with me ever since, namely that good and evil are relative to the natures of animals, irreversible in that relation, but indifferent to the march of cosmic events, since the force of the universe infinitely exceeds the force of any one of its parts."[11] That is to say, good and evil are simply accidental modes of existence that do not really disclose anything about the nature of reality.

Here then is the outcome. According to Royce, everything that happens is necessary. If so, what does it mean to speak of evil? According to Santayana, everything that happens is accidental. If so, what does it mean to speak of good? This leads us to the issue as it was put by Boethius long ago: "If there is a God, whence come evils? But whence come goods, if there is none?"[12] Thus we confront "The Problem of Good-and-Evil" as

---

[8]John Stuart Mill, *Nature and Utility of Religion*, ed. George Nakhnikian (New York: Liberal Arts Press, 1958) 20-21.

[9]*A Philosophy of Religion*, 240.

[10]George Santayana, "A General Confession," *The Philosophy of George Santayana*, Library of Living Philosophers, ed. P. A. Schilpp (Evanston: Northwestern University, 1940) 2:10.

[11]Ibid., 2:11.

[12]Quoted in Brightman, *A Philosophy of Religion*, 292n.

Brightman emphatically identified it in chapter 8 of *A Philosophy of Religion*. The problem out of which Brightman's conception of God develops must be recognized as the problem of good *and* evil.

Another aspect of the issues needs to be clarified before we can pursue Brightman's treatment of the central problem. I am referring to the distinction between a religious solution to the problem of evil and a philosophical solution.[13] What is the religious problem of evil? The answer can, I think, be articulated in the form of a question: How am I going to handle a world in which such evils happen? When people cry, "Why did this have to happen to me?" part of what they mean is, "What am I going to do now? How am I going to cope or survive under these circumstances?" Hence, the religious problem is chiefly *practical*. What is the *philosophical* problem of evil? We can also express the answer here in the form of a question: How am I going to understand a world in which such evil things happen? What kind of reality, what kind of God, would such things reflect? Hence, the philosophical problem is chiefly *theoretical*.

The solution to the religious problem thus understood is the affirmation that whatever we may say about evil, the good is fundamental. However we may explain evil, the good is ultimate. Thus, the religious solution takes the form of an affirmation. Refusal to take any evil, for many even death, as final, as the last word, is characteristic. The religious person says, "In the day of evil, suffer not our trust in you to fail." Jews in the Warsaw Ghetto during World War II sang, "I believe that the Messiah will come. I believe that God is good, just, righteous." The good is ultimate, no matter what.

To show the necessity of grappling with the problem of evil, not only as a religious problem, but also as philosophical problem, let us look at some theological hesitancies that intensify the problem. The religious affirmation of the ultimacy of the good often seems to be independent of any theoretical explanation of evil. But what if a person cannot make the religious affirmation a basis for coping with evil? Many Jews, for example, confronting the monstrous evil of the Holocaust, find it impossible to make the religious affirmation. If no philosophical solution is able to provide a convincing explanation, the religious life is seriously in jeopardy.

---

[13]Cf. S. Paul Schilling, *God and Human Anguish* (Nashville: Abingdon, 1977) ch. 2.

As we have seen, in the perspective of religious experience, there is an overriding sense of the ultimacy of the good. This is not a denial of the occurrence or reality of evil. Simone Weil makes the perceptive remark that "religion, insofar as it is a source of consolation, is a hindrance to true faith: in this sense atheism is a purification."[14] I take her to mean that, if one uses religion as a consolation to the extent of denying or escaping from the reality of evil, one is being dishonest; hence, an atheistic facing of the realities of human existence is a purification of the religious attitude. In fact, it is usually the sense of real evil that calls forth the basic religious response and the resistance to evil that accompanies it. In spite of this, the assurances of "the faith," in some theological formulations, appear to render recognition of and resistance to evil inexplicable. The reason for this is, I think, that traditional Christianity has never resolved the problem of God's relation to and/or responsibility for nonmoral or natural evil. That is, Christian practice in facing evil has been better than the theoretical explanation of evil in Christian thought.[15]

There are several modes in which the theological dilemma reveals itself. One of them is to be found in serious tension between the doctrine of creation and theodicy. This tension is rooted in the basic problem of theological dualism: Supernatural reality, which is perfect, eternal, and unchanging, creates natural reality, which is imperfect, temporal, and changing. Insofar as evil is recognized, it is associated with the natural world. "Change and decay in all around I see, O thou who changest not. . . ." In spite of the inferiority of the world and the flesh, it is held that the lower order is created *by* God. But no matter how transcendent God may be considered to be, God is responsible for the world *if* God's will produced it. The degree of transcendence does not affect the divine responsibility for God's creation.[16]

---

[14]Simone Weil, *Gravity and Grace,* trans. Emma Crawford (London: Routledge & Kegan Paul, Ltd., 1952) 168.

[15]Cf. Immanuel Kant, "On the Failure of All Attempted Philosophical Theodicies," in Michael Despland, *Kant on History and Religion* (Montreal: McGill-Queen's University Press, 1973) 283-97.

[16]Brightman, *A Philosophy of Religion,* 246-47, makes this point.

The mainline theodicy purports to resolve this problem. The traditional Christian explanation of evil has been twofold. (1) Evil is the result of misuse of freedom by created human beings. In this view, most, if not all, evil is moral evil or sin and the consequence thereof, namely, divine discipline or divine punishment for sin. In one version, natural or non-moral evil is subsumed under moral evil: the curse of God on nature is the result of human (Adam's) sin. For Augustine, for example, "natural evils are divinely ordained consequences of the primeval fall of man. . . . [Thus] 'there are two kinds of evil, sin and the penalty for sin.' "[17] (2) The second aspect of the traditional explanation of evil is this: what appear to be genuinely evil aspects of our experience (other than moral evil and its consequences) are really due to the larger purposes of God, which we do not yet understand. This, I think, is DeWolf's view. In short, evil as we understand it is not really evil. Suffering, therefore, is ultimately part of God's plan for goodness. As Brightman put it, "God wills what we call evil, and sees that it is good."[18] It should be clear that Brightman does not accept this view for reasons I shall soon be considering. I mention here, however, one fundamental problem with this view. If what seems really evil to us is not evil, perhaps what seems really good to us is not good. We are then left with a relativity of good and evil and can only appeal to the purpose of God, of which we are ignorant. Since the purpose of God is inscrutable to us, we do not have access to the only way of knowing not only what is really evil but also what is really good, unless, of course, we claim inside information of some sort.

There are two other modes of theological hesitancy I will merely identify. One of them has to do with the theory that evil is merely privation of the good. Augustine draws heavily on this theory in his explanation of evil. The logic of this position is very close to that which Brightman criticizes in the view that "evil . . . is incomplete good."[19] The second of

---

[17]John Hick, "The Problem of Evil," *An Encyclopedia of Philosophy*, ed. Paul Edwards (New York: Macmillan Publishing Co., Inc. and the Fress Press, 1967) 3:137.

[18]*A Philosophy of Religion*, 303.

[19]Ibid., 264. In this context, ch. 8, sec. 8, Brightman canvasses several other proposed solutions of the problem of evil.

these hesitancies is that related to the place of the devil or Satan in relation to an omnipotent God in traditional theology.

THE MEANING AND CRITERION OF EVIL

Many of the issues raised in the preceding section implicate the concept of evil. We need to clarify the meaning and criterion of evil if we are to have a foundation for theological formulations later on. Analysis of value and disvalue is an indispensable condition for further fruitful inquiry. Furthermore, if we cannot define evil, then it follows that we cannot define good: they have a reciprocal relation. There is, however, a notable asymmetry: evil cannot be defined independently but only with reference to a definition of good. Whatever our principle of value, our judgments of disvalue are relative to it. That is, evil is that which conflicts with, contrasts with, threatens, endangers, damages, or destroys good. If, for example, value is satisfaction of desire, disvalue is frustration of desire. This is another way of documenting Brightman's insistence that we are dealing with the problem of good-and-evil.

Two important insights follow from what has just been said. (1) Failure to take evil seriously also involves the correlative good and jeopardizes the distinction between good and evil. If I deny that X is really evil even though it radically opposes what in my own view is really good (Y), it is hard to avoid the conclusion that Y is not really good. Any theory that explains evil away, treats evil in a cavalier fashion, or does not face the occurrence of evil, undermines that without which there would be no problem, namely, a firm principle of value and the distinction between good and evil. (2) The second consequence of failing to recognize the correlative meaning of good and evil is this: if there is no principle of value, there is no concept of God. For, as Brightman has argued so powerfully, ''only the source of value is God.''[20] If God is the source of value, what becomes of God if value is undermined by assumptions we make regarding good and evil. The conclusion is clear: if we are to take good seriously and the God who grounds good, then we must take that which, on the same terms, is evil equally seriously.

---

[20]Ibid., 135.

As a proposal in this direction, based on the personalist principle that persons are centers of genuine worth, let me state a normative criterion of evil: The thwarting of the possibilities of the development of persons is genuinely evil. Since values are "in, of, and for persons," damage to or destruction of persons is truly evil.[21]

Related to the analysis of the meaning of evil are two distinctions Brightman develops in *A Philosophy of Religion*. I mention them briefly. The first is the traditional distinction we have already had occasion to note, namely, that between moral evil and nonmoral (or natural) evil. Moral evil is attributed to human freedom, while nonmoral evil is that which cannot be ascribed to abuse of human freedom or its consequences. Brightman considers this distinction helpful but not nearly sufficient.[22] Schilling carries this point much further in his *God and Human Anguish*.[23]

The second distinction is that between intrinsic evil or good and instrumental evil or good.[24] Intrinsic evil is the actual experiencing by some person or persons of evil, that is, whatever experience contradicts or prevents the realization of good in a person or persons. It is the state of suffering or the condition of hurting or damaging actual goods in human life. Instrumental evil is whatever condition, event, or process contributes to an intrinsic evil. Intrinsic evil is the actual state, the negation of good as such, while instrumental evil is the means contributory to intrinsic evil. The most important point about this distinction as it applies to evil is this: any intrinsic evil is always as such evil, but a particular intrinsic evil is not final; that is, it may be used and controlled for a later good. This, however, does not make the initial evil intrinsically good. The fact that we can overcome some intrinsic evils does not mean they ever become intrinsically good. It is rather a testimony to the creative goodness that refuses to take any evil as final, the last word. Thus, the fact that we rise above evil does not make it non-evil. It does, however, show that an intrinsic evil may become an instrumental value, an occasion for a later good. As William Blake said,

---

[21]Cf. Brightman, *A Philosophy of Religion*, 244.

[22]See *A Philosophy of Religion*, 243.

[23]See his provocative treatment of this issue in chs. 9 and 10.

[24]See *A Philosophy of Religion*, 241-48.

"evil must be given a form so that it may be cast out." Thus, artistic form may transform an intrinsic evil into an instrumental good.[25]

THE CONCEPT OF OMNIPOTENCE

We turn now to the concept of omnipotence, a concept that bulks very large in Brightman's treatment of the problem of evil. The concept is, however, so ambiguous in use that it behooves us to clarify its meanings as a basis for understanding why it figures so prominently in Brightman's critique of the traditional conception of God. In one sense, the term omnipotence may reflect the indiscriminate verbal ascription of every quality in the nth degree to God. Is this the metaphorical exaggeration of the religious attitude? Or is it the abstraction of theology? Or both?

Omnipotence may also be used in a nonliteral sense altogether. For example, a critic of Brightman's theistic finitism said, "For some this destroys their conception of God as omnipotent and superior to human beings." The context and language suggested that the critic was using "omnipotent" as equivalent to "superior to human beings." If so, it is a rather loose usage.

Literally, "omnipotent" means "all-powerful." Taken abstractly by itself the literal meaning is vague. Even for traditional theists, whom Brightman refers to as theistic absolutists, omnipotence (as all-powerfulness) is qualified in two ways. (1) God's power is limited by divine reason. Divine reason is not a product of the divine will or power. Although God's power does not create the principles of reason, God approves them. (2) God's power is limited by delegation of power (free will) to created beings, this being a divine self-limitation. Neither of these limitations is considered to qualify significantly God's fundamental omnipotence.

In a more important sense, omnipotence may mean "all the power there is." That is, originally, ultimately, God has all the power there is.

---

[25]Brightman's concept of "the dysteleological surd," a type of intrinsic evil "which is inherently and irreducibly evil and contains within itself no principle of development or improvement" (A Philosophy of Religion, 245-46), deserves more attention than I can give it here. Some questions have been raised about this concept. It is, nevertheless, a way of highlighting the intensity or magnitude of some intrinsic evils, and it is not essentially an exception to the characteristics of intrinsic and instrumental evil noted above.

There is no power other than that which resides in God's being. Thus, God is uncreated and absolute. On this basis, "omnipotent" is just another way of saying "infinite" or "absolute" or of expressing the unity and ultimacy of God. *In this sense,* Brightman's God is omnipotent.

In the technical theological context of the orthodox/traditional view, omnipotence, however, means something more. It means that God's will exhausts God's being, except for the divine reason. That is, there is nothing in God's nature but will (or power) and reason. God is thus will-reason. Hence, for the Scholastics there was the problem of the relation of will and reason (or existence and essence) in the divine nature. It is this sense of omnipotence that Brightman denies. For Brightman, though he does not use this locution, God is the only power there is (except that which God delegates in creation), but the divine will or purpose (plus reason) is not all of God's being. Brightman's formula, however, "finite in power and infinite in will for good," does not bring out fully enough how his concept of omnipotence does and does not differ from theistic absolutism. There is another dimension of the divine being that has to be recognized if we are to do justice to the personality of God. In the next section, I will attempt to make Brightman's position more precise.

In my judgment, it is misleading to fight out the battle of the problem of evil over the concept of omnipotence alone. The issues are much more fundamental than the formulation of one attribute, important as it may be in context. The problem can be dealt with only on the plane of metaphysics. Consequently, our solution, if we find one, must be gained by probing further into the problem of the nature of God.

When we do we find, to begin with, as Brightman argues, that "goodness is more fundamental than power: . . . There is nothing worthy of worship in power as such; only the power of the good is adorable, and it is adorable because it is good rather than because it is power."[26] Support for this point comes from disparate sources. A. C. Bouquet, a British historian of religion, maintains that power for good is religiously more significant even among religions recognizing some power for evil. Furthermore, he writes, "it may be doubted whether [the] 'good sacred' is supreme in the absolute sense, or merely 'powerful,' thus providing only a measure and

---

[26]*A Philosophy of Religion,* 319.

margin of security to the 'good.' "[27] From George Santayana comes a very different kind of support. Speaking of what he calls "one of the most important and radical of religious perceptions," he says that "the spirit . . . has perceived . . . that altogether, at every instant and in every particular, it is in the hands of some alien and inscrutable power. Of this felt power I profess to know nothing further. To me, as yet, it is merely the counterpart of my impotence. I should not venture, for instance, to call this power almighty, since I have no means of knowing how much it can do; but I should not hesitate, if I may coin a word, to call it *omnificent:* it is to me, by definition, the doer of everything that is done.''[28] Finally, John Stuart Mill maintains that "those who have been strengthened in goodness by relying on the sympathizing support of a powerful and good Governor of the world have, I am satisfied, never really believed that Governor to be, in the strict sense of the term, omnipotent. They have always saved his goodness at the expense of his power.''[29]

We are now prepared to state the minimum conditions of a viable solution to the problem of evil. First, a viable solution will maintain that without which God would not be God, namely, goodness. Second, a viable solution will have to face realistically the harsh realities of human existence. Taken together, these represent the theoretical and practical urgency of squaring our faith and task with the travail and tragedy life confronts. A contemporary of Brightman, R. A. Tsanoff, puts the matter graphically when he writes, "This is a world of good *and* evil, however we may define the two. Wholesale and unqualified condemnation of the world, and likewise suave dismissal of evil as unreal are plainly at variance with the facts of life, are indeed self-refuting views. . . . Using the terms good and evil in the broadest sense to designate value positive and negative, we are bound to say that, if either is admissible, both must be. We have them both on our hands, both actual. Our problem is to understand the relation between them, and the essential character of the world which

---

[27]A. C. Bouquet, *Comparative Religion,* 5th ed. (Baltimore: Penguin Books, 1956) 101-102.

[28]George Santayana, "Ultimate Religion," *Obiter Scripta,* ed. Justus Buchler and Benjamin Schwartz (New York: Charles Scribner's Sons, 1936) 284-85.

[29]Mill, *Nature and Utility of Religion,* 27.

the perception of their relation serves to reveal."[30] We cannot, therefore, accept the assumption that a philosophical or theological solution requires that evil be shown to be not really evil. Why not? Because it results in making good not really good. Thus, the real question is: what view of reality most adequately interprets evil *and* the religious response to it?

THEISTIC FINITISM

Theistic finitism, in general, as I am using it, is a name for a type of theory in which God is viewed as limited in power and/or knowledge. The limitations are, as we have seen, usually introduced to avoid the difficulties traditional theism has in dealing with the problem of evil. It is sometimes thought that finitism is an accidental aberration of Boston Personalism and particularly of Brightman. Finitism, however, is more widespread both chronologically and ideologically than is usually realized. It is beyond my purpose to document this here.[31] Instead, I want to turn directly to Bright-

---

[30]R. A. Tsanoff, *The Nature of Evil* (New York: The Macmillan Company, 1931) 387-88.

[31]An extensive bibliography of literature regarding finitist conceptions of God could be compiled. I will only mention several relevant sources. Brightman himself supplies an illuminating historical sketch of theistic finitism in *A Philosophy of Religion,* 286-301. *Philosophers Speak of God,* ed. Charles Hartshorne and William L. Reese (Chicago: The University of Chicago Press, 1953), includes several finitists under its own classification. Bertocci's discussion of "The Explanation of Excess Evil" (ch. 17) in *An Introduction to the Philosophy of Religion* (New York: Prentice-Hall, Inc., 1951) 420-40, is worth consulting in this connection. Two illustrations of poetic allusions are worth noting. One is Edwin Markham's poem "The Nail-Torn God," which begins

> *Here in life's chaos make no foolish boast*
> *That there is any God omnipotent. . . .*

New Poems: Eighty Songs at Eighty (Garden City NY: Doubleday, Doran and Company, 1932) 58. The other is from Tennyson's *The Idylls of the King.* Arthur's great closing speech begins

> *I found Him in the shining of the stars,*
> *I mark'd Him in the flowering of His fields,*

man's theistic finitism.

Brightman defined theistic finitism as the view "that the will of God [faces] conditions within divine experience which that will neither created nor approves."[32] I must begin by saying that I have never much liked the terms finitism and finite God. I think that the view of the nature of God that finitism is used to name is basically sound. But the name itself is highly misleading, especially in view of current usage. Finitism does not mean that God is dependent on anything external to the divine being. Finitism does not mean that God comes into being. Finitism does not mean that God is a human being, even though God is believed to be a person.

In Brightman's conception, God is, in legitimate and prevalent senses: (1) infinite (that is, uncreated and unending); (2) eternal (that is, everlasting or omnitemporal); (3) absolute (that is, ultimate reality, unconditioned by any other reality); (4) omnipotent (that is, having all the power there is except that delegated to created beings); and (5) perfect (that is, completely and continuously committed to the highest values and concerned about persons as bearers of values). Finitism is thus not a good term for Brightman's view. It blurs these positive features of the conception and does not bring out effectively what distinguishes the view from traditional theism or what Brightman calls theistic absolutism. Already, however, by 1934, in *Personality and Religion,* Brightman was speaking of "A Finite-Infinite God"[33] as a partial corrective to the misleading connotations of "finite God." He continued to use theistic finitism as the term to characterize his conception of God, and I shall follow his usage in spite of any

---

> But in His ways with men I find Him not.
> I waged His wars, and now I pass and die.
> O me! for why is all around us here
> As if some lesser god had made the world,
> But had not force to shape it as he would. . . .

The Works of Alfred Tennyson (London: Kegan Paul & Co., 1878) 526. The contemporary drama *Children of a Lesser God,* which deals with the plight of deaf-mutes, appears to have drawn its title from Arthur's phrase "some lesser god."

[32]*A Philosophy of Religion,* 282.

[33]Edgar S. Brightman, *Personality and Religion* (New York: Abingdon Press, 1934) 71-100.

terminological reservations. I turn then to exploring the main features of this theistic finitism. Since for Brightman God is a person, I can do this best by examining the essential dimensions of the nature of God as a person as Brightman conceived them.

We should remind ourselves that for Brightman the personal model or analogy is the basis for his hypothesis about the existence and nature of God as a person. In his presidential address to the Eastern Division of the American Philosophical Association in December 1936, entitled "An Empirical Approach to God," Brightman elaborated this hypothesis impressively. The core of the argument is an extrapolation from the personal analogy. He wrote, "all experients [persons] and all entities, as far as we know or imagine, have three properties, which we shall call action, content, and form."[34] Brightman stated it as an empirical hypothesis that a person is "an actual complex of awareness,"[35] "a structure that includes, in every phase of it, some activity, some rational form, and some brute fact [or content]," to use his language in *A Philosophy of Religion*.[36] He then maintained that not only "every moment of actual experience" but also "every concrete real object to which our experience can refer, is a complex which can be analyzed into the same three factors—activity, form, and content."[37] These factors parallel respectively Plato's Demiurge, Ideas, or Pattern, and Receptacle of becoming, except that for Brightman these are integral aspects of the complex unity of a cosmic person, while for Plato each is a separate order of being.[38] Thus Brightman concluded, "If God is

---

[34]In *The Development of American Philosophy*, 2d ed., ed. Walter C. Muelder, Laurence Sears, and Anne Schlabach (Cambridge MA: Houghton Mifflin Company, 1960) 317, where Brightman's presidential address is reprinted. Brightman's hypothesis is, of course, elaborated at considerable length in *A Philosophy of Religion*, especially chs. 9 and 10, and in *Person and Reality*, particularly chs. 16-18.

[35]*The Development of American Philosophy*, 318.

[36]*A Philosophy of Religion*, 319.

[37]Ibid., 319-20.

[38]See ibid., 338-39. Brightman also alludes to "a rather remarkable parallel . . . found in the Yoga analysis of rajas, sattva, and tamas, which mean energy, intelligence, and materiality, and correspond closely to will, reason, and content." Ibid., 340.

the supreme experient, his content would include awareness of all qualities in the universe; his form would include all possible relations; and his activity would select from among the qualities those of ideal value and would direct the cosmic process toward their realization."[39]

To elucidate this structural analysis of the nature of person and hence of the divine person, let us picture three concentric circles (with apologies to Bowne for indulging in picture-thinking). We will label the innermost circle *Will*. It is the activity principle, what Plato calls the Demiurge or cosmic Artisan. The second circle is labeled *Reason* or the principle of form and order, what Plato calls the Ideas or Pattern. Brightman uses the technical term Rational Given for this aspect of the divine nature. The Rational Given "consists of the eternal, uncreated laws of reason."[40] The outer circle is that of *brute fact* or the principle of content. Brightman speaks of this dimension as the Nonrational Given, and I will return to it shortly.

There is, of course, no significance to the size of the circles in our imagined diagram, and it cannot be emphasized too much that the three aspects represented by the circles never exist separately. Any concrete event, any actual person, involves all three inextricably interwoven. Thus the divine person is *unitas multiplex,* a unity of three dimensions. Art supplies an analogy that may suggest how this interplay functions. The creative energy and effort (the first circle: activity) of the artist gives form (the second circle: reason) to the content or raw material, such as sounds, colors, and words, of his/her experience (the third circle).

As I have already noted above, traditional theism (or theistic absolutism) recognizes only the first two of these aspects, that is, will and reason, as intrinsic to the divine nature. Brightman agreed with traditional theism that will and reason are necessary properties of God. But because will and reason alone do not constitute an intelligible model of the person and because traditional theism's conception of God did not provide an adequate explanation of evil, Brightman felt that will and reason were not sufficient to interpret the nature of God. On the basis of a broader, more empirical conception of person he recognized a third dimension, which he called the Nonrational Given. It is this concept that is most distinctive and most controversial in Brightman's view.

---

[39]*The Development of American Philosophy,* 318.

[40]*A Philosophy of Religion,* 337.

The Nonrational Given, according to Brightman, consists of ''eternal and uncreated processes of nonrational consciousness which exhibit all the ultimate qualities of sense objects (*qualia*), disorderly impulses and desires, such experiences as pain and suffering, the forms of space and time, and whatever in God is the source of surd evil.''[41] Like the Rational Given, the Nonrational Given is not a product of the divine will but is inherent in the nature of the divine being. Since God is ultimate reality, nothing exists or is real except the complex of will, Rational Given, and Nonrational Given. Let me make several comments on the place and import of the Nonrational Given in this complex.

(1) The Nonrational Given is not another will, not another focus of power, over against the divine activity or will. It would be better conceived as a kind of *primordial inertia*. As such it would express itself as a law of mechanics: objects at rest tend to stay at rest; those in motion tend to remain in motion. It is in polarity with the will, as activity and passivity are in polarity. The Nonrational Given can thus be recalcitrant or it can be an impediment, but not because it *chooses* to resist God's purposes. Its resistance does not consist in doing, but in not doing. It always needs to be energized, activated. It ''operates'' as a passive ''drag,'' to use R. A. Tsanoff's term;[42] it takes the line of least resistance. The Nonrational Given rests con*tent;* it is *con*tent.

(2) The Nonrational Given is not, however, a positive evil as such, a common misrepresentation of Brightman's view. Nor is the Nonrational Given as such irrational. Evil is not equal to or coextensive with the Nonrational Given. Evil ''involves'' all three dimensions of the divine person, which does not entail a moral fault of God's will. Evil results when content ''refuses'' intended form or when controlled content ''reverts'' to a lower order of control. Cancer cells may be a biological case of this. It is also interesting to speculate about entropy in this connection.

(3) Experientially any immediate datum is nonrational. No immediacy tells its own story. It is always a problematic situation that needs to be

---

[41]Ibid.

[42]Tsanoff, *The Nature of Evil,* 27: ''There is drag in the universe, and there is likewise an urge; the drag and the urge appear to be conflicting factors, but they are factors of one cosmic process, and the true philosophy is one that can take account of both.''

set in some context by something other than itself before it becomes meaningful. Any given needs to be coordinated with, related to, or integrated into the total context of experience before the problem it poses can be solved. If the given is integrated, an achievement has occurred. To the extent that an achievement takes place, value occurs. To the extent that the given resists integration (or is slow in becoming integrated), there is the danger of fragmentation, disunity, and disvalue.

(4) The Nonrational Given is abstractly best conceived, in my judgment, in terms of time and space or space-time. Plato's Receptacle, which corresponds to the Nonrational Given, is, to put it in Brightman's words, "the primordial chaos of space, discordant and disorderly motion."[43] Actually the Nonrational Given would be better spoken of not as disorderly motion but as unordered or not-yet-ordered motion. Time per se is also nonrational. There is no "reason" for it; it just goes on. At the same time it is not in itself bad or irrational. It is the "material" of all activity and the condition of every achievement. Wasting time does not make time bad but rather the one who wastes it. The only way to get the better of time is to use it, not to get out of time. To get out of time is to give up being. By contrast, in the traditional view of God as will and reason, time is hard to place. Even though will is presumably something that acts (and hence takes time), the traditional view conceives of God as timeless and unchanging. For Brightman, the notion of a person is inescapably the notion of a being who acts and who takes time in the process. And if God is not characterized by a temporal dimension intrinsic to the divine nature, what it means to speak of God as a person is inexplicable. We have no analogy whatsoever for what a nontemporal person would be.[44]

(5) Is the Nonrational Given in God similar to that in human persons? The answer to this question is at least implicit in the preceding comments. Let me make the answer explicit: Yes, as persons God and human beings have the same tridimensional structure. The Nonrational Given performs the same function in human beings that it does in God.[45]

---

[43]*A Philosophy of Religion*, 339.

[44]Cf. one of Brightman's most important articles, "A Temporalist View of God," reprinted in *Person and Reality*, 323-31.

[45]Note, however, the differences for Brightman between divine and human persons; see *A Philosophy of Religion*, 362-69.

I cannot complete my consideration of Brightman's theistic finitism without raising several questions. These questions will enable me to deal with some objections of critics of Brightman's view[46] as well as to gain a better understanding of the theory.

(1) Does not Brightman's theistic finitism create a dualism within the nature of God? This charge is undoubtedly the most common and possibly the most serious objection. Knudson stated it pointedly: finitism results in a dualism of "the divine nature and the divine will." It, therefore, "compromises the divine unity and so fails to meet the rational demand for a basal monism."[47] Brightman rejects this charge: no, finitism is not a dualism. God is a unified being with different aspects, as we have already seen. No one of these aspects exists except integrally in context. God is *unitas multiplex.*

It may be helpful to note what seems to me to be the background and assumption of this question, namely, the traditional distinction between the supernatural and the natural. Many theologians are so conditioned by this distinction they suppose that Brightman has simply imported the natural into the supernatural being. They fail to see that Brightman seeks to transcend the terms of this distinction. Hence, the question misses the point (that personality is the ultimate inclusive category) and/or begs the question (by assuming as final the theological distinction of supernatural and natural). An illustration is found in what is called "the lump theory of the Given." This theory, and the objection based on it, assumes that the Non-

---

[46]The most prominent personalist critics are A. C. Knudson and L. Harold DeWolf. Criticisms of Brightman may be found in *The Doctrine of God* (New York: The Abingdon Press, 1930) 254-75, where Knudson deals with the idea of a finite God and omnipotence. In his later book, *The Doctrine of Redemption* (New York: The Abingdon Press, 1933) 204-12, Knudson lists seven specific objections to Brightman's theistic finitism, on some of which I will have occasion to comment. L. Harold DeWolf, *A Theology of the Living Church* (New York: Harper and Brothers Publishers, 1953) 133-37, and *The Religious Revolt Against Reason* (New York: Harper and Brothers Publishers, 1949) 94-96, 168-74, 183-85, contain his assessment of Brightman's position. Note also Brightman's two articles, both entitled "The Given and Its Critics," *Religion in Life* 1 (1932): 134-45, and *Religion in Life* 11 (1941): 19-20.

[47]*The Doctrine of Redemption,* 205, 206.

rational Given is per se the natural world. But Brightman is emphatic in maintaining that Matter or Nature is *not* as such the Nonrational Given. Nature involves the interpenetration of all three aspects of the cosmic person. This, I take it, is what Brightman meant when he wrote on a handwritten 3 x 5 card to me in 1952: "The Nonrational Given is not that *out of which* God creates (for me), but rather is the set of conditions under which he creates." Finally, the tendency to equate God's being predominantly, sometimes exclusively, with the divine will also figures in the criticism behind the question.

(2) How does Brightman's theistic finitism solve the problem of evil? Knudson says that "there is nothing in the nature of the Given that gives us the slightest insight into the reason why its resistance to the divine will should lead to any specific evil."[48] Brightman provides more concrete intelligibility to the dynamic interplay of the three aspects of the divine nature. His view does not, however, purport to explain why the real is real or why reality is the kind of reality it is. It does claim to provide a theory of reality that renders intelligible all aspects of experience, including the occurrence of evil. Furthermore, for Brightman, evil is not an intended product of the divine will. In his *Principles of Moral and Political Philosophy* (1785), William Paley has what appears to be a remarkable anticipation of Brightman in this regard.

> Contrivance proves design; and the predominant tendency of the contrivance indicates the disposition of the designer. The world abounds with contrivances: and all the contrivances which we are acquainted with, are directed to beneficial purposes. Evil, no doubt, exists; but is never, that we can perceive, the object of contrivance. Teeth are contrived to eat, not to ache; their aching now and then, is incidental to the contrivance, perhaps inseparable from it: or even, if you will, let it be called a defect in the contrivance; but it is not the object of it. This is a distinction which well deserves to be attended to.[49]

Brightman would go on to say that God is continually seeking to control events in such a way as to prevent evil and in cases where it occurs to overcome it.

---

[48]Ibid., 212.

[49]Quoted in Alburey Castell, *An Elementary Ethics* (New York: Prentice-Hall, 1954) 31.

Knudson also argues that God must have approved evils that he foresaw would arise in his creative activity; hence, they are not evil; they are willed as part of the whole.[50] Brightman acknowledged that God anticipates that evil and suffering will occur. God does not, however, approve specific evils, but he accepts the conditions under which evil occurs because they make the creative enterprise possible. Consider an analogy of parents in relation to their children. A husband and wife could refuse to have children because they anticipate the problems, obstacles, and suffering their children will inevitably have to face. A husband and wife could have children and be entirely indifferent to their fate. A husband and wife could have children knowing what the children will probably have to face and endure but not desiring or approving such suffering as may occur. The parents will nevertheless accept the world in which evils occur and the risks the evils involve, for themselves and their children *jointly,* because of the new values that can thus be attained. The parents share with, suffer with, and sustain their children in the enterprise. In such a situation, suffering and evil are not eliminated, but they may be surmounted. There is, however, no guarantee that disaster and defeat may not thwart all the joint efforts. Consequently, though an analogy of parents and children offers a constructive explanation of how Brightman's view solves the problem of evil, it seems to me to call for a doctrine of immortality to complete it.

(3) How can we believe that God is and will remain in control? According to Knudson, "if it was metaphysically impossible for [God] to prevent the evils of life, there is no good ground for believing that he will be able to redeem men from them."[51] Though Knudson's conclusion is debatable, it is certainly true that there is no absolute assurance, no unconditional guarantee, no theoretical certainty that God will remain in control. There are, however, two factors that support our confidence. First, long-range perspective on the history of the universe to the present reveals no massive breakdown of order and shows cumulative development of complexity and organization. I am referring here chiefly to the natural order. Second, in the human enterprise, the testimony of the indomitable human spirit, the affirmation of life and value in spite of every obstacle, supports the conviction that God is not a God of unfinished business. I recommend

---

[50]See *The Doctrine of Redemption,* 207-208.

[51]Ibid., 207.

Schilling's chapter on "The Cross at the Heart of Creation"[52] as a moving documentation of faith in divine control and divine destiny.

(4) What is the end or goal of God's purpose? There is no final stopping point. The process goes on ad infinitum. The end of time is the death of reality. The end of time is emptiness, not fulfillment. Only if God commits suicide will time end. The Nonrational Given cannot be eliminated without eliminating God. To ask for a final end is to pray, "O Reality, be not real." The only way to overcome nonrational content is to give it a rational form. In this sense, every moment is for God an end, a consummation *and also* a beginning, a commencement. Every goal reached (an intrinsic value) becomes an instrument of further achievement. The surest way to lose what has been gained is to rest content with it, to freeze the status quo. Brightman has an eloquent passage on God as "Controller of the Given," from which I quote:

> The Given is, on the one hand, God's instrument for the expression of his . . . purposes, and, on the other, an obstacle to their complete and perfect expression. God's control of The Given means that he never allows The Given to run wild, that he always subjects it to law, and uses it, as far as possible, as an instrument for realizing the ideal good. Yet, the divine control does not mean complete determination. . . . God's control means that no defeat or frustration is final; that the will of God partially thwarted by obstacles in the chaotic Given, finds new avenues of advance, and forever moves on in the cosmic creation of new values.[53]

(5) Does not theistic finitism sacrifice "the complete rationality of God"? DeWolf argues that it does.[54] But what is "the complete rationality of God"? Does it mean, in the words of D. S. Robinson, that "God in his essential being has no problems"?[55] Or does it mean that the divine will seeks to maintain and increase values by controlling what needs to be con-

---

[52]*God and Human Anguish,* ch. 11, 235-60.

[53]*A Philosophy of Religion,* 338. See also *The Problem of God* (New York: The Abingdon Press, 1930) 183.

[54]See *The Religious Revolt Against Reason,* 94-96.

[55]D. S. Robinson, *Crucial Issues in Philosophy* (Boston: The Christopher Publishing House, 1955) 117.

trolled? What point would there be in willing to be rational for a being who is essentially "complete rationality"? As DeWolf himself says, "The rational alone is normative";[56] that is to say, the rational is *what ought to be* in an actual situation, which is not all that it ought to be, and hence contains something on which the rational will must act if what ought to be is to be realized.

DeWolf uses another locution in this connection: the nonrational cannot be made intelligible.[57] Or to put it in the words of a student: "I do not see how anything meaningful can come out of the meaningless." The implicit exclusive bifurcation between rational and nonrational, between meaningful and meaningless is highly misleading. The logical negation between nonrational and rational is not necessarily equivalent to the distinction between irrational and rational. The logical negation between nonmeaningful and meaningful is likewise not necessarily equivalent to the distinction between meaningless and meaningful. The argument is thus largely verbal, that is, an equivocation between nonrational and irrational. As a matter of fact, nearly everything rational comes out of the nonrational, as the achievements of both science and art overwhelmingly demonstrate. Indeed, it seems that the meaningless may be transformed into the meaningful: "Though your sins are like scarlet, they shall be as white as snow."[58] I turn now to a brief conclusion.[59]

CONCLUSION

It is not my intention to offer an evaluation of Brightman's courageous grappling with the problem of good-and-evil or of the radical conception of God that is his response to this problem. I have attempted to bring out fairly the dialectic of Brightman's position. In the course of the

---

[56]*The Religious Revolt Against Reason,* 129.

[57]See ibid., 183-85.

[58]Isaiah 1:18 (RSV).

[59]It would be interesting to pursue two other questions: (1) Is there any Biblical basis for theistic finitism? (2) Does theistic finitism have any practical applications? On the first, Schilling, *God and Human Anguish,* is most helpful. On the second, see Brightman, *The Finding of God* (New York: The Abingdon Press, 1931) 144-46.

exposition, however, issues about and criticisms of his theistic finitism have naturally surfaced. Even though I am convinced that Brightman's theistic hypothesis is highly credible, as I have attempted to show, there is no doubt that the theory has weaknesses, that it is, we might say, not sufficiently well-tempered. For this reason, thinkers interested in Brightman's personalism as well as those concerned with his theodicy should continue to assess and modify, where necessary, his theistic finitism. It is a mark of his impact, a measure of his contribution, that his conception of God has initiated a constructive process of rethinking the Western theological tradition.

There are those, however, who hold that Brightman's finitism is a project in presumption. To probe the psychology of the divine nature is to transgress the limits of human knowledge.[60] But how long will we continue to discourage or punish Promethean creativity from seeking to understand the sources from which it springs? What are the limits of responding to God by seeking to decipher the ongoing revelations of the divine message? Martin Buber said, "The relation with man is the real simile of the relation with God; in it true address receives true response; except that in God's response everything, the universe, is made manifest as language."[61] If so, Brightman's philosophical exploration is also an act of genuine piety.

Our century has been the arena of a polarity between a religious tradition that has been for the most part satisfied to consolidate its doctrinal position and powerful antitheistic forces that simply reject the religious tradition. Brightman would not accept such polarization. When the course of history breaks down this polarity, as it surely will, Brightman may come to be appreciated as a pioneer in the unfinished task of reconstructing the human spiritual dimension.

---

[60]See, for example, DeWolf's relatively moderate formulation of this charge in *The Religious Revolt Against Reason,* 168-74.

[61]Martin Buber, *I and Thou,* 2d ed., trans. Ronald Gregor Smith (New York: Charles Scribner's Sons, 1958) 103.

Bishop Francis J. McConnell and Social Justice

Paul Deats

From Francis J. McConnell's biography of Borden Parker Bowne I learned as much of McConnell as of Bowne and came to a new appreciation of McConnell's significance in the Boston Personalist tradition. Although the focus of these essays is on the academic succession of those who taught at Boston University, it would be an error to overlook a pastor who became college president and bishop, whose life was centered in the church—Methodist and ecumenical—and in, literally, the world, not just this country's public affairs. With all his responsibilities he still found time to write at least a dozen books, many of them originally lectures, and numerous articles.

LIFE[1]

Francis J. McConnell was born on his grandfather's farm in Ohio in 1871; he retired in 1944 to a nearby farm, where he died in 1953. His fa-

---

[1]See F. J. McConnell, *Borden Parker Bowne: His Life and Philosophy* (New York: Abingdon Press, 1929); *By the Way: An Autobiography* (New York: Abingdon-Cokesbury Press, 1952); and Earl Kent Brown, "Liberal in the Land," in Earl Kent Brown, *Ohio Biography Series* (North Canton OH: Bicentennial Commission of the East Ohio Annual Conference of the United Methodist Church, 1984) 71-88.

ther became a Methodist minister after his son was born; the son describes him as widely read and as an evangelist. The father died at age forty-three, in Massachusetts, leaving his family to return to Ohio, where the mother put three sons through Ohio Wesleyan Seminary, and into the Methodist ministry. One son, Charles M. ("Pat") was a legendary professor of rural church at Boston University. There are fascinating stories about how the mother refused to share in any money-raising events that were held *in* the church itself, and how she kept her tithe money in the coffee mill drawer (causing the Lord's money to be perfumed if not "tainted").

McConnell came from Ohio Wesleyan to Boston University in 1894, receiving his S.T.B. degree in 1897 and the Ph.D. in 1899. In 1897 he married Eva Thomas, about whom he wrote in his autobiography,

> There is often an unconscious assumption on the man's part that he himself is something remarkable, and the best thing he can say of his wife is that she helped make him so. . . . I gladly admit that my wife has done more for me than my most discerning friends could ever have imagined possible, but I am most concerned here in saying something about what she is in herself.

He went on to describe her "enduring and persistent idealism" and her refusal to compromise, both wedded to her "clearheaded practical sense."[2] McConnell served churches in Massachusetts and in Brooklyn, New York, until 1909, when he became president of DePauw University. He was elected a bishop of the Methodist Episcopal Church in 1912 and served in an active capacity for thirty-two years. He was president of the Methodist Federation for Social Service (now "for Social Action") and of the American Association for Social Service. When he was president of the Federal Council of Churches (1929-1933), Rabbi Stephen S. Wise introduced him to Al Smith as "the Protestant pope."[3] He gave leadership to the church committee investigating the Steel Strike of 1919; the strike dealt with such issues as the twelve-hour day and employment of women and children.[4] As bishop he presided over the Methodist conferences in Mexico in 1913-

---

[2]*By the Way*, 80.

[3]Ibid., 213.

[4]Walter G. Muelder, *Methodism and Society in the Twentieth Century* (New York: Abingdon Press, 1961) 96-103.

1919 and toured China in 1921 and India in 1930. McConnell opened a
chapter on "Bishops at Close Range" with a delightful story of the exercise of episcopal authority in thwarting a radical editor, but then went on
to tell how the then dean of the B. U. School of Theology told the bishops
that what was wrong with the choice of books for ministerial candidates
was that it was in the hands of the bishops.[5]

CONTINUITIES IN PERSONALISM

McConnell's wide reading is reflected in copious references, seldom
with footnotes; but his genius is in anecdotes, especially as these came out
of his international experiences. He never dodged philosophical issues.

> I regret the metaphysical nature of some of my discussion, though I do
> not see how metaphysical questions can be handled without metaphys-
> ical discussion. The most confirmed metaphysicians—and the most
> harmful—are those who disavow metaphysics.[6]

PERSONALISTIC THEISM

McConnell insisted that the impersonal world is not independent but
must serve the personal.[7] He thought of God as spirit, as mind, as moral
in essence. It is not as though the material universe were God's body, but
God's spirit is active throughout the universe. "I think of God as Mind,
not because I see specific marks of design in the world but because I find
the world intelligible at all."[8] Brightman thought McConnell held to
Bowne's personalism, treating persons as keys to reality. McConnell shared
Bowne's understanding of realism as involving "belief in a real and substantial self confronting an order which it did not make, but found." He
was neither a mystic nor at home with aesthetics; for him ethics was fundamental; he came to see that "the logic of personalism is essentially so-

---

[5]*By the Way,* 224-25, 250.

[6]*Is God Limited?* (New York: Abingdon Press, 1924) 11.

[7]*Christianity and Coercion* (Nashville: Cokesbury Press, 1933) 49.

[8]"The Eternal Spirit," in Joseph Fort Newton, ed., *My Idea of God: A Symposium of Faith* (Boston: Little, Brown, 1926) 253.

cial."[9] This intellectual development was congruent with his own life. Earl Kent Brown confirms this view.

> From an early age, he took a deep interest in social issues. His father had been a strong supporter of the anti-slavery stance and had a deep interest in the career of Abraham Lincoln. In later years, his father had been ardently prohibitionist as well. Long before women had the vote nationally, his mother would harness up the family horse and go forth to round up votes on issues which she thought Christians should see were socially and religiously significant. She often spoke with disdain of the "soft heads" she had found—i.e., "the good people who didn't believe that religion had anything to do with political and social questions." She could not understand at all a woman who would not vote when she had the chance, because "my citizenship is in heaven." Francis himself worked one summer in a large cotton mill in Lawrence, Massachusetts . . . 60 hours a week. . . . It was, perhaps, this experience that made him so interested in labor questions.[10]

A LIMITED GOD

There is a section on "The Limited God" as early as 1919. The first argument is that God had to choose self-limitation if persons were to be given freedom. The second argument hinges on the moral responsibility of the exercise of power, which applies to God as well as to human persons. God is not free to run the universe arbitrarily; God is the most obligated being there is. McConnell did not subscribe to "current doctrines" of a finite God, linked to "pluralists" such as H. G. Wells.[11] But human freedom requires that we limit the doctrine of divine omnipotence. There is also the possibility of God, or the capability of God to feel and experience emotion.

> The most limiting experience that we know is pain. If pain reaches to the center of the universe, we have seriously limited God.

---

[9]Edgar S. Brightman, "The World of Ideas," in H. F. Rall, ed., *Religion and Public Affairs* (New York: Macmillan, 1937) 167.

[10]Earl Kent Brown, "Liberal in the Land," 84.

[11]McConnell, *Democratic Christianity* (New York: Macmillan, 1919) 4-7; "The Eternal Spirit," 255-58; and *Christianity and Coercion,* 119.

And if God does *not* share our pain, God is even more limited.[12]

Brightman thought McConnell was more realistic about evil than was Bowne. J. Neal Hughley, on the other hand, evaluated McConnell as sharing "the central trait" of the Social Gospel movement—an undisturbed optimism and confidence. But McConnell warned against a fatalistic optimism that refuses to face the consequences if humans cannot learn to live together.

> An unregenerate patriotism will inevitably burn up the riches of the earth, destroy the race, and leave a blackened globe—a cosmic pile of ashes— as a monument to human fatuity, imbecility, and selfishness.

This quotation is from 1923. Three decades later he looked back and saw "large reason for pessimism as to the prospects for religion in such a world as this," reason for discouragement if not despair.[13] But his autobiography closed a few pages later with a word of hope in the deeds of simple folk.[14]

MORAL LAWS

I find at least an implicit formulation of five of Brightman's Moral Laws, from books published in 1923 and 1932. There is the obligation to pursue self-imposed ideals or goals; the requirement that one consider consequences of an action; the necessary attention to be given to the most inclusive end; the need to specify the good particular to a situation; and the injunction to cooperation (the last foreshadowing the communitarian laws).[15] Since Brightman published *Moral Laws* in 1933, I can only as-

---

[12]*Is God Limited?* 120. In *By the Way,* McConnell tells of the influence on Bowne of Professor Lorenzo Dow McCabe of Ohio Wesleyan and his theory of "divine nescience," which Bowne never accepted.

[13]J. Neal Hughley, "Religious-Democratic Reformism," in J. Neal Hughley, *Trends in Protestant Social Idealism* (Morningside Heights NY: King's Crown Press, 1948) 66. *By the Way,* 266. *Living Together* (New York: Abingdon Press, 1923) 166.

[14]*By the Way,* 269.

[15]*Christian Materialism* (New York: Friendship Press, 1936) 32; *The Christian Ideal and Social Control* (Chicago: University of Chicago Press, 1932) 3, 37; *Living Together,* 30-38, 46.

sume that Brightman's systematic statement grew out of his continuing discussions with McConnell and others.

RECURRENT THEMES
IN MCCONNELL'S THOUGHT

I turn now to a number of themes in McConnell's writing that anticipated, in one way or another, the systematic statement of the communitarian laws by Walter Muelder and Harold DeWolf in 1966 and 1971.[16]

The first theme is democracy, in which McConnell gave credit to A. D. Lindsay in several places. He wrote in *Democratic Christianity* of democratizing institutions in a way that reminds one of Walter Rauschenbusch. He even suggested the democratizing of the idea of God.

Closely related to this appreciation of democracy is his positive understanding of government. He held that society as a whole has created some values, that it is entitled through government to take those values, but that we have not yet come to terms with this idea. Thus, society allows too much profit to go "as prizes to private pockets," ostensibly to encourage private initiative, but probably because each of us hopes our time will come to get prizes.[17]

> The question today is not whether government shall more and more concern itself with business (in reply to an objection about government interference in business), but whether government's concern shall be in behalf of this or that special interest, or in behalf of the widest human interests.[18]

Government should be responsible for social welfare. There is an important role for voluntary associations. One finds arguments for gun control and against capital punishment. He started the latter argument by writing that "Society has a right to insist that nobody shall gain by anti-social conduct." He went on to dismiss as outdated a notion that individuals can use

---

[16]Muelder, *Moral Law in Christian Social Ethics* (Richmond VA: John Knox Press, 1966); DeWolf, *Responsible Freedom* (New York: Harper and Brothers, 1971).

[17]*Christian Materialism,* 15, 21.

[18]*Living Together,* 155-56.

death-dealing weapons at their discretion. If we are to allow any killing to be done, it must be at the hands of the state. Then he noted,

> There is something so horrible even about a legal execution of a human being that we may well question whether a state has a right to ask one of its officials to take charge of an execution even if the criminal richly deserves the penalty.

The responsibility of the state is to aim at the public good.[19]

Especially in democracy is social sentiment or public opinion important; and the sentiments can be either good or destructive (as fanatical nationalism in wartime). At points this concern extends to creation of an ethos or moral climate that enables good choices and does not put too great temptations before us.[20]

We have already noted Brightman's suggestion that McConnell developed the social implications of personalism more than had Bowne. McConnell thought Bowne did not take sufficiently into account "the degree of reality which attaches to institutions as such" and their impact for good or ill on persons.[21] Jesus' stress on persons was set against the background of the Hebraic organic understanding. Too much stress on individualism, even in evangelism, might lead a convert to passionate devotion to a wholly wrong cause. It is possible for personal unselfishness to serve group selfishness (here he foreshadowed Reinhold Niebuhr's *Moral Man and Immoral Society*). But individuals must repent and be born again in social relationships. Sin is collective and repentance can be collective (*now* he corrected Niebuhr).[22]

Even McConnell is not wholly consistent in this attitude. His trust was still typically individual conscience rather than social regulation. Products must not be socially harmful, but he did not share Vida Scudder's idea of "corporate responsibility," which is over three decades in advance of the

---

[19]See *Christian Materialism,* 17, 51, 75; and *Christianity and Coercion,* 43, 105; the quotation is from page 51.

[20]*Christian Materialism,* 39.

[21]"Bowne and the Social Questions," in E. C. Wilm, ed., *Studies in Philosophy and Theology* (New York: Abingdon Press, 1922) 135.

[22]*Living Together,* 11-12, 40-41; see *Christianity and Coercion,* 83; *The Christian Ideal,* 4, 7.

organized movement in this direction. There were still calls for conversion of institutions and of individuals in institutional relations.[23]

Hughley seems to criticize McConnell because he possessed "no doctrinaire socialism" and goes on to say "no militant pacifism, no Marxian economics." "His is a more or less negative, piecemeal criticism which tends to apply Christian principles and insights in *ad hoc* fashion to any and all problems demanding attention." This judgment is qualified a few pages later when Hughley notes that "McConnell seems to waver between a compromising, non-violent democratic reformism and an out-and-out socialism."[24] Hughley admits that the bishop is "anti-capitalist." It is true that McConnell is not doctrinaire and not a socialist, certainly not in the sense of being "a party man," as Brightman indicated. McConnell told of looking for books on socialism with Bowne and noted his teacher could not be a socialist. He had only scorn for what he calls "parlor socialists" and mainly praise for the British Labor Party; and he would not intentionally be doctrinaire on any issue, mainly because circumstances change. He did spell out how society shared in the creation of values and should be entitled to some return for its creation. He had only harsh words for a competitive society and refused to trust "the private initiative of present-day capitalism" to deal justly with the rights of "noncivilized peoples."[25] Socialism does "tend to absolutism" (written in 1919), but its doctrines do not necessarily imply atheism. He acknowledged the difficulties in building socialism in one country by itself.[26] In 1933 he knew that the U.S.S.R. had stern dictators, but they held their power because of the "general conviction that they are seeking to serve the mass of the people." Still in 1933, he saw more danger of a dictatorship "of moneyed groups than of socialist groups" in the U.S.[27] Muelder concurs that the bishop "anticipated the anticommunist hysteria that was to come later," quoting McConnell that

---

[23]*Christian Materialism,* 5, 27, 28.

[24]Hughley, "Religious-Democratic Reformism," 55-56, 61.

[25]"Bowne and the Social Questions," 133; *Christian Materialism,* 8-15; "Ethics," 198; "Economic Incentives," 345-46; *Living Together,* 239-40.

[26]*Democratic Christianity,* 49, 51; *Christian Materialism,* 3.

[27]*Christianity and Coercion,* 81, 43.

if fascists were to conquer Britain and move here, they could capture "our materialistic tories" whether there was danger of communism or not.[28]

Hughley's criticism extends to McConnell on coercion and war, where the bishop is judged to be as confused as he is on socialism.[29] My sense is that McConnell was not confused but still refused to be an absolutist in the sense that he judged what pacifism of that day was. With all his passion for democracy, he knew that "all society, and almost all social institutions, depend upon some form of coercion, even though that coercion may not rest on force or the threat of force."[30]

His most sanguine judgment about war itself came in 1919 and had to do with the responsibility of God, who "must do his part to bring about a worthy outcome" in the "Great War," for God cannot be unconcerned about human struggles. Under the heading "Making the World Safe for Democracy," he wrote of "justifiable war." The only war to be justified is one that will do away with war. But in the same section, he acknowledged, "If there is to be another war on a large scale civilization may as well give itself up for lost."[31] Two decades later he wrote, "The deadliest form of atheism is acceptance of the war policies and of the war spirit." He thought that there was no way to humanize war and that the church must not bless war.[32]

McConnell's refusal to identify himself as a conscientious objector to war had several sources. One is that even God cannot be absolutely non-resistant.[33] Conscientious objectors annoyed the bishop also because of their biblical literalism, for we would be in trouble if we took all of Jesus' words literally. But CO's are "the best present-day exemplars of prophetic genuineness even if at times they do lack judgment." McConnell admitted he was not enough of a martyr to be a CO, and his sternest words were for

---

[28]Muelder, *Methodism and Society*, 181.

[29]Hughley, "Religious-Democratic Reformism," 62.

[30]*Christianity and Coercion*, 10-11.

[31]*Democratic Christianity*, 8, 58, 68-69.

[32]*Christian Materialism*, 154; *The Christian Ideal*, 118; *Christianity and Coercion*, 19.

[33]*Democratic Christianity*, 46. Note, this is not nonviolent resistance.

what he called the "unconscientious objector, the coward calling loudly for war and objecting to any risk for his own skin, searching for safe quarters from which to urge others to death."[34] He did seem to approve of vocational pacifism.

McConnell's illustrations from his broad international experience both reveal some insensitivities and at once demonstrate his consistent respect for and solidarity with other peoples. The insensitivity is evident in his references to "backward peoples," "non-adult" groups, and stages or levels of evolution or development; however, these labels were often put in quotation marks as "so-called." And the respect shines through. He was opposed to imperialism, qualified in his endorsement of Western evangelization, and in favor of the indigenization of leadership in the younger churches. It is better for such peoples to "return to the old ways of tribal war and slaughter than to have them ruled over by outsiders." It is not now so easy to see "the Christian nations [as] the agents of salvation." Only exceptional human beings are wise enough to have authority "in spiritual concerns over a native in another country."[35]

Respect is not enough; there must also be economic justice among nations. And there must be self-determination. It is very hard for an American Christian to respect any democracy except the Anglo-Saxon variety, even though not "all forms of democracy or morality or religion are on the same plane of value."[36] After eight years of presiding over Mexican Methodism, McConnell knew that the Mexican people had "first claim over their own resources." He had high regard for the pro-Indian writings of Las Casas, an early Spanish priest who was critical of the conquest.[37]

His 1933 words about revolutions have a peculiar poignancy in these days of concern with Central America.

> The only means of stopping revolutions at the start would be in going back through the years and stopping whatever tends to depress human values.

---

[34]*Living Together*, 140; *The Christian Ideal*, 129; *Living Together*, 147, 149.

[35]*Living Together*, 243, 207, 273.

[36]*The Christian Ideal*, 70-76; *Living Together*, 210, 213.

[37]*Democratic Christianity*, 66; *By the Way*, 135.

Revolutions are not necessarily bloody.

> The amount of blood spilt in a revolution is likely to bear some ratio to
> the amount spilt in the oppressions which have led up to the revolution.

The crucial question about revolutions is whether they lead to better human conditions.[38]

H. F. Rall, in the essays written to honor Bishop McConnell, provides the most telling statements of the bishop's moral judgment on U.S. policy in Latin America, quoting at length from his report to the Congress on Christian Work in Montevideo in 1925.

> It would be folly not to recognize the obstacle to foreign missionary work
> in Latin America created by the real or supposed policies of the United
> States toward her neighbors to the South.

The report detailed the seizure of Panama, the taking over of Santo Domingo's custom houses, the conquest of Haiti, the Pershing expedition to Mexico in 1916.

> The tragic situation at the present day in Latin America deserves careful
> consideration, country by country, where the United States exercises
> control. Control, moreover, always develops resentment and enmity
> among a people, though their officials may approve it.

He then referred to "a group of countries controlled through display of force": Cuba (with a navy base threatening our intervention), Haiti, Santo Domingo, Panama, Nicaragua (where Marines have been since 1912, opposed by most of the people, "but which is favorable to American bankers"), and Honduras.[39]

In a few pages one cannot do justice to the full range of McConnell's ideas or his institutional leadership, to his articulation of social ideals or to his formulation of theological and ecclesiological argument. I do not always, personally, agree with his social judgments, as, for example, on nonviolence. But I live in a later time, and I am amazed at how much of his writing is contemporary.

He took seriously the institutional dimensions of social problems. He sought justice in labor struggles, argued for a less imperialistic and more

---

[38]*Christianity and Coercion,* 38-39.

[39]Rall, *Religion and Public Affairs,* 21-24.

human rights-oriented U.S. policy in Latin America, reformulated mission strategy, wrestled with the inevitability and limits of coercion in institutional life. He knew conflict was endemic. He did, as Brightman wrote, develop—and embody—the social logic of personalism. And, at the same time, he continued work on the theological/philosophical problems of a limited God and of God's immanence and transcendence. I am tutored by his life and his thought; he has helped me understand why I am a personalist.

Georgia Harkness as a Personalist Theologian

I. Philosophical Theology, Dianne Carpenter
II. Theology and Ethics, Rolaine Franz

I. PHILOSOPHICAL THEOLOGY

Georgia Harkness has a significant place in the story of twentieth-century personalistic philosophy and liberal theology. From 1921 until 1974, a formative period in the development of American philosophy and theology, she grappled with theoretical and systematic issues in order to answer the call to a Christian witness in the midst of social change. There has been little research on her work and to begin to remedy this situation is no easy task. In 1939 Harkness wrote, "For many years the philosopher and the theologian in me have been, not exactly at war, but in friendly rivalry . . ." She was very articulate about her stand within liberal Christianity, all the while very capable of seeking to reform it through a critical review of weaknesses. While the second portion of this essay addresses her articulation of liberal Christianity, the task of this first portion is to identify Harkness with the philosophical school of Boston Personalism.

Her philosophical theology is profoundly personalistic; however, her metaphysical thought shows development and incorporates some other contemporary hypotheses about the reality of nature. In his preface to *Per-

sonalism in Theology, Brightman pointed with enthusiasm to differences among personalists as a ''healthy sign of growth.''[1] Harkness, nevertheless, defies identification with any established philosophical position. She used her metaphysical perspective to adopt the label of ''theistic realist.'' While one must take very seriously her self-chosen identification, in her writing personalism and not realism became the warrant for her moral philosophy. Her experience of the personal God turned the tide of her own dilemma in favor of classification first as a liberal theologian and second as a personalistic philosopher.

Recognizing that personalistic philosophical theology is most vulnerable to criticism in its explanation of evil, she explored the possibility of a metaphysical reality that is ''dualistic in a qualified . . . sense.'' However, ultimately, it is organic personalistic monism that informs her moral philosophy.

In order to defend this thesis, I will briefly outline the social and educational influences on Harkness's life and thought, compare her position on critical issues in philosophy of religion, metaphysics, and moral philosophy with that of Brightman, and conclude that she is a woman whom personalism can proudly claim as one of its own.

Social and Educational Influences

Georgia Harkness was born 21 April 1891 to J. Warren and Lillie (Merrill) Harkness in Harkness, New York. The town had been named in honor of her grandfather, and her family was a prosperous part of this small rural community. She grew up on a farm that had belonged to her father's family since 1801, when her Scotch-Irish forebears had migrated to the Lake Champlain region.

The youngest of four children, Georgia Harkness attended the town's one-room school, which also housed the Methodist congregation to which her parents belonged. Once a year the traveling revivalist came to the town, and around the age of nine she resolved what she claimed was the only crisis of faith of her life. She joined the church at the age of fourteen and maintained her membership there as well as strong ties to the people of Harkness for the rest of her life.

––––––––––––––

[1]Edgar S. Brightman, ed., Foreword to *Personalism in Theology* (Boston: Boston University Press, 1943) viii.

After graduating from high school in Keeseville, New York, she attended Cornell University, where she joined the Student Christian Association and the Student Volunteer Movement and pledged her life to service as a foreign missionary. The Social Gospel's vision of human progress combined with the deep personal piety of her childhood to shape her underlying faith.

She received her A.B. from Cornell in 1912 and taught in high schools until 1918 in order to be near her parents. The experience of teaching was not satisfying, and she was delighted to learn of a new profession that opened theological education and church employment for women. She graduated from Boston University with a master's degree in religious education and an A.M. in 1920.[2]

In 1921 Georgia Harkness's first book, *The Church and the Immigrant,* was published. There she was identified as an instructor at the B. U. School of Religious Education and Social Service. In the book Harkness challenged the church to take up the neglected cause of the immigrants flowing into the United States.

> We have applied to him unpleasant epithets, and have frequently placed upon his shoulders the blame for all our present social and industrial unrest. If we have permitted him to be the victim of exploitation and greed, if we have denied him the opportunities for education and Americanization that are his due, can we wonder that he sometimes pays us back in our own coin?[3]

She highlighted the need for education that "foreign-born" people could perceive as useful, advocated mediation between labor and management, and showed particular sensitivity to the plight and needs of immigrant women who were occupied at home, isolated, and pressed to comprehend the influence of their newly available suffrage.

In this year she must have also begun her doctoral studies in philosophy with Edgar Brightman, who had arrived at Boston in 1919 to teach.

---

[2]"Harkness, Georgia Elma," in *Notable American Women: The Modern Period,* ed. Barbara Sicherman, Carol Hurd Green, Ilene Kantrov, and Harriette Walker (Cambridge MA: The Belknap Press of Harvard University, 1980) 312-14.

[3]Georgia Harkness, *The Church and the Immigrant* (New York: George H. Doran Co., 1921) 15.

Knudson's work in personalism and theology was just beginning to take shape. While Harkness recognized her debt to Brightman in all her early works, it is not until 1955 that she referred to her "two greatest teachers, Edgar S. Brightman and Albert C. Knudson."[4]

In 1922 Harkness went to Elmira College in New York as an assistant professor of religious education. She received her Ph.D. in philosophy from Boston University in 1923 with a dissertation on "The Philosophy of Thomas Hill Green with Special Reference to the Relations Between Ethics and the Philosophy of Religion." That year she returned to Elmira as professor of philosophy and remained there until 1937. During her years at Elmira, she wrote *Conflicts in Religious Thought*. It is Georgia Harkness's first full-length philosophical discussion of religion. Looking back she wrote in 1939,

> At 10:00 on the evening of February 8, 1929, I put the last words to the writing of *Conflicts in Religious Thought*. At the awareness that at last the long job was done I felt a wild exhilaration such as makes one want to "paint the town red." Being thoroughly conditioned to sobriety, I went to bed. . . . There is nothing in *Conflicts in Religious Thought* that I wish to retract. Were I writing it now there is much that I should wish to add. . . .[5]

She repeated this confidence in what she had written when she had the opportunity to revise it in 1949.

The year 1937 was significant for several reasons. In that year her father died, she was appointed professor of religion at Mount Holyoke, and she completed one year of study at Union Theological Seminary. Looking back on this time she stated,

> I have profited from the currents coming out of continental Europe and too superficially called Barthian. These have come to me through books, but more through the forceful personalities of Reinhold Niebuhr and Paul Tillich—men with whom I do not agree very far but by whom I am stirred to rethink my faith. They have come at Oxford and Madras through

---

[4]Georgia Harkness, Foreword to *Foundations of Christian Knowledge* (New York: Abingdon Press, 1955).

[5]"A Spiritual Pilgrimage," *The Christian Century* 56 (15 March 1939): 348.

wrestling with continental theology for the liberalism which I believe to have the truth.[6]

Her contribution to a 1941 symposium on Reinhold Niebuhr's *The Nature and Destiny of Man* stressed two points at which she believed his work went astray. One was an "over-identification of religious liberalism with the secularistic liberalism of bourgeois culture." Her second argument stated, "A more basic error lies in an almost complete identification of the term *Biblical* with *Hebraic-Pauline.*"[7] Due to these two "differences in standing-ground" her view of Christian democracy and Christian social action, both based in Jesus' view of human beings, parted company with Niebuhr at numerous points.

Standing firmly with the liberal theological position, Harkness was also its critic.

> This does not mean that I have seen nothing in liberalism that needed correction. We are in danger of selling out to science as the only approach to truth, of trusting too hopefully in man's power to remake his world, of forgetting the profound fact of sin and the redeeming power of divine grace, of finding our chief evidence of God in cosmology, art or human personality, to the clouding of the clearer light of the incarnation.[8]

She took seriously the limitations of "finding our chief evidence of God in . . . human personality" when she wrote *The Recovery of Ideals,* also published in 1937.

Conflicts in Religious Thought and *The Recovery of Ideals* are critical to an analysis of the development of Georgia Harkness's philosophical theology. The former was written under the influence of her personalistic training and her position as professor of philosophy. It was revised in light of her movement to a dominant theological liberalism. The latter was written in light of Barth, Niebuhr, and Tillich's theologies, ecumenical dialogue, and the philosophical work of pragmatism, the process school, and

---

[6]Ibid., 349.

[7]"A Symposium on Reinhold Niebuhr's *Nature & Destiny of Man,*" *Christendom* 6 (1941): 568-69.

[8]"A Spiritual Pilgrimage," 349.

critical realism as expounded by James, Whitehead, and Pratt, respectively.

Comparison with Edgar S. Brightman

Personalistic idealism in the Brightman tradition has no simple definition. It works out of an epistemic dualism, recognizing the hypothetical character of all philosophical propositions. It holds a radically empirical view of the self, which is characterized by both unity and freedom in its knowing and valuing. Ultimate reality is viewed as personal and pluralistic in the sense of a society of persons, with an organic rather than atomistic understanding of the relation of the persons. Central attention is paid to axiology, with the objectivity of values affirmed.[9] Harkness worked generally within this framework, testing it at certain points to be noted below. *Conflicts in Religious Thought* (in both editions) and Brightman's *A Philosophy of Religion* exhibit a great deal of similarity in regard to philosophy of religion. This should not surprise us since Harkness studied with Brightman. Both are scientific and historical in their approaches. Harkness asserted as the major thesis of her book "that faith and reason when rightly envisaged are harmonious, not conflicting." She recognized the value of scientific method and identified its distinguishing feature as a "working hypothesis," which she equated with faith from the religious perspective; Brightman noted the same affinity of faith and hypothesis.

Discussing the various types of faith she concluded that

> the faith of religion gives a transcendent grasp of a power by which to achieve new heights of self-mastery and peace. . . . the faith of theistic religion is a personal confidence in a loving Personality. The faith of philosophy combines the search for facts with the search for meanings; only in religion do we find these values applied to human life and made warm, dynamic and effectual through the grip of personal fellowship with the divine. . . . Religion is rational. Its intellectual substructure ought to be justified by reason, and it can be.[10]

In this text, Harkness analyzed all the possible avenues to truth and concluded that coherence, a Brightman concept, is the criterion of truth.

---

[9]Walter G. Muelder, Christina Sears, and Anne Schlabach, *The Development of American Philosophy* (New York: Houghton Mifflin Co., 1960) 211-21.

[10]*Conflicts in Religious Thought,* rev. ed. (New York: Henry Holt, 1949) 47.

This theme was reaffirmed in several places in this text and later works. This scientific, coherent, hypothetical approach to religion, along with a warning against those who would claim to have found the absolute truth, kept her well within the liberal tradition. She did affirm that there is an absolute truth grounded in the nature of things and in certain eternal logical principles. This affirmation of an absolute truth points to an Absolute Mind,[11] and the reality of eternal logical principles will be important in considering her moral philosophy.

Having pointed the way to an Absolute Mind, Harkness examined the obstacles to belief in God and the evidences for belief. Of the obstacles, pain and suffering loom largest.

In 1929, the considerations that she recognized as the most valid grounds for belief in God were:

(1) the unity and interacting harmony of the physical universe;
(2) the existence of human personality;
(3) the rationality and ''mind-like'' nature of the world;
(4) the evidences of a guiding purpose;
(5) the religious experience of humanity;
(6) the nature of values.[12]

In her 1949 revision she added to this list ''the revelation of God in Jesus Christ,'' and her treatment of this ground for belief is her major revision. It is a revision that shows her hand as a philosopher turned theologian. However, it does not deny an underlying personalistic theology. In both editions she moved boldly into her central proposition, that God is a Supreme Personality who is creative, intelligent, purposeful, and good. This Supreme Person, like human persons, is a self-conscious being consisting in the total complex of experience and being unified about a center. A person is not corporeal because personality is not linked to the physical body. Human and divine personality is mental.

To complete her philosophy of religion she addressed human suffering, prayer, and immortality. Reflecting continuity with the philosophical thought of Brightman, Harkness advocated a melioristic position toward suffering. She also addressed human freedom and the problem of sin. Prayer

---

[11]Ibid., 72.

[12]Ibid., 107-108.

is the rubric under which she alluded to organic pluralism and the responsibility to express altruism, in this book and in *Dark Night of the Soul*.

Keeping the paradigm of personality central, Harkness stated that first among all the facts that make immortality a necessary postulate in a universe that is reasonable and good is the supreme value of human personality. Immortality conserves the abiding place of values for Harkness just as it does for Kant. However, defending the suggestion that personality is the essence of the self, she stated that it is personality that is immortal. In 1949 the philosophical statement of human moral worth was replaced by a theological statement of created human worth. Again we have the personalistic theologian Harkness evolving from the personalistic philosopher.

The philosophy of religion Harkness outlined and discussed is most congruent with the tenets of personalistic philosophy. In its revision it went no further than the personalistic theology of Knudson. It is significant that the details of personalistic metaphysics that support Brightman's theory of a finite God were addressed in neither the original nor the revised Harkness work. This theory is a part of Brightman's *A Philosophy of Religion*. Inasmuch as he spoke for a finite God, he footnoted Harkness as supporting this concept.[13] However, in the argument that she proposed we find her self-defined philosophical position to be that of the "theistic realist." The argument is first found in *The Recovery of Ideals* where she stated,

> I was reared in the personalistic tradition which holds that God and human persons are the only metaphysical realities. Such a view does not, of course, make physical nature an illusion. It makes physical things the acts of God. That is, it regards nature as an eternal system of divine activity; not something God has created, or still creates, but something God *causes* with consistent regularity. Human persons, being relatively independent real units of existence, are created; physical things are caused.
>
> To this view I still assent in part, but only partially. My present view comes closer to a form of theistic realism. I now see no valid sense in which it is possible to say that only persons are metaphysically real.[14]

---

[13]Edgar S. Brightman, *A Philosophy of Religion* (New York: Prentice Hall, 1940) 325-28.

[14]Georgia Harkness, *The Recovery of Ideals* (New York: Charles Scribner's Sons, 1937) 165.

As I present her metaphysical position there will be similarities of thought between her position and terminology used by Whitehead and Tillich. However, I will finally turn to the epistemology of Critical Realism to understand her position that she is a theistic realist.

In *Recovery of Ideals* Harkness expressed the view that she was less optimistic of humanity's ability to help remedy suffering than she had been in 1929. This is important because in 1929, like a thoroughgoing personalist, she had believed that the only metaphysical realities were human and divine personality. If there was suffering it had to be ultimately attributable to one or the other. If suffering were to be alleviated, it must be changed by divine or human personality. In fact, if God was ultimately good, and omnipotent, why did God make a world where suffering exceeded the explanation of human sinfulness? In 1929 she went no farther than the explanation of suffering as instrumental. Suffering is an occasion for human cooperation in God's moral purpose through development of ''moral ruggedness.'' She stated, ''Progress comes ever through conflict, and if suffering urges us toward the goal, it serves a useful purpose.''[15] This is a functional, theological explanation of suffering. It avoids the hard metaphysical question of who or what is responsible for suffering. It threatens our concept of an ultimately good, divine and omnipotent personality and at best shrouds the topic in the mysteries of faith. The only other explanation available to the rational, religious human being is that God is finite, limited by something inside or outside of God's self.

Faced with this dilemma, Brightman placed the limits within the divine personality. Harkness, on the other hand, proposed a ''qualified dualism.'' She identified at least three other types of interrelated realities separate from persons—events, things (living or inanimate), and eternal forms. She suggested that God, like human beings, may be limited by circumstances that these three realities present. She made a comparison of her concepts with Whitehead's definitions of ''actual entities'' and ''actual occasions.'' The limitations for God of the separate reality of *things* she identified as inertia and/or recalcitrance, while the limitation created by *events* is chance. She linked her thought to a view of the created universe as an ''eternal process—the never-beginning and never-ceasing ac-

---

[15]*Conflicts in Religious Thought,* 216.

tivity of an immanent yet transcendent deity,''[16] which is apprehended by us as product not process.

Harkness developed her definitions of events, things, and eternal forms, continuing to two further proposals. First,

> The world *as created* is a process in which God has priority over the world in the sense that he makes the world and is not made by it. But this does not mean that God, at any point in time, created the world out of nothing.[17]

There is a noticeable similarity here with Whitehead's process thought. Bertocci dealt with the concept of creation-ex-nihilo by affirming that God created human personality where there was none before. In this sense Harkness might concur if she had been asked.

The more difficult proposal is to define the nature of events, things, and eternal forms as they exist without created personality. This second move appears to be based in the epistemology of Critical Realism, which was being developed independent of Harkness's work. Critical Realism suggests that there are selves and objects in the world. However, the selves do not perceive the objects directly. Rather, they perceive the objects as experienced. This concept of the object as experienced grants real status to the derivative power of interpretation by persons.

In the 1938 article ''The Abyss and the Given,'' Harkness articulated these same views of God's limitations.

> My metaphysical position, stated in the *Recovery of Ideals,* is shamelessly ontic. It is monistic in its foundations and fruition, dualistic in a qualified though not ultimate sense in its theory of God's relation to the world. With the personalists I regard nature as the eternal activity of God [stated in 1929, p. 267]. But I do not equate it with an aspect of God's consciousness. Both human and physical nature are the product of God's creative will, and in both there is an interweaving of what Tillich calls freedom and fate, though to escape panpsychism I prefer to use the terms spontaneity and order for physical nature, but not all the juxtapositions of circumstance which arise within the given, uncreated structure of possibilities. God is limited, therefore, both by human wills and the element of chance which emerges within nature and history. There are some

---

[16]*Recovery of Ideals,* 161, 169.

[17]Ibid., 169.

circumstances which God cannot prevent, but there are none which cannot be transcended through God's limitless power to enable men to triumph over tragedy.[18]

In the discussion of personalistic idealism referred to earlier, Muelder explained,

Personalists have opposed Neo-Realism quite fully. They have been congenial to the basic contention in the epistemology of Critical Realism. They have noted with sympathy the organic philosophy of Whitehead. They have been friendly to the voluntarism of pragmatism but have been critical of its ontology. They have seen in naturalism, as ordinarily interpreted, their chief opponent.[19]

We conclude that Harkness's thought is congruent at each point.

Harkness did deal with whether reality is "mental" in the Berkeleian sense. Muelder's review of "The Idealist Tradition" notes James E. Creighton's careful distinction between "mentalism" and the "speculative idealism" with a focus on concrete experience. Harkness's early work, *Conflicts in Religious Thought*, developed the hypothesis that human and divine personality are mind and not matter. Regarding the physical world, Harkness in *Recovery of Ideals* alluded to the possibility of creation from preexistent matter but did not work this out as a hypothesis. She was primarily concerned with the independent reality of the experienced meaning of interrelated created selves, matter, eternal forms, and events. Most personalists have attributed this qualified, derivative reality to human or divine mind. Harkness attributed God's limitation to the reality of the derivatives of the Divine Mind and the created world, thus a "qualified though not ultimate" dualism. Her choice of theistic realism as a metaphysical position is one Brightman could include within personalism. Harkness let her philosophical hypothesis remain in the shadow of the theological affirmation that God's presence in the midst of suffering was the real issue.

The relationship of personality to the corporeal has been one of the debates within personalism. Harkness modified the view proposed by William James in her 1929 discussion of immortality. She suggested that the

---

[18]"The Abyss and the Given," *Christendom* 3 (1938): 519-20.

[19]Muelder, et al., *The Development of American Philosophy*, 219-20.

relationship of brain to mind is instrumental or expressive rather than productive.[20]

While Harkness used the epistemology of Critical Realism in identifying the realities that limit God, she explored her own epistemology, which
she identified as "synoptic supernaturalism." She thus continued the epistemic dualism adopted by Brightman. Linking this epistemology to the
revelation of God, she was concerned with a dimension of reality not addressed by realism. She took a concept crucial to Brightman, that of coherence, and contributed to its development, thereby enhancing the
expression of personalism in the same way that Muelder's work contributed in another direction. Harkness and Muelder represent, respectively,
the more theological and more philosophical development of the concept
of coherence. Harkness also dealt with faith and the term *supernaturalism*
in a very different sense from that of neo-orthodoxy or process philosophy,
in a manner more compatible with personalism.[21]

Moral Philosophy

Out of deep ties to personalistic philosophy and to Christian faith,
Harkness developed her moral philosophy in relation to the responsibility
of moral choice. In *Conflicts in Religious Thought,* under the rubric of
prayer, she alluded to organic pluralism and the responsibility of altruism,
stating, "Our obligation to pray for others is a consequence of our duty
both as Christians and as members of a social universe."[22] Her major work
in this area, in *The Recovery of Ideals,* bears a comparison to Brightman's
development in the *Moral Laws.* In general, Harkness's work is very similar to Brightman's, with the notable exception that it is far less structured.
In the chapter "Barriers to Religious Living," she advocated the position
of "triumphant religion as a norm" and "creative idealism," which was
the underlying theme of the entire book. Harkness asserted that revelation
is incomplete until it is appropriated, and she identified the "triple curses
of modern society as racialism, nationalism and economic exploitation."
At this point she moved into a discussion of how we are to know ideals are

[20]*Conflicts in Religious Thought,* 295.

[21]*Recovery of Ideals,* 91-92, 97. W. G. Muelder, *Moral Law in Christian
Social Ethics* (Richmond: John Knox Press, 1966) 153.

[22]*Conflicts in Religious Thought,* 277.

directed toward right ends. We need two measures: "an objective criterion of what is good" and "a comprehensive and unbiased knowledge of probable consequences of any projected act." She further stated, "Such a good is found in inclusiveness of values as they contribute to the enrichment of personality." Realizing that we must often choose between evils she asserted,

> Living in the kind of world we do, the only thing we can do in these situations of conflicting values is *to do the best possible under the circumstances.* The "best possible" has to be judged by a wide survey of all the possible results. Having made the survey and formed the judgment, the thing to do is *to act,* undaunted by the awareness that the ideal is unattainable. It is better to attain it partially than through indecision or inertia to attain it not at all.[23]

Viewed in light of her various and scattered comments concerning logical consistency and coherence, her obvious reliance on the principle of autonomy, and the above remarks, I find her advocating the essence of Brightman's original set of moral laws, with the possible exception of the Law of Specification. Her tendency to subscribe to a "Jesus ethic," which was developed later, as I shall mention, tended toward a perfectionism that may be inconsistent with the implications of the situationalism that can be read into the Law of Specification.

Harkness's discussion of moral choice lacks the structure of Brightman's earlier work, as well as the terminology of laws or principles. However, her philosophical theology depends, for its coherence, on these eternal laws she mentions in her 1929 text. Moral laws are the logical result of thinking within personalistic philosophical guidelines.

After becoming more theological, Georgia Harkness wrote three books in the 1950s that have to do with morality and ethics. The first was historical: *The Sources of Western Morality* (1954). The second was *Foundations of Christian Thought* (1955), which she identified as Christian apologetics and in which she assembled the most comprehensive selected bibliography including by far more Boston Personalists than she had ever referred to in her pre-1950 texts. The third was *Christian Ethics* (1957) in which she attempted to return to a "Jesus ethic" and devoted a chapter to "Duties to Self and Society" that introduced the concept that motivated

---

[23]*Recovery of Ideals,* 99.

the addition of the communitarian laws to the original moral laws. She also devoted half of the book to "Problems of Social Decision" including Marriage and the Family; Economic Life, the Race Problem, Conscience and the State; War, Peace, and International Order; and Culture.

II. THEOLOGY AND ETHICS[24]

Georgia Harkness resolved the rivalry between herself as philosopher and herself as theologian in this way: in her words, she taught philosophy but wrote religion.[25] As mentioned earlier, 1939 was a decisive year in this resolution. Sensitive to the fact that the Barthian expressions of neo-orthodoxy challenged her theological liberalism and wrenched by the social upheavals of the 1930s, she thought her way through to a position of Christian apologist or evangelical liberal. Her father, from his deathbed in 1937, gave her an intensely personal motive for abandoning the quest for "an ideal of philosophical objectivity" as he urged her to "write more about Jesus Christ." Fortuitously, her faith stance was supported professionally by the invitation, still in 1937, to teach religion at Mount Holyoke College, and two years later, to become professor of applied theology at Garrett. In 1950 she agreed to teach applied theology at the Pacific School of Religion in Berkeley, from which she retired in 1961—but retired only to continue her scholarly work. In those retirement years she wrote almost a book a year and spoke her mind quite emphatically on ecclesiastical and social issues. Shortly before her death in 1974, at the age of eighty-three, she asked an interviewer not to emphasize her age because she did not want people to stop asking her to do things.[26]

She could not overcome the philosophical objections to her theological stance, but she remained with her theological commitment till the end

---

[24]I draw on the following published assessments of Georgia Harkness: Dorothy C. Bass, "Harkness, Georgia Elma," in *Notable American Women: The Modern Period*, 312-14; Margaret Frakes, "Theology Is Her Province," *The Christian Century* 69 (24 September 1952): 1088-91; Georgia Harkness, "A Spiritual Pilgrimage," *The Christian Century* 56 (15 March 1939): 348-51; and Helen Johnson, "Georgia Harkness: She Made Theology Understandable," *United Methodists Today* 1 (October 1974): 55-58.

[25]"A Spiritual Pilgrimage," 349.

[26]Johnson, "Georgia Harkness," 58.

of her life. Still, her philosophical training and research kept her honest in surprising ways. Though she regretted not including a chapter on Christ in *Conflicts in Religious Thought* (1929), she remedied that in the 1949 edition and in some works of the 1950s when she dealt with *Christian Ethics* (1957) and its precursor volumes, *The Sources of Western Morality* (1954) and *Foundations of Christian Knowledge* (1955).

Her theological stance is not a denial of her former self but an expression of her faith. In *The Dark Night of the Soul* (1945), faith itself is a gift and a task. In good Wesleyan mode, she recognized the imperative to bear fruits of the spirit, and for her the fruits were a variety of teaching styles. She distinguished herself as a scholar, and a common methodology for her was to trace the historical roots of an issue, to establish a context that extended beyond intuition.

She was also a "theologian for the common reader"—again in good Wesleyan mode, recalling Albert Outler's assessment of Wesley as a folk theologian, committed to "plain truth for plain people."[27] Georgia Harkness commented in a 1974 interview, only a month before her death, "I have not become a big name in theology. My talent, if I have one, lies in making theology understandable to people."[28] She minimized her importance as a systematic theologian—which indeed makes the task of identifying her personalism more difficult—but we must guard against the judgment that the recognition of her accomplishments is a token of condescension that recognizes reluctantly the need to create an inclusive society, a society that acknowledges the role of women at all levels of critical and creative activity; that clearly was not the case. But she did make theology understandable; her touchstone was that only "in Christ is revelation ultimate and unequivocal";[29] and ultimately her understanding of Christian ethics is that we must center on the ethics of Jesus, not of Paul, or Luther, or Calvin—not even of Wesley!

There is a simplicity about much of her work that disarms some critics, and they deride her writing as "simplistic." It *is* unnerving to read her

---

[27]Albert C. Outler, ed., *John Wesley* (New York: Oxford University Press, 1964) vii.

[28]Johnson, "Georgia Harkness," 55.

[29]"A Spiritual Pilgrimage," 349.

books, particularly *Mysticism* and *Dark Night of the Soul,* with their references to popular magazines such as *Good Housekeeping, Time,* or the *New Yorker.* For Harkness there is a crucial theological issue in emphasizing the importance of the laity and correlating doctrine with experience. It is an inductive approach—not usually the approach of a systematic theologian—to begin with human experience and wrestle with it in terms of the doctrine of the church. In addition, one of Harkness's themes is the challenge to a "ministry of reconciliation." Consequently, while an imperative of the Christian faith is to go to the ends of the earth to proclaim the Gospel, the first part of that proclamation will address human need. There begins to form an image of a woman very much engaged in life, and not just at academic levels. Her vulnerability, as she wrote about it, can scare us. The absence of much deliberate autobiographical writing, even raw data, is lamentable. There is only a piece written for the Pacific Coast Theological Group during the 1950s and existing in manuscript form at Garrett. However, she revealed herself in all her writing and especially in her poetry, which she called her "spiritual autobiography."[30] Her poetry is a way of looking at Georgia Harkness's stand on several issues—theological, ecclesiastical, and social.

Harkness never considered herself a poet, but thought of her poetry as another way of expressing her commitment to the kingdom of God in this world. It may be helpful to think of her poetry as another form of folk theology, etiologically based, confronting some of humankind's enduring questions. Most of her poems were published in the *Christian Century,* and many reflect her delight in the beauty and peace of unspoiled nature, reminiscent of her childhood in rural New York, the home to which she returned on school vacations.

She began writing poetry in 1931, and in 1935 *Holy Flame,* the first of several devotional books, was published. She described the title poem as her first serious poem. Almost in sermon style, it declares the text from Isaiah: "And I heard the voice of the Lord saying, 'Whom shall I send, and who will go for us?' Then I said, 'Here I am! Send me.' " The poem itself has all the formality and dignity and depth of a sonnet.

> *Isaiah mourned the passing of the king,*
> *And to the temple came to muse and pray.*

---

[30]Georgia Harkness, *Grace Abounding* (Nashville: Abingdon, 1969) 13.

Dark was the kingdom's future on that day,
Beset with greed and every evil thing.
No spokesman of the Lord was there to sting
The conscience of the mob, or lead the way
To gallant victories in Jehovah's fray
With sin and strife, with self and suffering.

God gave Isaiah then the vision high;
His unclean lips were purged with sacred fire.
Out of the smoke a Voice in challenge came;
Unhesitant, he answered, Here am I.
Again the days are dark, the outlook dire;
Lord, touch Thy prophets now with holy flame.[31]

Her early optimism is gone. The poem, written during the days of the Great Depression, recognizes ugly and destructive elements, even in the natural order, which—in her own comment—"had not yet been subdued to human good."[32] This poem is the beginning of Georgia Harkness's personal struggle with suffering and evil in a world we believe to have been created by a good God.

Edgar S. Brightman posited a finite God, ever struggling against the Given within God's nature, limited in power but not in goodness. Georgia Harkness, on several occasions, disclaimed any sympathy with this position of her "honored professor";[33] instead, she makes the distinction that there are "recalcitrant" evil elements in the world that God has commissioned us to subdue.[34] The Book of Genesis records the first commissioning—to be "fruitful and multiply, and fill the earth and subdue it." That God's purposes will be fulfilled, that the earth will be subdued, that the outcome of this whole process of living is foreordained—these are assertions to be tested. Some would argue that such is the stance of faith. Georgia Harkness assumed more than that; she wrote, "I believe that God in infinite wisdom has limited himself by a mode of creation that precludes any quick and easy victory, but has not surrendered his ultimate con-

---

[31]Ibid., 125.

[32]Ibid.

[33]Ibid., 184.

[34]Georgia Harkness, *Stability Amid Change* (Nashville: Abingdon, 1969) 138.

trol.''[35] Is that a satisfying explanation of the poem ''The Divine Patience''?

> *God strives.*
> *Before the firmament was formed, the Eternal One*
> *Envisaged all, and saw a battle to be won.*
> *Through countless aeons of creative pain and toil*
> *He shapes his world with everlasting moil.*
> *God strives.*
>
> *God feels.*
> *The God who hears the gunfire of eternal war,*
> *And smells the stench of sin, must suffer with and for*
> *Humanity. The God who heals with conquering power*
> *Must know himself the pangs of grief when shadows lower.*
> *God feels.*
>
> *God waits.*
> *Man lights a torch: in feverish haste he goes about*
> *His task. He sees the light burn low: it flickers out.*
> *The ever-striving, ever-suffering God relights*
> *The torch, and labors on through agelong nights.*
> *God waits.*[36]

The theme of the ''ever-striving, ever-suffering'' deity is underscored in another poem as she imagined God to be a ''Master Poet.''

> *For he too makes, and sings in endless strife,*
> *Struggling to mold the world that is to be.*[37]

Is the poet at war with the theologian? Does the energy of these lines reflect a realism that acknowledges real risk in thinking of our world as a place in which we have a crucial responsibility to participate with God in continuing creation of the kingdom—even on this earth?

We have noted Georgia Harkness's acknowledged debt to both Reinhold Niebuhr and Paul Tillich—an indebtedness not of imitation but dialogue. In rising to the challenge of Niebuhr's neo-orthodoxy, she

---

[35]*Grace Abounding*, 184.

[36]Ibid., 182-83.

[37]''The Maker,'' *Grace Abounding*, 186.

recognized that liberalism had underemphasized sin, judgment, and divine grace. This profound sense of sin, newly incorporated into her theology, perhaps altered the tenor of her personal faith. She would not echo Tillich's words about the "courage to be in the face of non-being," but she would root her faith unequivocally in the personal God of her "ultimate concern."

The period between 1939 and 1945 was one of pain and change for Georgia Harkness. She suffered a severe fever and later a back injury as well as insomnia and depression; in *Dark Night of the Soul* she wrote about suffering and its religious meaning. Still, she was somewhat self-conscious to include a later poem on "accidie" in one of her books, reluctant to acknowledge her "shadow side."[38] "Toiling over much" could well describe Georgia Harkness, who once wrote that she was "by nature more of an activist than a mystic."[39] The work of reconciliation—of individuals to God, to each other, and to society—is such that she often "saw no increment" for her efforts. Once her chosen task was accomplished, however, she determined that the efforts of others be recognized; in this she herself is a striking example of the selfless giving that she identified as the high standard of the ministry of reconciliation.

The strength of self that enabled her to distinguish her self from her work also helps us understand her reservations about the possibility of mystic experience. In her 1973 book entitled *Mysticism*—having taught a course in "Mysticism and the Devotional Classics" at both Garrett and the Pacific School of Religion—she defined the mystical relationship with God as communion rather than union, partly so as not to restrict mysticism to quietism. "But," she queried, "is the human soul, or self, ever actually merged with God in such a manner as to lose its own identity even for a transient moment?"[40] And she answered, "I cannot think so." "Yet," as one reviewer remarked, "it is clear from the writings of the mystics that this is exactly what happens. If you will, the God within us, the Self of the self, the capacity for love is released in the mystic experience and is uni-

---

[38]"Accidie," *Grace Abounding,* 164-65.

[39]"A Spiritual Pilgrimage," 349.

[40]Georgia Harkness, *Mysticism: Its Meaning and Message* (Nashville: Abingdon, 1973) 23.

fied with its Creator.''[41] When Georgia Harkness averred, finally, that Jesus was not a mystic, she did so on grounds that discourage us from making Jesus the exemplar of our own main concerns. She urged us to look to the spirit of Jesus the universal man as a guide for our times—whether the issues be pacifism, civil rights, labor relations, ecumenism, or women's ordination. I will move now to a consideration of her position on some of these issues.

Georgia Harkness became a pacifist in 1924, when she visited a war-ravaged Europe with a Sherwood Eddy seminar. At the time of the signing of the armistice treaty, she had been a student at Boston University, and she recalled the enthusiasm with which students gathered at Faneuil Hall ''to celebrate the end of this and supposedly all wars''; then, ''a pacifist position that would oppose all wars on grounds of Christian conscience did not occur to me.''[42] During the summer of 1924 she became convinced, from what she saw and heard on that European tour, that personal renunciation of war was the only answer to international discord; her position was reinforced years later by Reinhold Niebuhr's *Moral Man and Immoral Society.*

She held to the pacifist position in the 1930s as war broke out in Europe and threatened America; the *Christian Century,* in particular, provided a forum for her views during those years. The Korean War was more problematic for her, however. She offered to withdraw her membership in the Fellowship of Reconciliation at that time because she thought that international police action under the United Nations might be justified. Upon advice, she continued her membership, sure that nation should never lift up sword against nation. She anchored what many would call a utopian vision in at least one historical fact: one of her few narrative poems, ''The Treaty,'' recorded the amicable agreement between the colonist William Penn and the native Indians.[43]

In 1950 the Dun commission of the Federal Council of Churches formulated a statement, ''The Christian Conscience and Weapons of Mass

---

[41]Paul G. Dimmitt, ''Unity with the One,'' *The Christian Century* 90 (2 May 1973): 512.

[42]*Grace Abounding,* 130.

[43]Ibid., 128-30.

Destruction.'' Georgia Harkness signed a minority statement that took exception to the majority's approval of the use by the United States of "atomic weapons or other weapons of parallel destructiveness" in retaliation for the use of such weapons against the U.S. or its allies.[44] One observer noted, "It was characteristic, however, that after the inevitable debate over that portion of the Dun Report broke out, she did everything she could to center attention on the parts where all the commission members were in agreement, and to encourage moderation in the discussion of differences."[45]

Some persons would be impatient with such an approach to controversy. Georgia Harkness held in delicate balance the call to be a peacemaker and the call to stand for truth and right. She did this more easily than Emil Brunner, for example, who needed to distinguish between love and justice; Georgia Harkness understood justice as an instrument of love. So, with Paul, she counseled us to "have this mind among yourselves, which you have in Christ Jesus," to work carefully, knowledgeably, perhaps even more slowly than our zeal would lead us, and to begin the work of reconciliation with individual persons. For, though peace or civil rights or fair labor practices may be legislated, it is only when individual lives are conformed in attitude consonant with such legislation that the recognition of the equality and dignity of all persons will take hold in our society. As an example, "One may be conscientiously a Christian pacifist, but if this is one's only approach to the problem of peace and war, he will do less for the cause of peace than if he works for peace and world order side by side with other Christians who are not pacifists."[46] A nonpacifist once said of her, "She is the only pacifist I ever met who was *pacific* in argument."[47]

In her condemnation of the Vietnam War and the struggles in Biafra, she became increasingly wrenched by the suffering of innocent children. That concern extended to all innocents who suffer, and who suffer not only the devastation of war but also the pain of hunger, malnutrition, and need-

---

[44]As quoted in Frakes, "Theology Is Her Province," 1090.

[45]Ibid.

[46]Georgia Harkness, *The Ministry of Reconciliation* (Nashville: Abingdon, 1971) 139.

[47]The nonpacifist is not named, only quoted in Frakes, "Theology Is Her Province," 1091.

less disease. Her poem "The Innocents" makes more horrible and immediate the biblical story of the slaughter of the innocents.[48]

Pacifist though she was, Georgia Harkness worked untiringly on behalf of the "church militant"—a phrase that did, indeed, appeal to her. As a child she delighted in the hymn "Onward, Christian Soldiers." In 1939 she commented on her later dislike of the military metaphors and, even more, "its bombastic assertion of what seemed flat falsehood":

> *We are not divided,*
> *All one body we,*
> *One in hope and doctrine,*
> *One in charity.*

"Was there anything the church more obviously was not than 'all one body'?" she asked.[49] She changed her mind in 1937, when she attended the Oxford Conference on the Life and Work of the Churches as a consultant. Her obvious enthusiasm justifies quoting her own account of the Oxford Conference.

> There were enough divisions in hope and doctrine, if not in charity, at Oxford to tear any group in the world asunder. Yet this group was knit together in unity. The conviction was borne in upon me, as upon many others, that the foundations on which the church rests are not of this world, and that the Body of Christ is more than a time-honored phrase.
>
> Within the church as it is, with all its division, its compromises and its pettiness, Christ's true church is working. It encompasses some of the most strategic social action of our day, as it has in every day. Because it is a supra-national fellowship, it is the only truly international organism. When almost everything else trembles it is least shaken of all our major institutions. Into a world of strife and gloom it brings brotherhood and light. Both because of its foundations and its mission, the gates of hell cannot prevail against it. The Christian can be confident that whatever the outcome of the present turmoil, the church will survive and will go forward "with the cross of Jesus going on before."
>
> This vision of the church came to me at Oxford.[50]

---

[48]*Grace Abounding,* 133-34.

[49]"A Spiritual Pilgrimage," 350.

[50]Ibid.

The vision was strengthened by her participation in the same year, 1937, in the Madras International Missionary Conference. In later years she was a delegate to several World Council of Churches meetings.

In preparation for the 1954 Evanston assembly of the World Council of Churches, the Hymn Society of America sponsored a competition to secure an appropriate hymn. The prize went to Georgia Harkness; the hymn is number 161 in the current *Methodist Hymnal*, its title—"Hope of the World." Written some fifteen years after the vision at Oxford, the language is strikingly different from that of "Onward, Christian Soldiers"; the first stanza provides sufficient example:

> *Hope of the world, thou Christ of great compassion,*
> *Speak to our fearful hearts by conflict rent.*
> *Save us, thy people, from consuming passion,*
> *Who by our own false hopes and aims are spent.*[51]

Her ecumenism supported her pacifism. The unity of Christians across national boundaries, she argued, enabled the church to preach reconciliation to the world.

Her ecumenism also supported her concern for women's rights. In a paradoxical way this happened precisely because some ecumenists used the ecumenical movement to discourage the ordination of women. As early as the Madras International Missionary Conference, a request was made to include in one of the reports a statement encouraging women in ministry, whereupon the Bishop of Winchester asked to have the request denied "because such a move would cause barriers to the ecumenical movement and in particular to church union."[52] It was denied. Wrote Georgia Harkness, "Repeatedly since that time I have heard this argument used. It seems not to occur to those who use it that the argument can be reversed—if the ministry of women is supported by the ecumenical movement, more churches will embrace it and thus the total ministry of the churches will be enlarged."[53] At the 1948 meeting of the World Council of Churches, she debated for full participation of women in a memorable exchange with Karl

---

[51]*The Methodist Hymnal* (Nashville: The Methodist Publishing House, 1966).

[52]Georgia Harkness, *Women in Church and Society: A Historical and Theological Inquiry* (Nashville: Abingdon, 1972) 132.

[53]Ibid.

Barth. Twenty-four years later she took heart that the Plan of Union of COCU (the Consultation on Church Union) provided for the ordination of women. More importantly, she pressed this point: "Church *unity* in Christian fellowship and cooperative service is a far more vital movement in our time than the organic union of denominations, which hinges on so many factors that it is inevitably a slow process."[54]

Harkness thought that if she, as a loyal Methodist, were going to speak up for equality for women in the church, then she ought to demonstrate her concern in every way she could. Her studies at Boston University were considered the equivalent of a full seminary course, and so in 1926 she was ordained a local deacon in the Troy Conference in the Methodist Episcopal Church. In 1938 she received her local elder's orders. She knew her own vocation was to teach, but she argued forcefully against the restriction that prohibited full membership in annual conference—and therefore the assurance of an appointment—for women.[55]

She did not see the Methodist church hampered by theological objections to women's ordination, but by practical aspects of its connectional system. In her own church she never had to dispute (officially, at least) with those who argued for the exclusive ordination of men because Jesus was a man or because he chose twelve men to be his disciples. Because of her historical sense she recognized the cultural/social restraints on women in Jesus' time. Yet she betrayed her impatience with the line of reasoning that restricts ordination to men by suggesting that perhaps every twelfth Christian needs to be a Judas.

She, more than any other one person, is credited with the final vote of full ordination rights for women in the Methodist church in 1956. When the vote came at General Conference that year, it was typical of Georgia Harkness that, having done the groundwork, she sat in silence, letting the record of women who were already serving as accepted supply pastors speak for itself, and letting "able" and "discerning" men carry the issue.[56] This is not scheming in its negative sense but, again, a reflection of her com-

---

[54]Ibid.

[55]"Local" ordination in the Methodist church allowed for the exercise of most ministerial functions but denied membership in annual conference.

[56]*Women in Church and Society,* 30.

mitment to the ministry of reconciliation. The work done, Georgia Harkness never asked for full membership in her annual conference, and therefore attended six General Conferences as a lay delegate.

In terms of today's concern for the use of inclusive language, Georgia Harkness believed that official documents of the United Methodist Church should avoid sexist language. But about the language of worship and historical Christian faith she said the following:

> It seems to me we had better accept the fact that our language uses the word *man* not solely as male but in a generic sense as human. I believe because Jesus spoke of God as Father, so should we. I am certainly not going to call God "she," and if you don't say "he" or "she," then the only alternative is "it." I am not going to use that.
>
> I don't believe in making the Bible over to try to change language solely on a sexist basis. Consequently, I'm not much in sympathy with some of my sisters' desire to eliminate all of the *hims* or to revamp the male pronouns to be nonsexist, not even if some of the leaders of the women's liberation movement may call me a back number![57]

And so they may! No one would argue against Georgia Harkness's own disclaimer that she was not a militant feminist.

Georgia Harkness's commitment to women's rights, especially those of ordination, was consistent with her support for a ministry of the laity. Her book *The Church and Its Laity* (1962) was part of the movement, sparked in the 1950s by Hendrik Kraemer's *A Theology of the Laity,* which argued for the ministry of all Christians. Ten years later she saw the same questions argued in another context. She herself wrote that "as a fresh interest in women's liberation in secular society and the ordination and ministry of women in the churches has come upon the scene, there is renewed opportunity to grasp the meaning of priesthood of believers."[58] She continued,

> To the degree that women's liberation is able to open more and richer opportunities for service in any field, and uses methods of dignity in pressing toward such goals, I am ready to give it my blessing. Yet there are fields of responsible service to God and humanity within the churches

---

[57]Johnson, "Georgia Harkness," 56.

[58]*Women in Church and Society,* 226.

which need greatly to be opened and to be accented where open. It is this enterprise with foundations in Christian truth and justice which is my major concern.[59]

In the 1939 article that was part of the *Christian Century* series "How My Mind Has Changed in This Decade," Georgia Harkness noted the modifications to her theological liberalism, but declared that her social philosophy had undergone less alteration than any other aspect of her religion. That assessment still held at the end of her life in 1974. The positive change in her conception of the church was a watershed mark in 1939, and we have noted some of the results for the church in the ensuing years. Primarily, her progress has been a spiritual progress. One of her frequently reprinted books of poems, *Grace Abounding,* echoes in its title John Bunyan's autobiography, *Grace Abounding to the Chief of Sinners.* Said Georgia Harkness, "I have shamelessly appropriated the title, though I prefer to leave it with the Lord as to who may be the chief of sinners."[60]

Her sense of social sin is more like Walter Rauschenbusch's understanding of social sin than it is like Reinhold Niebuhr's, partly because of Niebuhr's depersonalized Christ as well as his position of love as an impossible possibility—a dichotomous view that, observes one critic, "in fact elevates justice rather than love as the determining principle of social ethics."[61] Because Harkness was known for her quest for social righteousness as well as her appeal to the "common reader," the Division of Human Relations and Economic Affairs of the General Board of Christian Social Concerns asked her to summarize "for general study purposes" its four-volume project on Methodism and society.[62]

---

[59]Ibid., 226-27.

[60]*Grace Abounding,* 11.

[61]James H. Burtness, review of *Christian Ethics,* in *The Lutheran Quarterly* 10 (February 1958): 74.

[62]Georgia Harkness, *The Methodist Church in Social Thought and Action,* ed. Board of Social and Economic Relations of the Methodist Church (Nashville: Abingdon, 1964) 12. The original four volumes are Richard M. Cameron, *Methodism and Society in Historical Perspective;* Walter G. Muelder, *Methodism and Society in the Twentieth Century;* S. Paul Schilling, *Methodism and Society in Theological Perspective;* and Herbert E. Stotts and Paul Deats, Jr., *Methodism and Society: Guidelines for Strategy.*

The central question in this study concerns whether Georgia Harkness was and remained a part of the Boston Personalist tradition. We are now prepared to answer that question in the affirmative. She became a theistic realist and thought this put her outside the tradition. However, she continued to work with the philosophical method of Brightman, relying on the criterion of coherence. She had serious questions about Brightman's concept of a limited or finite-infinite God, but so did such personalists as DeWolf and Knudson. She retained her belief in God's respect for human personality and freedom. She had no reason to disavow the statement made in 1937: "To say that man cannot save himself is a position both empirically and theologically defensible; to say that God saves men either contrary to, or in the absence of, human volition is to defy all that we know of human and divine nature."[63]

---

[63]Georgia Harkness, *The Recovery of Ideals,* 192.

Developments in My Thought

S. Paul Schilling

Two words of caution occur as I approach the topic assigned. First, I assume that one's thought is integrally related to the rest of one's life. Reference to the experiences out of which thinking arises seems to be especially important in understanding personalism. Second, I do not take development here to mean a gradual, almost automatic unfolding from bud to blossom of ideas already implicitly present—the simple unwrapping suggested by the etymology of the term. I use it rather to connote the appearance of changes representing insights or emphases that to some degree are for the thinker new and different. Lest these two cautions seem to point in opposite directions, I fully recognize that all our ideas, however novel, reflect the influence of our previous thinking and living. Yet the Spirit, like the wind, blows where it will (John 3:8). I shall examine six stages of my life and thought.

PRECRITICAL INERTIA, 1904-1925

Immanuel Kant is not the only thinker who needed to be awakened from dogmatic slumber. Slumber is a physical, mental, or moral condition like sleep; to slumber is to be in a state of suspended animation, dormant, quiescent, unaware. Such words describe fairly accurately my own situation until two years after my college graduation. Possibly a better term than slumber would be inertia, the property by which matter (or mind!) remains at rest or uniform motion in the same direction unless acted on by some outside force. Perhaps also my condition was not precisely dogmatic. However, it did entail a set of beliefs, and it was precritical, unawakened, involving acceptance without serious question of the opinions prevailing in my immediate environment.

I was born and raised in the mountains of western Maryland, a part of what is now often called Appalachia. Located on the upper Potomac River, Cumberland was a railroad junction in a region marked by mining and small industry. My father wanted to study law, but he was financially unable to pursue his formal education beyond high school. He worked first as a carpenter, then for almost forty years in the postal service, initially as a mail carrier and later as a clerk. My mother was the oldest child in a large family. Needed at home to help care for the younger children, she left school after the eighth grade. They were both devoted and responsible members of the church, filling various leadership roles. My own early commitment to the Christian life was a natural result of their precept and example.

My grandfather Schilling was a Civil War veteran who often attended encampments of the Grand Army of the Republic. During my boyhood he took me with him to two such reunions in Gettysburg and Washington, and I absorbed a good deal of his patriotic fervor. My mother was active in the Women's Relief Corps of the G.A.R., which decorated the soldiers' graves each Memorial Day. My father was for many years financial secretary of a fraternal order that stressed patriotism as traditionally understood. As a Boy Scout, I won a medal for selling ten war bonds to support World War I—the only member of my troop to reach this goal.

Both the schools and church I attended were racially segregated. The only black adults I knew were janitors or barbers. Black families lived near our home, and occasionally I played outdoor games with some of the boys on summer evenings, but the white assumption that Negroes were inferior prevented me from forming friendships with black children, who attended a separate school at the edge of town.

The serious question as to whether I would be able to attend college was resolved when a full scholarship (tuition, room, and board) to St. John's College in Annapolis became available for the fall of 1919, and I placed first in the competitive examination that determined the appointment. St. John's today is a distinguished college committed to the high standards of the great books program conceived by Robert M. Hutchins, but in the 1920s it was a small and little-known military school. I graduated in 1923 as a second lieutenant in the U.S. Army Reserve, believing that the best way to peace and security for America was preparedness for war through a strong national defense.

Participation in various extracurricular activities provided valuable experience in working with other people. Especially noteworthy was the opportunity to serve during my senior year as editor-in-chief of the college weekly, the *Collegian*. This led me, after much uncertainty, to plan for graduate study in journalism, to be financed by savings from several years of secondary school teaching.

Accordingly, I became a teacher of English, one year in the public high school in my hometown, and one year in a military boarding school in Kentucky. In the latter I had the title of captain, and like other faculty wore the appropriate olive drab uniform. In both schools I was instrumental in founding and advising the staffs of successful biweekly newspapers. These associations with English communication exerted a lasting influence on me.

Far more significant, however, was the deepening religious awareness that came in these first two post-college years. During the first I taught a church school class of fifteen-year-old boys, and during the second I served as superintendent of the Southern Methodist Sunday school. Twice I represented my home church as delegate to a young men's conference connected with the Baltimore Annual Conference of the Methodist Episcopal Church. My interest in journalism was declining as I began to consider the possibility of a church-related vocation. So when at the youth conference in 1925 Bishop Henderson challenged us to resolve, "Whenever, whatever, wherever thou wilt," his words came to me as a call from God, and I responded. Learning through Charles F. Boss, Jr., then Baltimore Conference Director of Religious Education, of the excellence of the Boston University School of Religious Education, I came to Boston in September 1925 as a candidate for the M.R.E. degree.

AWAKENING, 1925-1932

When I came to New England I had never heard of the Great Awakening, but these words aptly characterize the experience that soon began. Precritical slumber was mercifully superseded by a growing awareness of reality that was at once intellectual, ethical, and religious. Still a racist and a militarist at heart, I was ripe for change and welcomed it enthusiastically when it came.

I took my first course in philosophy, followed by one in metaphysics, both taught by Earl Marlatt and based on Brightman's *Introduction to Philosophy*. Marlatt dictated his lectures—a teaching method not calculated to inspire—but he wove in enough poetry and anecdotes to maintain interest, and for me the content of both class discussions and reading was so new and relevant to my needs that I quickly came to love philosophy. Probably because I had been a secondary school teacher, Earl Marlatt asked me to serve as his reader that year. This experience sharpened my critical faculties and helped me to weigh alternatives. I learned what personalism was and was favorably disposed toward it.

That year I also undertook for the first time a scholarly study of some of the biblical writings. I was excited by the opportunity for an open-minded, truth-seeking exploration of the teachings of the prophets, and by the discovery that biblical and scientific accounts of human and cosmic beginnings could reinforce and complement rather than contradict each other.

Experience in a summer pastorate in 1926 led me to decide on the pastoral ministry, and hence to transfer to the School of Theology in the fall. Continuing study and life in Boston brought two radical changes in my ethical attitudes. For the first time I came to know black students as classmates, as well as candidates for the Christian ministry. One night in Malden I heard Countee Cullen read from his own poems. Deeply moved by his insights, aware of the anguish that gave them birth, and touched by the beauty of his language, I was forced to acknowledge that I could not write poetry of such quality. One Sunday in Symphony Hall I heard Roland Hayes sing. Lifted by the mellow richness of his voice and the depth of the spirit it expressed, I had to admit that such singing was far beyond any capacity of mine. At Ford Hall I heard W. E. B. DuBois speak of the injustice and oppression suffered by black people in America. Chastened by experiences like these, I surrendered all my shallow claims of white supremacy and asked the mercy of God on me, a sinner.

Having accumulated at the School of Religious Education thirty credit hours that would not be needed for the S.T.B. degree, I decided to use them toward an A.M. degree. Having begun by this time to question my military assumptions, I decided to explore in my thesis the relation of Christian faith to the problems of war and peace. I examined critically the attitudes toward war of ten American Christian leaders from 1914 to 1926. The views I encountered ran the gamut from radical pacifism to reliance on armaments to defend Christian values. The sweeping change that resulted in my own convictions is best indicated by two actions that followed completion of my thesis: I resigned my commission in the U.S. Army Reserve and joined the Fellowship of Reconciliation—a membership actively maintained ever since.

Theological studies opened many areas that called for serious exploration, which I undertook with zest. When it became apparent that three years would not be enough time for the quest that now beckoned, I determined to go on as a candidate for the Ph.D. My goal was a pastorate in a college community where I might minister to the intellectual and spiritual needs of students and faculty as well as townspeople. Challenged by the thought and teaching of Edgar S. Brightman, I made philosophy of religion my major field. The proximity of Harvard University afforded opportunity for exposure to the teaching of William Ernest Hocking, Ralph Barton Perry, and Alfred North Whitehead.

June 1930 was an exceptionally important month in my life. On 8 June I was ordained into the ministry of the Methodist Episcopal Church. On 18 June I married Mary Elizabeth Albright of Piedmont, West Virginia, my beloved companion of the ensuing fifty-five years. On 26 June we sailed for Germany for study at the University of Berlin. The year 1930-1931 made possible courses with scholars like Adolf Deissmann, Arthur Titius, and Wolfgang Koehler. I was also able to continue regular contact with Brightman, who spent his sabbatical leave in Berlin writing the sequel to his book *The Problem of God*.

In Berlin I read *auf Deutsch* the whole of Kant's *Kritik der reinen Vernunft* and began research for my dissertation on "The Empirical and the Rational in Hegel's Philosophy of Religion." A new critical edition of the three-volume *Religionsphilosophie* edited by Georg Lasson had just been published, so I was able to utilize it along with many other important sources available in Berlin. Dissertation research continued during another year in Boston and was completed in 1934, when the degree was conferred by Boston University.

PASTORATES, 1932-1945

In 1932 I began my pastoral ministry in the Baltimore Annual Conference. By that time the United States was deeply mired in the world economic depression. Wesley Foundations were forced to reduce drastically their work on college and university campuses. There were no opportunities for the kind of ministry for which I had prepared, so I accepted those that were available. The result was that I spent thirteen years as pastor of typical local churches.

After seven years in academe, I had much to learn regarding the day-by-day lives and religious needs of ordinary people and the communities they compose. As we shared the lives of the families of artisans, farmers, business and professional people, and government employees, we came to understand the foibles and strengths, the hopes and fears, the perplexities and sensitivities of garden-variety Christian people, as well as the weakness and promise of the church. I also discovered that the years invested in interpreting the meaning and truth of religious faith contributed constructively to my work as pastor. Though time was limited for scholarly pursuits in the strict sense, I learned that lay persons were responsive to preaching and educational activities that challenged their thinking and helped them to understand and clarify their faith in its relation to the personal and social problems they faced daily. Another form of learning occurred during these years through the birth of our children, Robert (1933) and Paula (1937), who lifted the lives of their parents to new levels of joy and responsibility.

During the Depression years in Baltimore, when Social Security legislation was still unknown, many thousands had no work, and public relief was pitifully inadequate, I worked with the interracial People's Unemployment League to try to reduce hardship and joined a few other clergymen in drafting and presenting to a committee of the Maryland legislature a plan of unemployment for the state. I was involved twice in guiding the religious youth of Baltimore, Christian and Jewish, white and black, in staging Armistice Day peace parades, with over a thousand marchers. In Washington I had the arduous task of ministering during World War II to a congregation that had ninety of its young people in military service. During the same wartime years I chaired the Baltimore Conference Commission on World Peace and the Washington Federation of Churches Committee on a Just and Durable Peace, both of which joined the Maryland-Delaware Council of Churches in 1943 to hold an ecumenical conference attended by several hundred Christians seeking ways to end the scourge of war. During these years the nation's capital was teeming with vastly increased numbers of government workers in a new and strange environment. The need and the opportunity for informed evangelism were great, and pastor and people learned together as they sought to bear a persuasive Christian witness.

TEACHING AT WESTMINSTER, 1945-1953

In 1945 I was invited to become professor of systematic theology and philosophy of religion at Westminster Theological Seminary. The only theological school of the former Methodist Protestant church, it had only four full-time faculty members in addition to the president, but the chance to devote all my energies to teaching and scholarly work exerted a strong appeal, and I accepted.

The school was small, with limited facilities, but it also had strong potential. A survey by the Methodist Episcopal University Senate pointed out its weaknesses and raised serious questions as to its survival. Nevertheless, it weathered the storms, doubled its full-time faculty, and under the leadership of Bishop G. Bromley Oxnam set in motion efforts that led in 1958 to its move to Washington, D.C., where it changed its name to Wesley.

For me personally the years at Westminster were a time of retooling. The demands of busy pastorates had allowed relatively little time for philosophical and theological research, and I had not kept abreast of the major movements of religious thought. Now it was imperative that I fill in the gaps. Westminster afforded me the opportunity to learn how to teach, to understand the personal, intellectual, and spiritual needs of theological students, and to become acquainted with the main currents of Christian thought in the mid-twentieth century. Teaching in various pastors' schools, leadership in summer courses for lay people, and five years as president of the Baltimore Conference Board of Education provided valuable experience in relating theology to the church at work. The preparation of articles for theological journals and symposia laid the groundwork for later, more substantial writing.

In the meantime the growth of Boston University School of Theology created the need for faculty expansion, and I was invited to join Harold DeWolf in the department of systematic theology. I rejoiced in the opportunity to return to the school and the university that had been so formative in my student years.

TEACHING IN BOSTON, 1953-1969

Since there was a strong department of philosophy in the Boston University Graduate School, I never taught philosophy of religion in the School of Theology. However, I did offer seminars several times on Kierkegaard, Thomas Aquinas, and the Christian interpretation of history, as well as a course in personalism. I never felt any opposition between theology and philosophy. My work in Christian thought has always gone forward with openness toward the beliefs and practices of other religions, though constantly informed by my central Christian commitment. I should mention also that though personalism appeared in the title of only one course, personalistic convictions have been influential in much of my teaching, and personalistic philosophy was an important part of courses in Philosophical Backgrounds of Christian Theology, offered at both Westminster and Boston.

Three projects involving research and writing were particularly influential in shaping my thought during the Boston years.

Methodism and Society

In the late 1950s the Methodist Board of Social and Economic Relations requested our faculty to investigate the role of Methodists in social thought and action. The faculty named seven of its members to fulfill the assignment in cooperation with a committee of the Board. My own chief responsibility was the writing of the third volume of the four-volume MESTA series, *Methodism and Society in Theological Perspective* (1960).

The volume examined the central doctrinal emphases of John Wesley; the status of Wesleyan doctrines in Methodism today, with particular reference to their social significance; the interpretations of ecumenical Christian beliefs found in Methodist theologians and official church pronouncements, with their implications for social thought; and the findings of a churchwide questionnaire on the religious, ethical, and social beliefs of Methodists—an instrument prepared by the entire team. Against this background, part two of the book proposed that a sound theology of society, true to the New Testament gospel, Wesley's thought, and the implications of a broad spectrum of Christian beliefs, can be founded on an extension of the meaning of salvation from the individual to human social relations as a whole. Christian social concern is implicit in and an outgrowth of the Christian's experience of redemption, and the social task of the church is part of its ministry of reconciliation.

The goal of Christian social thought and action is then what may be properly called social salvation: the deliverance of groups, and of society as a whole, from the conditions, attitudes, and activities that blight life and obstruct the divine purpose; and the establishment of group relations that express and encourage the concerns of persons for one another's welfare, make possible the realization of their highest potentialities, and facilitate their entrance into a transforming experience of the love and power of God.[1]

For me personally participation in the MESTA project was important because it clarified the relation between two long-standing concerns, theology and social justice, helping me to see Christian responsibility in and for society as unavoidably involved in a holistic understanding of Christian faith.

Contemporary Continental Theology

Acutely aware of my need for broader and deeper understanding of contemporary theology, I decided to use my first sabbatical leave in 1959-1960 to gain as far as possible firsthand knowledge of the main theological currents on the continent of Europe. With headquarters in Heidelberg, my wife and I were able to visit and interview thirty-six representative thinkers in seven countries—a fascinating pilgrimage of friendship and learning. By the end of the year I was clear regarding the broad outlines of the picture, but far more work needed to be done in the voluminous writings of individual theologians. After returning to Boston I devoted as much time as possible to the project, but the demands of teaching and graduate studies administration were such that it was 1965 before a manuscript was ready for the press. *Contemporary Continental Theologians* was published by Abingdon in 1966 and simultaneously by SCM Press in England.

The book expounded, compared, and evaluated the systematic theologies of eleven thinkers. Eight Protestants formed three broad groups: (1) theologians of the Word of God, whose perspective was predominantly

---

[1]From *Methodism and Society in Theological Perspective* by S. Paul Schilling. Copyright © 1960 by Abingdon Press, 214-15. I am indebted to Abingdon Press for permission to incorporate in my account several passages from three of my books. These appear on this page and pages 198, 202.

Barthian, represented by Barth himself, Hermann Diem, and Josef L. Hro-
mádka; (2) theologians influenced decisively or conspicuously by existential modes of thinking, typified by Rudolf Bultmann, Friedrich Gogarten,
and Gerhard Ebeling; (3) theologians who found in either the Lutheran
confessions or Luther himself definitive guidance in interpreting the faith
of the Scriptures, represented by Edmund Schlink and Gustaf Wingren. I
was unable to give to Roman Catholic or Orthodox theologians the attention that their critical and creative contributions deserved, but I did devote
chapters to the Catholics Yves M.-J. Congar and Karl Rahner and the Greek
Orthodox Nikos A. Nissiotis. This work greatly increased my understanding and appreciation of the divergent emphases encountered as well as of
the underlying unity of purpose often apparent. Contacts made during this
and a later sabbatical leave paved the way for visits and lectures at the
School of Theology by Guenther Bornkamm, Anders Nygren, Gerhard
Ebeling, Helmut Gollwitzer, Jan Lochman, and Yves Congar.

Theism and Atheism

In 1960 our visit to Prague and contacts with teachers and students of
the Comenius Faculty of Protestant Theology made me acutely conscious
that many Christians today are living and witnessing in lands where the
Christian church and its faith, though tolerated, are officially regarded as
enemies of truth and justice. Succeeding years heightened the awareness
that many Marxists and others quite honestly and thoughtfully reject any
theistic view of reality. I found myself asking, Why? What are the grounds
of the deep erosion of faith that is so widespread today? Are they to be found
partly perhaps in the failure of Christians themselves to make clear in their
words and actions the meaning of God in human life? Can believers learn
something from the serious objections raised by atheists? Just what are they
rejecting when they deny God? Such questions led me to undertake, beginning with my second sabbatical leave in 1966-1967, a critical examination of the thought of contemporary atheists, and in the light of their
critique to seek a clearer understanding of the divine reality.

Research in published sources was augmented by personal interviews
with about twenty-five Marxist and Christian leaders in East and West
Germany, Holland, Czechoslovakia, and Switzerland, including Helmut
Gollwitzer of West Berlin, Hendrikus Berkhof of Leiden, Ernst Bloch of
Tuebingen, Olaf Klohr of Jena, and Jan Lochman and Milan Machovec of
Prague. It was especially revealing to hear Machovec speak of the two main

grounds of his atheism: the suffering and death of millions of men, women, and children in the Holocaust and the indifference to social justice he had observed in Christian congregations. I felt drawn to him by his earnest commitment to the same human values that claim my devotion. His concern for the real well-being of persons puts to shame the apathy of many professing Christians I have known.

Against the background of nineteenth-century sources (Feuerbach, Marx-Lenin, Nietzsche), I identified and investigated six present-day varieties of atheistic humanism: Freudian psychoanalysis, Marxism, existentialism, scientific humanism, linguistic philosophy, and so-called "Christian atheism" of the death of God. Published writings and conversation disclosed the following bases of unbelief: (1) Belief in God can be explained as an objectification of purely human ideals, wishes, longings, or needs. (2) Theistic faith is in one way or another inconsistent with scientific method and the scientific view of reality. (3) The term *God* lacks clear, univocal meaning that can be unambiguously communicated. (4) Faith in a God of power and goodness cannot be reconciled with the extent and intensity of human suffering. (5) Belief in the sovereignty of God is inconsistent with recognition of the worth, freedom, and full responsibility of human beings. (6) Theistic belief produces passivity in the presence of injustice and opposition to social change. (7) Multitudes of persons, including many who are seriously committed to the highest human values, have no personal awareness of God.

Obviously, some features of the composite image of God that emerge from this critique can and should be upheld by intelligent Christians. Some represent a parody of the views endorsed by the most thoughtful believers or reflect conceptions accepted in the past but no longer widely held. But some of the most questionable and repugnant aspects of the notion of deity encountered are deeply imbedded in the thought of revered theologians and the beliefs, worship, and practice of millions of devout Christians today. It is therefore imperative that we take a new look at the notion of God we have somehow communicated to unbelievers, and similarly at our own understanding.

My inquiry led to eight proposals: (1) Our thought of God must be related intelligibly to all relevant knowledge gained from secular sources. (2) Christian thought should affirm unmistakably the intimate relation of God to the world, which finds in God the ground and source of its unity, its manifold activity, and its ultimate meaning. (3) Our conception must maintain the real freedom and responsibility of human beings and the importance of their contributions to cosmic and historical processes. (4) Nevertheless, God should be understood as other than and transcendent to all finite reality. (5) God should be conceived eschatologically as the activity that opens before women and men a future, gives them a hope that outruns every present, and leads them toward the fulfillment of ever new possibilities. (6) Christian thought should now add to its affirmation of God's eternity a frank acknowledgment of divine temporality. (7) Christian faith should maintain belief in God as Creator, with emphasis on continuing divine creativity and recognition of human responsibility to share in creation. (8) God should be thought of as participating in the pathos and tragedy of existence, nevertheless keeping human beings in invincible love and through suffering fulfilling divine ends.[2]

As I sought to take account of all these needs in rethinking the meaning of God, I found four conceptual models particularly serviceable: being, creative process, love, and personality. We must, of course, guard resolutely against making God a mere copy of ourselves, since the ultimately real must far transcend the limitations of knowledge, power, and goodness that mark finite persons. Nevertheless, understanding is advanced if we conceive of God as possessing characteristics somewhat akin to what we experience as self-consciousness, reason, purposiveness, discrimination among and ability to realize values, and capacity to enter into and sustain relations with other persons.

However, the personal analogy should be used in close relation with the other three. Each supplies something essential, and none is sufficient by itself. Taken together, they provide a diversified yet unified conceptuality that incorporates the major positive proposals stimulated by the atheistic critique. We are thus led to think of God as the dynamic personal love at the heart of reality, as the creative, energizing actuality of the personal life who in love animates and interpenetrates all that is and seeks to realize what ought to be, or as the loving personality in process who is the ultimate ground of all being and becoming and who for Christians is supremely manifest in Jesus Christ.[3]

---

[2]From *God in an Age of Atheism* by S. Paul Schilling. Copyright © 1969 by Abingdon Press, 139, 147, 152, 158, 164, 170, 174, 179.

[3]Schilling, *God in an Age of Atheism,* 215.

POST-RETIREMENT YEARS, 1969-

The Unrecognized Presence of God

God in an Age of Atheism, reporting the conclusions just described, was published in August 1969. By that time I had retired from the faculty of Boston University and was in the midst of a one-year visiting professorship at Union Theological Seminary in Manila. In the meantime I had begun to ask myself whether the conceptualization I had reached corresponded to anything encounterable in the daily lives of flesh-and-blood people. Is there evidence that human beings can and do enter into genuine relationships of trust, worship, and commitment with God understood in the fourfold manner I had outlined? Such questions claimed my attention in Boston, in the Philippines, and during a three-year teaching assignment at Wesley Theological Seminary in Washington.

For many people today, God, however conceived, is hidden or absent. Their searches lead to no conscious disclosure of the divine presence. At the same time, in a wide variety of unexpected quarters one finds repeated evidence of pervasive activities that transcend both individuals and society as a whole, and that men and women do not produce or fashion according to their wishes but confront. This wide recognition of transcendent reality suggests that what is involved may be the actual presence of God, as it were, incognito.

In *God Incognito* (1974) I found in the works of contemporary psychologists, sociologists, artists, novelists, and poets, and in the data of ordinary life accessible to all thoughtful persons, evidence that in our time God may be acting in creative and liberating ways in experiences that are not recognized by those who have them as indicative of the divine presence. I did not bypass religious experience as conscious awareness of God but focused major attention on a variety of phenomena that point toward a transcendent dimension not ordinarily identified as God: the depth in existence, human dependence, the search for meaning and wholeness, the call to personal and social responsibility, and the pull of the not-yet.

Critically evaluated, such intimations of transcendence may be coherently ascribed to divine activity. They may be reasonably regarded as manifestations of an actual relationship of men and women to the dynamic personal love that sustains and permeates the whole of our existence.

God and Evil

These reflections led me almost irresistibly to inquire into the relation of the God I now believed in to the evils so destructively active in God's world. At the age of fourteen, while picking peaches in a mountainside orchard in West Virginia, I was shaken when a twelve-year-old co-worker was killed by lightning. With others I asked, why this fine lad alone out of a work force of about fifteen? Similar questions arose through the years as other tragedies occurred. I was never able to accept the explanations most frequently given—that God sent such events to punish wrongdoing or to build strong character.

I therefore welcomed enthusiastically Brightman's hypothesis of a Given within the divine nature that limited God's power to actualize God's perfectly good will. Acceptance of this conception, initially stated in *The Problem of God* (1930), was confirmed during my year of graduate study in Berlin, when Walter Muelder, Jannette Newhall, Ewart and Martha Turner, and my wife and I were privileged to meet weekly with Edgar and Irma Brightman as he read chapter-by-chapter the manuscript of *The Finding of God* (1931) and invited us to raise questions. Usually he resisted our criticisms initially, then opened the next session by reading the revision our wise comments had occasioned! During the years in the pastorate and teaching I continued to find in this theory the most coherent interpretation of the data, though I could not brush off some of the objections lodged against it.

By the early 1970s, in the context of my other recent investigations, I felt an urgent need to address the problem anew, in the hope of clarifying my convictions and reaching a view I could fully support. The resultant research led to the publication in 1977 of *God and Human Anguish,* in which I stated and evaluated nine historic responses to the problem of suffering and formulated the conclusions I reached.

Basic to my own interpretation is the conviction that the God whose creative activity permeates and sustains our world is seeking to form a community of mutually supportive persons who strive with God and one another for the maximum realization of values. The process through which this venture is being carried out is unfinished; we live in a world in the making.

Four features of this endeavor shed special light on the universality of suffering:

1. The very possibility of life and value fulfillment requires a physical world marked by constancy, regularity, and predictability; but such a determinate natural order entails hardship and pain when sentient creatures fail to observe its provisions, whether intentionally, carelessly, or ignorantly. This stable order is the setting for the changes of the evolutionary process—a vast experiment in which every stage involves incompleteness and deficiency needing to be overcome, hence widespread struggle and suffering. But the resulting ills could be eliminated only by a drastic alteration of the process that would destroy its positive potentialities.

2. Responsible exercise of real freedom of choice is indispensable if men and women are to become true persons rather than automata; yet freedom produces suffering when it is deliberately, thoughtlessly, or ignorantly misused. It is a precious but perilous gift. We cannot enjoy its benefits without risking the distress that our abuse of it occasions in ourselves and others, and without causing anguish in God also when we oppose God's righteous will. Also pertinent is a degree of freedom in subhuman animals, which, together with atomic indeterminacy, brings about some organic instability and so contributes to evil as well as development in sentient beings.

3. The interdependence of our world, manifest in intermeshed human relationships, interaction in the physical order, and close interconnections between human life and its total environment, is essential to life and responsible for some of its richest fulfillments, but it makes persons vulnerable to the errors and wrongs of others and the frequently disruptive impact of the natural order.

4. Further comprehension of evil is gained if we discard the traditional notion of divine omnipotence, conceiving the power of God as ultimate and incomparably great, yet less than infinite or absolute. God is who and what he/she is, not something else that we might prefer. Possibly eternal, uncreated limits are intrinsic to divine power. If so, though God's love is unbounded, God's creative activity involves costly travail over long periods of time, and human beings are exposed to ills that God does not choose, but works ceaselessly to remove and prevent.

Two additional conclusions belong to this synopsis: suffering, though not ordained by God, often contributes to the growth of character; and the travail of evolution and the concrete historical disclosure of God's suffering love in the cross and resurrection of Jesus Christ suggest that God intimately shares the pain and pathos of creation. Strictly speaking, these affirmations are not answers to the theological question of why there is so much suffering. Nevertheless, both of them help us to meet and overcome evil and hence to reduce its terror. To that degree they lessen the theoretical problem also, since they serve to diminish the human anguish that needs to be reconciled with the character of God.[4]

Returning now to my fourth suggestion regarding the *why* of suffering, let me try to clarify what I mean by limited divine power. I agree with Brightman and Peter Bertocci in discarding the traditional notions of absolute divine sovereignty. Four considerations argue persuasively for this rejection: (1) the pain, travail, and waste of evolution, suggesting a God who is creating experimentally and hazardously, ever willing and perhaps needing to change courses and explore new possibilities; (2) the subatomic indeterminacy disclosed by quantum mechanics and the randomness, unpredictable novelty, mutation-producing instability, and spontaneity found in the physical order, which are not readily attributable to an all-determining divine will; (3) the presence of much purposeless, ''nondisciplinary,'' gratuitous, inequitably distributed evil that exceeds what might conceivably be needed for character formation and instead often warps and embitters human lives; (4) the biblical witness that God's creative and redemptive work requires strenuous, sacrificial effort.

I therefore find it reasonable to think of God as limited by something within the divine nature. However, I no longer find very illuminating the notion of a nonrational Given, involving an impediment or recalcitrant aspect (Schelling, Bertocci) or a retarding factor (Brightman) in God. Strictly speaking, this is not a dualistic concept, since it is internal to God and nonmoral rather than evil. Nevertheless, impediments or retarding obstructions within God do not readily cohere with the one world known to the sciences and our experience as a whole.

Derived from the Latin *impedire* (to shackle or entangle the feet), the word *impediment* designates anything that hinders or blocks normal functioning, something abnormal, a defect. Applied to deity, it intimates that because of it God is internally torn by opposing tendencies, lacking in harmony of aim and execution. The adjective *recalcitrant* is derived from a Latin verb that means literally to kick back or strike with the heels. Hence to be recalcitrant means to be obstinate or stubbornly rebellious, implying

---

[4]From *God and Human Anguish* by S. Paul Schilling. Copyright © 1977 by Abingdon Press, 261-63.

to some degree an actively defiant tendency. Applied to God, it suggests an activity that refuses to cooperate with God's eternal purpose. This is certainly not what either Brightman or Bertocci intends, but in spite of all disclaimers the term has dualistic overtones. A God who must suppress a recalcitrant element within the divine being hardly qualifies as the Ground of the *uni*verse we experience or the ultimate Source of healing and wholeness in the personal and social life of fragmented human beings.[5]

I also find it misleading to use the term *nonrational Given* to denote only hindrances to God's power. What is given—eternal and not produced by the divine will—is God's power itself. More accurately, the datum, that which is granted or assumed when we consider nonrational aspects of the divine experience, is the *whole* of God's being.

God does not choose how much power to have; it simply is what it is, however immense or limited. Or, rather, since power is not a separate entity but an aspect of the integral wholeness of the divine life, we might better say that God is what he/she is, hence not something other that we might prefer. For God to have any positive nature at all is a form of qualification; it means that God is this and not that.

It is therefore beside the point to ask why the ultimate Ground of all being and becoming is not different. Included in the kind of reality God is are the quality and extent of divine power. Whether that power is greater or less than we might wish, like other facets of God's essential character it is eternal and uncreated, not willed or chosen from among various possibilities. If the evidence of our total experience suggests that it is less than infinite, we may soundly regard this limitation as inherent in God's eternal, uncreated nature. Finiteness of power may be itself ultimate, a frontier beyond which human thought cannot go. If we can free ourselves of preconceptions of what God must be, it should be neither shocking to us nor debasing to God to think of divine power as bounded in this way. The ultimate reality experienced in religious faith is what it is—ultimate.

I recently came across two items that may help to make clear the view I am advancing. One is a statement of Harris F. Rall in a review of Brightman's *The Problem of God* in the *Garrett Tower* (November 1930). Rall found in "the conditions which seem to belong to the very nature of creation as a process of becoming and achieving, the real clue alike to divine

---

[5]Schilling, *God and Human Anguish,* 243.

limitation and the presence of evil . . . in the world.'' The other exhibit is from an utterly unexpected source, a cartoon by Bill Hoest in *Parade* (12 February 1984). The drawing shows a woman who is obviously dissatisfied with all of the sample colors the redecorators have daubed on the wall for her decision. Frustrated, one painter declares, ''You understand, of course, lady, that our colors are limited by the spectrum.'' May we not say that the colors of God's creative activity are limited to those present in the ultimate, uncreated spectrum of the divine life? That structure is not willed by God; it is.

This means that God, in order to achieve the goods of this created order, must experience the risks and negativities of a stable, interdependent, open-ended universe in which persons made in the divine image may grow in responsible freedom. The Creator embarks on and continues in this costly venture, knowing that it will involve suffering, yet choosing in love to create for the sake of the community of shared values that such a world makes possible.

Inevitably objections may be and have been raised to this conception. The most serious difficulty, in my view, is this: if evil arises partly because of an ontological limitation of God's power, what basis is there for expecting the ultimate triumph of good? Thus William H. Becker, in a review of *God and Human Anguish,* asks how a God who cannot prevent the suffering of *individual persons* can be expected to bring them to the victorious end affirmed by Christian faith. More broadly, if God is not unqualifiedly omnipotent, what ground is there for my confidence, shared with Calvin, that God is at the helm of the universe?[6] Frederick Sontag makes the same point when, looking backward instead of forward, he insists, ''Any God who possesses the power necessary to save us must have been powerful enough to design the world differently at the beginning, had he wanted to.''[7] Albert C. Knudson criticized Brightman in similar fashion. Religious faith, he asserted, demands an objective goodness that is linked with power to accomplish the ends willed; if God cannot prevent ills there is no reason for believing that they can be overcome.

---

[6]William H. Becker, ''Review of *God and Human Anguish,*'' *Interpretation* 33 (1979): 103.

[7]Frederick Sontag, ''Does God Play Russian Roulette?'' *Circuit Rider,* June 1981, 6.

In response to this criticism I offer two comments. First, whether God's power is absolute or limited, belief in the triumph of divine purpose is a matter of faith. Simply to assert God's unbounded power does not validate the assertion. Abraham Lincoln once told the story of the man who asked a friend, "If you call a tail a leg, how many legs has a dog?" "Five," was the answer. "No," replied the questioner, "four. Calling a tail a leg don't make it one." To call God omnipotent does not impart the power asserted. The basic question is, "What does the evidence justify?" There are difficulties with either view. The verdict should depend not on what faith requires, but on what faith finds more intelligible in relation to our experience as a whole.

Second, nothing in the judgment that divine power is less than infinite implies that God is weak or puny. If the power of the eternal Person is not absolute, it is nevertheless utterly unparalleled, and it is prodigious. Its greatness is attested by the magnitude, orderliness, and marvelous complexity of the cosmos. As the ultimate reality, God is the source, ground, and possessor of all the power there is.[8] Hence, there is ample warrant for believing that divine striving for the conservation and advance of values will ultimately succeed and that on the way the divine presence can give to those who suffer the strength needed to endure.

However Christians may differ as to the extent of divine power, they are one affirming God's boundless love. That love, whatever hazards it may encounter, has its own unique strength. When Charles Birch speaks of a "cross pattern deeply woven into the very fabric of creation,"[9] he is using a New Testament symbol that can never be separated from its sequel, the Resurrection. Amid all their ambiguities and contradictions, the Resurrection narrators speak with one voice in declaring that the God disclosed in Jesus Christ emerged victorious. The suffering love they had experienced in him had triumphed over sin, pain, and death. The birth of the Christian community and the experiences of multitudes of its witnesses through the centuries bear testimony to the uncoercive power of sacrificial love to

---

[8]Schilling, *God and Human Anguish,* 248.

[9]L. Charles Birch, "Creation and the Creator," *Science and Religion: New Perspectives in Dialogue,* ed. Ian G. Barbour (New York: Harper Torchbooks, 1968) 214.

achieve divine ends. To affirm the adequacy of such power is an act of reasonable trust.

Theology in Hymnody

During the past several years, while continuing active work on the problem of evil, I have devoted major attention to the theological content of Christian hymns. This was the theme of courses taught at Andover Newton Theological School (1978-1981) as visiting professor there, and at several local churches. Since this interest has concerned me for more than three decades, it does not signify, strictly speaking, a new development. However, it does represent a new dimension. *The Faith We Sing,* published in March 1983, is my first book-length project to integrate systematic and practical theology and to relate critical theological reflection to the worship of the church. I refer to it here also because many hymns— notably those that sing of God, providence, Jesus Christ, salvation, the Christian life, and life eternal—voice the response of faith to human anguish.

Every hymn witnesses to some aspect of religious experience and belief. Yet worshipers frequently pay little attention to what they affirm when they sing, and they may even be led by appealing tunes to sing lustily what they don't believe at all. In the context of historical and contemporary Christian thought, the book attempts to identify, interpret, and evaluate the theological convictions raised in representative hymns now in use. It utilizes some sixty Protestant, Roman Catholic, ecumenical, and independent hymnbooks, encompassing the treasures of historic hymnody and numerous new hymns of strength and beauty.

I began with a concern to point out the important role of theology in hymnody. In the process I learned that hymns in turn frequently illuminate theology. Religious verse cannot match the precision of carefully formulated theological treatises, but spiritually sensitive hymnists through poetry and metaphor often express deep insights with a clarity and vividness that may elude prosaic language.

For example, a hymn by W. H. Vanstone (b. 1923) conveys in lucid simplicity the heart of my understanding of God's suffering love. Vanstone writes that the nails and crown of thorns of one who hangs helpless on a tree "tell of what God's love must be":

Here is God: no monarch he,
throned in easy state to reign;
here is God, whose arms of love,
aching, spent, the world sustain.

Reflections on the Experience of ''Oughting''*

Peter A. Bertocci

SOME TURNING POINTS

I was born in Gaeta, Italy, 13 May 1910. Soon after my birth my mother brought my older brother, Angelo, and me to join my father. At the turn of the century, he had left his fisherman's nets to come to Somerville, Massachusetts, and had finally decided that it was a good risk to settle his family in this country. He was to spend most of his life as a low-paid laborer in the meat packing industry that was the center of a slum in-

---

*For a more complete account of issues raised and positions taken in this essay, see Peter A. Bertocci and Richard M. Millard, *Personality and the Good: Psychological and Ethical Perspectives* (New York: David McKay, 1963); Peter A. Bertocci, *The Person God Is,* part 2; *The Goodness of God,* chs. 2-5.

I gladly acknowledge my debt to my teacher, Edgar S. Brightman, whose work *Moral Laws* (New York: Abingdon, 1933; Millwood NY: Knaus Reprint, 1978) is the larger framework for this discussion—although I cannot claim that he would wholly approve of the noncognitive view of oughting I have stressed.

habited mainly by Italians.[1] I was to be the second of six children (another brother and three sisters).

My parents were not strict Roman Catholics and did not forbid Angelo and me from being increasingly lured into the Protestant Mission, whose varied ministry was carried on mainly by part-time workers of different denominational persuasions, who went more than the second mile "in Jesus' name."

It would take pages to sketch the preadolescent factors that led me, during an Evangelical Crusade held, as I recall, in a Methodist church, to go "up front" and "accept the Lord, Jesus Christ, as my Saviour." Much to my amazement, it took. My favorite teachers at the Mission and the shining example of my brother, Angelo, nourished my "new life in Christ," and in such a way that in 1927 I was registering at Boston University's College of Liberal Arts at 699 Boylston Street, again following my brother's footsteps.

Angelo had already come under the influence of Professor William Aurelio's "modern" teaching of the Bible and of Edgar Sheffield Brightman's approach to problems of philosophy and religion. Their "devilish" teachings were almost responsible for a break between my brother and me. Our major arguments were about the infallibility of the Word of God as revealed in the Bible. How hesitantly did I give up "the foundation of my faith," the literal inspiration of the Bible! I finally did, and my lifelong struggle with the relation of faith and reason began in earnest. How many of my classes have heard me say, overdramatically I fear, that if I were to be exiled, I would beg for two books, the Bible and Plato's Dialogues, since together they face one with the problems involved in one's search for the things that matter most.

I majored under Brightman in philosophy and minored in psychology; and I gradually decided that I wanted to teach college students and participate in the life of the church as a teacher. Also, with Brightman's encouragement, I crossed the Charles River in 1931 and earned my M.A. at Harvard in 1932, coming under the influence especially of A. N. Whitehead, R. B. Perry, W. Ernest Hocking, and C. I. Lewis. Since Brightman

---

[1]See Angelo P. Bertocci, "Memoir of My Mother," *Harpers Magazine,* June 1937.

had taken his sabbatical during my senior year at CLA, and since I wanted to study further with him and also to have the opportunity to be in Albert C. Knudson's classes in the School of Theology, I came back to Boston University to work for my doctoral degree in philosophy under the approved plan at that time and take one third of the course requirements at Harvard. So I spent 1933 and 1934 shuttling back and forth between Boston University and Harvard. The high point, however, especially in the midst of the Great Depression, was the further good fortune to work, during 1934-1935, on my dissertation, under Brightman's constant guidance and the direct supervision of Frederick R. Tennant at the University of Cambridge. My dissertation, "The Empirical Argument for God in Late British Thought," focused on the place of the person and of personal values in the interpretation of the universe; and Tennant wrote a most generous foreword when it was published.[2] In June 1935 I walked down the aisle with my good friend L. Harold DeWolf, as both of us were hooded for the Ph.D.

Who would have dreamed that my first teaching position was to depend largely on my undergraduate work in psychology and the fact that F. R. Tennant, in two volumes of *Philosophical Theology* (1928, 1930), selectively presented, reinterpreted, and revised the work of James Ward, *Psychological Principles* (1918)? At Bates College, from 1935 to 1944, almost two-thirds of my courses were to be in psychology. In September 1944, having been honored by the call of my alma mater, I began teaching in the department of philosophy (with part-time, for several years, devoted to teaching psychology).

Now I ask you to share considerations on the nature of moral experience that began to grip me during my days at Cambridge—indeed, as I was walking out of a lecture in a course in ethics by C. D. Broad. As you will see, I am still straddling the borderlines of psychology and philosophy, refusing to allow what are barriers of convenience to separate our thinking about the moral experience of the person.

---

[2]Peter A. Bertocci, *The Empirical Argument for God in Late British Thought* (Cambridge MA: Harvard University Press, 1938; Millwood NY: Knaus Reprint, 1970).

OUGHTING AS AN EXPERIENCE OF THE PERSON

I here assume that the person, as I have argued elsewhere,[3] is essentially a self-identifying being-becoming—a complex unity of irreducible activity-potentials: sensing, remembering, imagining, reasoning, feeling, wanting, willing, oughting, and aesthetic and religious appreciating. A person *is*, experiences himself or herself *as being*, these activity-potentials. A person is not an identical, unchanging being in and through them, but self-identifying as expressed in them. Every aspect of this conception is controversial, but I purposely restate it so that we shall not, despite our language in referring to these activities separately, forget that it is the person who senses, remembers, and so forth. I shall always be assuming that it is the person who experiences oughting within the complex of activities distinguished above.

My primary appeal, as I proceed, is to my experience of oughting as it appears in a larger context that I cannot elaborate upon here, but I hope that what I do distinguish will find favorable confirmation in your introspection and consideration.

THE OUGHTING SITUATION

I suggest that the activity-potential oughting appears in experiential situations like this: "I want experience x; I want experience y. I cannot have them both. On reflection I decide that x is better than y. I ask the critical question: Do I ever, having decided that x is better than y, also experience. I ought to do y?" (I assume that both x and y are within my power.) My answer is *never*. To expand this a bit: if I deliberately decide (the reasons for so deciding are another important matter, but not at issue now) that x is better than y I never find myself saying, "I ought to do y!" I add, if, on further deliberation, I change my mind and decide that y is better than x, I then experience: I ought to do (will, choose) y.

It is as simple as that. Elaboration will be forthcoming, but choice-situations—with no exceptions—lead me to conclude that I am an oughting person, that oughting is a built-in activity-potential that is aroused,

---

[3]Peter A. Bertocci, *The Person God Is* (New York: Humanities Press, 1970) chs. 2-6; and *The Goodness of God* (Washington DC: University Press of America, 1981) chs. 4 and 8.

evoked, whenever a person, having weighed alternative values presumably within reach, decides that one (*x*-value) is better than the other (*y*-value). I conclude: *One ought to will (choose) the best one knows.*

OUGHTING AND ITS RELATION TO ANY PARTICULAR VALUE

Further reflection on such choice situations leads me also to conclude that the person is an oughting person regardless of the means by which he or she comes to know *what value* (or system of values) is the better (the best). Oughting is not experienced because of what value one deliberately claims to be the best, but because, once one is capable (mentally mature enough) to consider alternatives, and once one can decide, in a choice-situation, *what* is best, oughting is aroused as an unlearned response to *that* best, as long as one considers it the best. Thus, the irreducible existence of oughting is not dependent upon any particular theory of value (or norm of value), any more than the irreducible existence of thinking depends upon a particular theory of truth. For example, the person who has given up the conviction that the standard of value is *vox dei* in favor of the relativity of values, or vice versa, still experiences oughting the best he or she knows. This does not mean that oughting is experienced without a value deemed best, for oughting is still a constitutive activity as the person changes his or her conception of the best. But, if I am correct, there is no experiential basis for the view that if one changes one's mind about the best, one is no longer under the moral imperative to choose the best among the alternatives one believes are open.

To summarize: oughting itself does not depend upon any cognitive, or noncognitive, *view of value,* but this does not mean that the person ceases to ought the best among the alternatives as he or she sees them. Again, a change in conception *about the value-object* does not result in a change in one's experience of oughting the best one knows. Hence, a person who decides that the exercise of sheer power is the best experiences oughting to will that goal; so does the person who holds that the Ten Commandments define the best, and so on.

THE AUTHORITY OF OUGHTING

At root, I think, it is the assimilation of oughting to any one conception of the best (or the good) that I strongly hesitate to grant—hesitate waveringly. Often, as when I review such views as those of Bishop Butler and Immanuel Kant, I am stirred by Bishop Butler's statement about the moral consciousness: "Did it [his word is conscience] have the strength, as it has the right; had it the power as it has manifest authority, it would absolutely govern the world."[4] In this context he adds that conscience "magisterially exerts itself" as intrinsic to the human constitution. But in his view conscience is *cognitively* linked to altruism. A consideration of Kant's categorical imperative also finds the *authority* of the ethical ideal exclusively in the *rational* will as autonomous.

However, both Butler and Kant, among others, have properly emphasized the *authority* of oughting in the person. As Kant put it, even if it turned out that persons live in a "stepmotherly" world, the "good will" would "shine by its own light."[5] This distinction between the authority of oughting and its power is of the highest importance if we are able to gain insight into the dynamics of a person's moral situation. Still, I think the authority of oughting must not be assimilated to a given source of values.

I suggest that the understandable concerns to know *what* values are best and *what* their status is in the universe have served to obscure, if not entirely conceal, oughting itself as an intrinsic dimension of the person. I am aware that oughting as authoritative in its own light, along with the irreducible quality of the cognitive ought, is disqualified by philosophers who argue that moral judgments are essentially a matter of acquired attitudes and therefore cannot be held to be true or false.

I shall confine myself, however, to the climate of opinion that prevails in our day that has roots in the psychosocial sciences. The "stern daughter of the voice of God" is now the product of acculturation; a person's "conscience" is the wholly learned outcome of one's struggle with socially imposed restrictions on one's instinctive urges. Some equivalent of Freud's "where the id is, there shall the ego be" (with its ego-ideal) presides. The word *ought* may survive linguistically, but it stands for the psychic accommodation: if I want *x*, then I had better, indeed, I *must*, do

----

[4]Bishop Joseph Butler, *Five Sermons,* sermon 2, section 8 (New York: The Liberal Arts Press Division of Bobbs-Merrill Company, Inc., 1950) 41.

[5]Immanuel Kant, *Fundamental Principles of the Metaphysics of Morals* (New York: The Liberal Arts Press Division of Bobbs-Merrill Company, Inc., 1949) 19.

y. But I do want *x,* and if, after all, I must join "them" to beat them, let me form a (largely) unconscious monitor (superego) that will minimize the loss of pleasure and fend off unacceptable displeasure in such predicaments. Much as I try, however, I shall undergo anxiety whenever I am uncertain of the power of my inner monitor to cope with these struggles between "them" and my persistent desires to gratify my needs.

WHY NOT REDUCE OUGHTING TO WANTING?

If I have caricatured, in this oversimplified presentation, this substitute psychosocial framework for "ought" and "oughting," I am less than apologetic. For, in essence, the drift in most academic, orthodox views (if the words *moral obligation* come up at all) is to derive oughting, and any specific ought, from the clash of the person's basic and learned wants with artificial social pressures. My essential defense against this annulment of oughting is to ask you to allow oughting to shine by its own light as experienced, as I continue to point to other inescapable features of oughting that are irreducible to wanting in any of its forms as experienced.

I am assuming that as long as *x*-value is deemed, for whatever reason, the better alternative, a person ought to choose it. Note, one may not *want* to choose it, but one experiences the imperative to do so as long as *x*-value is deemed better. I ask you to consider the difference between the *pull* of the strongest want and the *imperative* of the weaker approved want. In this same context, I ask you to inspect the difference between the *authority* of oughting and the experience of sheer power that is *authoritarian*. The unique imperative, the unique authority of the approved want, is, I suggest, never experienced *as* want, even the strongest want. True, the authority of the imperative may be overcome—alas, it so often is—but it makes itself felt as long as the person deems *x*-want to be better. "I ought to have chosen it" does not die. It is this magisterial authority, this imperative quality—as I experience it—that I can't understand as "wanting," or as amounting to a "must," that coerces.

I ask, then: can *want* plus *want* plus *want* produce anything but *want?* Surely, *must* plus *must* plus *must* can produce only *must!* (We should be aware that the urgency of *ought* and of *must* allows us often to exclaim: "I must do this!" But language is not the final judge here.) It is also the case that often what a person considered "a must" becomes "an ought" because reevaluation sees it as the better of the alternatives.

This conception of the imperative, of moral authority, helps to explain the dynamics of conscientious believing and conscientious objecting, as the reduction of oughting to wanting does not. For the person who only "mightily" wants x, there is no experience of the moral imperative even if the preferred want is now second nature. But the conscientious objector (or believer) is exerting a moral imperative in support of whatever powers one has at one's disposal. Indeed, one is now dealing not only with one's loyalty to a deeply entrenched value judgment but with the imperative beat of an inner drummer who exerts his moral authority over one— enough to sacrifice one's very life in carrying it out. The imperative of a Gandhi and a Martin Luther King, Jr., is not in itself different from that of a person who experiences the imperative to destroy them in pursuit of an imperative goal. The inner drummer marches to the best one knows, whether or not the best is held to be infallibly known.

Once we recognize the dynamics of the moral imperative, we cannot overemphasize the importance of doing our utmost *to know the best*. For, as stressed above, oughting the best, the imperative to the best, is not knowing the best. Oughting does not by itself make the person wiser! It does make a difference in one's experience as a person whose moral integrity sustains the noblest deeds—and the most ignoble! Hence, exploration of *what is best* takes on far greater importance even as a matter of prudence.

OUGHTING AND MORAL GUILT

Our explanation has touched only the tip of the iceberg as we now begin to inquire what one experiences if one does not follow one's imperative to the best one knows. I submit that the experience of *moral guilt* is not reducible to anxiety, although anxiety may accompany it. (Moral guilt is not identified with guilt in the eyes of the law, much as the law may be involved in the person's decision as to what is best.)

Guilt and *anxiety* are used so interchangeably by both scholars and nonscholars that I often think there must be something I am overlooking as I find myself unable to equate moral guilt with anxiety. No expert on Freud, I nevertheless have looked in vain for something clearly other than an interchangeable use of *guilt* and *anxiety*. Nor do I find the situation different in the literature of psychology of personality.[6] Why, then, do I per-

---

[6]Gordon W. Allport has found merit in my view of "oughting." See his *Becoming* (New Haven: Yale University Press, 1955) 74.

sist in my refusal to identify guilt with anxiety? Because anxiety is essentially uncertain fear; it often accompanies moral guilt, but it does not have the quality of guilt. Also, anxiety accompanies the *moral approval* a person experiences when he or she does follow an imperative at the cost of *social disapproval* and its consequences for the self and others associated with that self.

There is much more to be said about this differentiation, but I turn to reinforce my essential thesis by submitting that no others can make me experience guilt, however anxious they can make me feel about consequences of my decision. Guilt, however, is self-imposed, and though I "flee to the ends of the earth," it is there. And my experience of *moral approval* for having chosen what I deemed best is still mine even though I am sorry, to say the least, that even those I respect disapprove of my choice.

THERAPY FOR GUILT AND ANXIETY?

There are consequences for therapy, if anything like these views is correct. Moral guilt occurs because one has not chosen what one deemed best among alternatives. Anxiety occurs because uncertain fear of events (often related to deliberate moral choice) threatens what the person at the time holds dear. One's fears may turn out to be exaggerated and even unfounded, but in principle they may be allayed or increased by the course of events, and by the help of others, or both. But can guilt be allayed? If I am correct, it cannot. The guilty person chose not to take the course deemed best. Others may sympathize and help create situations in which one will not be encouraged to overemphasize one's guilt, but they cannot allay the guilt (nor can they decrease *moral approval*): one remains responsible for one's own choice, even when one can come to see it in a more illuminating light.

My underlying protest, therefore, is against those who identify guilt with anxiety and proceed to treat the guilty person and the anxious person in essentially the same way. How often, for example, is guilt treated as if it were solely the unfortunate emotional consequence of the person's having had the misfortune to follow "authorities" who, knowingly or not, actually misled that person into thinking y-value is evil, when as a matter of fact, as is now clear, it is not. Such being the source of guilt, it is treated only as an unfortunate accident that handicaps a person's development.

I applaud every effort to decrease and eliminate a person's handicapping anxiety, as well as helping persons see their oughting in proper perspective. Yet, I have claimed that oughting is not identical to any particular best, that it is not rooted in wanting, that it is not derived from, or an emergent from, introjected social norms. So, I keep asking as I inspect the quality of oughting: by what psychological alchemy does fear-anxiety become moral guilt (or moral disapproval)? What combination of "wants-musts" acquires the *moral imperative?* I am not satisfied by the explanation that explains this imperative *away.* I dare to persist that it is an intellectual scandal simply to disqualify oughting in terms of a biopsychosocial framework that is not based on the moral imperative as persons experience it. The imperative to the best is not defended here because it has high-sounding connotations. Knowledge of our own inner experiences, let *alone* even a superficial view of what horror as well as good has been done in the name of the moral imperative, may well lead us to reflect on the truly tragic (not, "it's just too bad!") in the situations resulting from "Here I stand, I can do no other!"

REFLECTIVE OVERVIEW

I close with a reflective overview of the oughting person. The importance of a comprehensive theory of the best (the good) and the constant review and evaluation of one's choices in the light of the best must not escape us. The imperative to the best is not *the* guide to the best; it is no inner compass that points unerringly to what is best. As noted above, the conscientious objector faces the conscientious believer and in the name of an imperative is too often willing to destroy the oughting person as well as the self if need be. Because oughting is, I suggest, the inner cry for quality at choice-point, its magisterial authority, even though it may sound like a whimper in the midst of conflicting powers, must be recognized in any view of the person as a whole. Yet, one person cannot bear or allay another's experience of moral approval or guilt; nor can either be erased or wiped away by the sacrifices of others, or by one's own actions. But I would suggest that further reflection on these facts, far from closing the way, opens the avenue to, indeed gives priority to, the ideal of persons responsive to, and responsible for, each other in a community of persons sensitive to the imperative as best they see it. Releasing persons from unnecessary anxiety cannot be substituted, however, for recognizing the quality of the imperative. For the imperative to the best is the beating heart of the person, especially as one becomes aware of the importance of one's evaluations of other oughting persons and their capacities and needs. At the same time, I cannot emphasize enough, at the end of this limited discussion, that the heart, never to be pampered, is *not* the whole person.

Ethical Implications for Criminal Justice

L. Harold DeWolf

It is no exaggeration to say that my journey to personalism began when I was born as the son of the Reverend Dr. Lotan R. DeWolf. My father was one of the best educated men in the large Nebraska Conference of the Methodist Episcopal Church. He was largely self-educated. Growing up on the frontier in the sandhills of Nebraska, he had the opportunity to attend school only in bits and pieces of time and for a total of less than a year before he was seventeen. Yet he had learned to read at an early age and he had read many books, often riding horseback on journeys of one to three days to borrow and later return the books.

Finally, he enrolled as a resident student at a preparatory school. After working, when possible, for ranchers and farmers, to put by some money, he attended Simpson College in Indianola, Iowa, until he ran out of funds after one year. Meanwhile, he had qualified for the Methodist ministry and had begun work. From my earliest memories, I, too, planned to be a minister. Even before finishing high school at age fifteen, I had read the entire Bible three times and also had read some of the books in my father's library. He was my idol, and we had many serious talks in his study, especially about the work of a pastor, of which he was a widely recognized master, and about theology.

The seriousness of his studies is exemplified by the fact that he had learned well both the Hebrew and Greek languages, the better to get at the intended meanings of the Scriptures. Indeed, when he suffered an eventually fatal stroke at age fifty-one, his Greek New Testament lay open on his desk where he had used it in his private devotions.

Among his favorite books, to which he often referred, were the works of Borden Parker Bowne and later Albert C. Knudson. Those two personalists and a third, Edgar S. Brightman, were the principal reasons that from an early age I assumed that when I had taken my bachelor's degree from Nebraska Wesleyan I would go to Boston University for theological studies. My father's especially well-chosen library, with its personalist center, became my most cherished part of his estate.

In personalism, especially as developed by Brightman and Knudson, I found a network of reason by which I could defend belief in a Christlike God. I agreed with Bowne that apodictic proof of God's existence could not be achieved. Even Brightman would not have disagreed, but his emphasis was quite different. He argued and stressed that more complete coherence with all human experience was to be found in Christian theism than in any other worldview. I was convinced by his argument. In Knudson I found a coherent elaboration of theism in terms of the principal traditional Christian doctrines, also a convincing critique of unworthy historical and contemporary additions to the authentic tradition.

In both philosophical and Christian ethics, Brightman, Knudson, and Bowne convincingly taught the basic personalistic principle that every human person, old or young, rich or poor, wise and knowledgeable or foolish and ignorant, even good or evil, is of sacred worth because he or she was created and loved by God, the supreme Person.

I welcomed the "Moral Laws" stated and supported by reasoned argument from experience in Brightman's book by that name. However, in my classroom lectures, and later in my *Responsible Freedom,* I proposed some changes. Since Brightman's so-called moral laws were not prescriptive statements of particular acts that ought or ought not be done, but rather statements of principles according to which we ought to make moral decisions, I call them "principles of moral decision." I also make some slight further changes in wording of some of the principles.

In my treatment of these principles, I note that they are philosophical rather than biblical or theological in their rational grounding so that they constitute a substantial portion of a natural law ethics. Yet in my presentation of them I carefully show how they harmonize with New Testament teachings that illustrate them and are mutually supportive of them.

With such supplementation and some minor verbal changes, I present the Formal Principles of Consistency and Personal Conscience; also the Principles of Evaluation, including Coherent Valuation, Foresight (comparable to Brightman's "Law of Consequences"), Best Possible, Situational Relevance (or "Specification"), Variety and Depth (or "the Most Inclusive End"), and Ideal Control. Then come the Principles of Choice of Beneficiary—Self-Realization, Altruism, and then Ideal of Personhood.

An important addition I have made to Brightman's "Moral Laws" is to take into full account the fact that individuals are not only affected by and are in turn obligated to other individuals, but are also in reciprocal relations with the communities of which they are members and also frequently with other communities.

Since all persons affect and are affected by communities, my Principles of Moral Decision "must include some directions for choosing our relations to the community and the kind of community to be developed."[1] The need for such principles and some further suggestions concerning them were first brought to my attention by Glen W. Trimble, then a graduate student in my classes. My personalist colleague, Walter G. Muelder, welcomed my formulation of them and thereafter used them in lectures and in writing on social ethics.

My latest formulation of Principles of Community distinguishes and defends three of them. The idea of the first had been included among Brightman's Moral Laws. As I have formulated it, this is the Principle of Cooperation: "Every person ought, when possible, to cooperate with others in the production and enjoyment of shared values."[2] Only thus may we hope to achieve and help others to achieve the maximum possible of personal values.

The second Principle of Community is the Principle of Social Devotion: "Every person ought to devote himself to serving the best interests

---

[1]L. Harold DeWolf, *Responsible Freedom* (New York: Harper and Row, 1971) 166.

[2]Ibid., 167.

of the group and to subordinate personal gain to social gain.''[3] A person concerned only with the cultivation of values for himself or herself cannot achieve a maximum of values even for self. We are by nature socially interdependent and need to subordinate our self-interest to the interests of various communities to which we belong.

Anders Nygren advocates the total denial of self-interest for the sake of another person. But this demand cannot withstand careful examination. If every person denied every value for self in order to give it to another, there would be no one to receive it. Yet, Nygren seems to be aiming at an important altruistic principle. The solution is to be found in the preferring of the community over the self.

The roots of this idea are to be found in the work of Bowne. He wrote, for example, "Not formal moral correctness, but vital fullness, is the deepest aim in life. We need not an abstract morality, but the morality of good homes, of good schools, of good farms, of good roads, of good cooking, of good management, of good literature, of good newspapers, of good libraries, of good health, of good politics, of good government, of good citizenship, and of good institutions generally.''[4]

Muelder believed that Brightman had intended that all I included in the Communitarian Principles should be understood from his moral laws. There is considerable evidence to support him both in Brightman's *Religious Values* and in his later *Moral Laws*.[5] However, Muelder agreed with me that it was important to recognize explicitly that "Groups have distinctive traits and generate distinctive problems.''[6]

The third and last of the Principles of Community is the Principle of the Ideal of Community. As I have formulated it, this principle reads as follows: "Every person ought to form all of his ideals and values in loyalty

---

[3]Ibid., 168.

[4]Borden Parker Bowne, "Morals and Life," in Warren E. Steinkraus, *Representative Essays of Borden Parker Bowne* (Utica NY: Meridian Publishing Co., 1979) 83. The essay quoted originally appeared in *The Methodist Review*, no. 169.

[5]Edgar S. Brightman, *Religious Values* (New York: Abingdon Press, 1925); *Moral Laws* (New York: Abingdon Press, 1933).

[6]Walter G. Muelder, *Moral Law in Christian Social Ethics* (Richmond: John Knox Press, 1966) 113.

to his ideal of what the whole community ought to become; and when possible to participate responsibly in groups to help them similarly form and choose all their ideals and values."[7]

The Christian's ideal of community, clearly, will be the conception of the Kingdom of God, so far as it can be realized on earth. This is in accord with Jesus' command as recorded in Matthew 6:32-33. Now, what has all this to do with my special concentration on crime in our society and on proper goals and procedures of criminal justice? Two different but related processes led me to this concentration.

First is the effort to minister to individuals victimized by crime and by our uniquely benighted system of criminal justice. Moved by New Testament teaching, reinforced by the personalist emphasis on the high value we are to place on all individuals according to their needs, I began early in my ministry to seek help for victims of crime and for offenders.

I observed that after a crime the law concentrated attention on the offender and rarely attempted to do anything for the victim. Whether in Nebraska, Massachusetts, Washington, D.C., and its vicinity, or Florida, I heard a great public outcry against the offender. When any attention was given to the victim and family, in public opinion, it was usually only to express and further foment anger against the offender who had caused the injury or loss.

When one visited a charged or convicted offender or the embarrassed and grieving family, the complaint was immediately that the visitor was forgetting the victim. Usually the complainants were doing nothing for the victim, but they seemed to feel that any attempt to assist the offender or the offender's family was showing a special callousness toward the victim.

This phenomenon seemed especially strange among professed followers of Christ who repeatedly enjoined his followers to visit the imprisoned. Indeed, Jesus himself, according to the account in Luke 23:39-43, even while undergoing the fatal torture of the cross, ministered helpfully to the repentant criminal on one of the crosses beside him. Moreover, Christians through the centuries have been taught the familiar word of Luke 23:34, concerning the crucifiers, "And Jesus said, 'Father, forgive them; for they know not what they do.' "

---

[7]DeWolf, *Responsible Freedom,* 171.

As I went into jails and prisons to visit individuals or to hold services of worship, I soon became acquainted with chaplains and also wardens and staff members. Since many of my visits were with men and women not convicted but still awaiting trial, I became increasingly interested in the laws and court procedures in which they were involved.

While I was becoming increasingly involved in personal ministry to victims and perpetrators of crime, another kind of activity was converging upon this whole area of interest. As a student of philosophical and theological studies, I encountered the problems of defining the meaning and proper goals of criminal justice. It seemed to me strange that in a time when crime and the actions of the police, the courts, the prison officials, and the parole boards were reported every day in the media, most scholars of ethics were giving little or no attention to the problem. Many years ago I determined that I would try to make some contribution to its solution.

I soon learned that some penologists and some judges were keenly interested in defining justice and wanted to be as helpful in my project as possible. Among penologists, Miriam Van Waters, Virginia W. McLaughlin, James V. Bennett, Norman A. Carlson, Winston E. Moore, and Jerome G. Miller made especially significant input of various kinds. One police officer, Larry J. Moss, stands out in my memory. Among judges, I was especially fortunate in receiving help and encouragement from such distinguished persons as Judge Marvin E. Frankel, Chief Justice Earl Warren, and Chief Justice Warren Burger. Other judges also made significant contributions to my thought and, like those named, were remarkably generous with their time and attention. Dean Roscoe Pound of Harvard Law School was helpful with his counsel and in helping me to secure financial aid. Gerhard O. W. Mueller, of New York University and Chief of the Crime Prevention and Criminal Justice Section of the United Nations, was helpful both in sharing basic ideas and in referring me to good consultants in Europe. Within Boston University, Albert Morris, criminologist, and Albert Beisel, professor of law, taught jointly with me a seminar on criminal justice, for me a valuable experience. A superior graduate student, Ms. Dean Hosken, who concentrated in this field, was also helpful.

It is certainly preferable by far to prevent crime rather than to deal with the offender and victim afterward. Moreover, the volume and seriousness of crime in a community depend much less on the criminal justice system than on other factors affecting the kind of community we have. One important condition determining the amount of serious violent crime is the availability of handguns. The relation between this availability and murders is clearly shown by the following figures brought together by the award-winning journalist Sydney J. Harris.[8] He writes, "In 1980 . . . (the last year for which we have accurate international statistics) handguns killed 77 people in Japan, eight in Great Britain, 24 in Switzerland, eight in Canada, 18 in Sweden, four in Australia—and 11,522 in the United States." In none of the other countries named can handguns be as freely sold as in the United States. The need for our states to join other industrialized nations in banning handguns from general public sale is obvious.

There are other characteristics of a society, also, that have important bearing on the crime rate. Wherever some segments of the population feel excluded from the opportunities and caring attention given to others, the crime rate will be high. It also tends to be high among people who feel themselves to be above the law, privileged to take economic and other advantages of their fellow citizens because of their greater wealth, aristocratic birth, or the like. If we want to reduce the rate of crime, then, our first attention should be given to eliminating discrimination on account of race or national origin. We need also to move against citizens who have defrauded or otherwise wronged others but commonly escape prosecution because of their economic, social, or political positions.

Moreover, all that can be done to knit our people together in mutually caring community will not only make life more interesting and pleasant for us all, but will also have the effect of reducing crime. I noted earlier that forming such community is mandated by both personalist ethics and the teaching of the New Testament, the latter especially in the familiar admonition to "seek first the kingdom of God."

It is sad to observe that the individualism of our predominantly capitalist society, especially under the presidency of Ronald Reagan, tends to move us away from the ideal of mutual caring and support. The popularity of Reagan's appeal has much to do with the fact that in the United States there is a much higher rate of crime, especially of violent crime, than in any country of Western Europe.

Weakening family ties is another factor in producing our high rate of crime. Studies by Sydney and Eleanor Glueck have shown conclusively that children from broken homes or homes with at least one parent who is

---

[8]*Lakeland Ledger,* 6 January 1984.

an alcoholic are especially likely to move into delinquent and then criminal behavior. There are few things we can do that are more helpful in lowering the crime rate than strengthening family life so that from early childhood, children have the guidance of parents in forming their values and habits.

As we move to consider our system—or nonsystem, as the American Bar Association calls it—of criminal justice, we soon observe a serious confusion of purpose. Some judges when they pronounce sentence are seeking one goal, other judges a different one. Legislators likewise differ widely regarding the proper purpose to be served by criminal justice, and public opinion differs even more.

Before we can intelligently decide what we ought to do with the system, we must decide what ends we should try to achieve. Is it education in the values that the state approves—the dominant purpose in the Soviet Union and often a part of the aim here? Is it retribution, or giving the offender his or her due, or, in popular parlance, "what one has coming to one"? Is it to establish an emphatic warning, a deterrent against repetition of the crime or of similar offenses by the same person or by others? Is it incapacitation, that is, making it impossible or excessively difficult for the offender to repeat?

Since most people incarcerated for crime in this country eventually go free, a goal of sentencing that is rising in favor is rehabilitation. If the danger of repeated offenses is to be avoided, the offender's motivations and attitudes must be changed.

And what of the victim? Should we not include in the goal of criminal justice some effort to compensate the victim of crime?

A purpose often included under rehabilitation is social readaptation. It is more than the changing of the individual. A crime is a sign that something has gone wrong in the relations between the offender and others in the society. Changes in the attitudes of others toward the offender may be required, as well as changes in the individual offender.

In order to appraise these different meanings and goals of justice we must appeal to the ethical norms of philosophical personalism and also, in a community striving to be Christian, we must observe New Testament teachings on the subject.

Education, it would seem, should be part of the goal we seek in dealing with many offenders. We must not look on this task as do the Soviet leaders. They regard the Communist state as the one exclusive authority in the establishing of values for all the people from childhood to death. In our democratic society we recognize various sources of guidance in the formation of ideal values for the individuals, including the family, the church, and literature. Only when, for whatever cause, the individual pursues values in ways that interfere with the lives of other people does the state have the right to intervene.

However, the need to educate or reeducate an individual is often made evident by a delinquent or criminal act. Moreover, some inmates of our prisons have never learned skills or work habits by which to earn an honest living. They obviously need occupational training. By providing this training the state both assists the individual offender and helps protect society against further injury by new offenses.

What of retribution? It is true that personalist philosophy recognizes the individual person as a responsible moral agent. It is sometimes claimed that to respect an offender as such requires that one can be punished according to one's deserts. But there is a non sequitur here. To suffer punishment is not to undo the results of one's wrongdoing. Such supposedly symbolic repaying to society for one's crime actually pays nothing of value. What is needed for that purpose is some kind of restitution to the victims of crime or, perhaps, required service to the community, the order and tranquility of which have been disturbed. The demand for retribution barely conceals an angry desire for revenge. Revenge has no standing in personalist ethics, because it in no way serves the good of persons or of community.

If it is protested that biblical ethics justifies retribution, indeed requires it, we are referred to the teaching in Leviticus and Deuteronomy about taking eye for eye, tooth for tooth, and life for life. For Christians this teaching has been directly cited by Jesus who then contradicts it by his teaching of inclusive love.[9] Jewish scholars interpret the old command as a provision to limit vengeance, later succeeded by more humane measures, for example monetary restitution.

The one truth implied in the doctrine of retribution is that there should be limits in criminal justice by a certain sense of proportion. The state should not busy itself in assessing measures even of deterrence or restitution for trifling offenses that everyone should simply overlook; and, when the offense is a little more serious but still of minor nature—like smoking where

---

[9]See Leviticus 24:20, Deuteronomy 19:21, and Matthew 5:38.

forbidden on a bus, for example—only minor measures should be used, like the assessment of a small fine.

Deterrence, to protect other persons and the community from future offenses of similar nature by the same person or by others, is a legitimate purpose with certain reservations. As far as special deterrence is concerned, that is, against repetition by the same offender, it should be recognized that incarceration with bad company and otherwise under conditions anything but uplifting often aggravates criminal tendencies more than it deters them. Often the embittered inmate only resolves that after release he will be more clever and avoid future arrest. General deterrence, that is, warning against similar offense by other persons, may lose effectiveness from the well-known fact that only a minor fraction of criminal offenses are ever solved by arrest and conviction of the guilty persons. Even when they are solved, the period between the criminal act and the actual serving of the sentence is often so long that the connection is likely to be dimmed in the public mind or replaced by association with the processes of law. When I have asked various prison inmates on what they placed the blame for their present unhappy plight, they have usually told me that they had lost "the game the lawyers play" in court, or used similar words to place the blame outside themselves.

When a person engages in a whole series of violent criminal acts, such as assault with a weapon or armed robbery, it may be clearly evident that the public must be protected by locking up the offender for a time, thus preventing further crimes. In fact, such a need may be evident even after police have arrested an individual for a single act if the offender displays an attitude that indicates the likelihood of repetition.

At the same time, it must be recognized that a person shut up for the sake of incapacitation, when released, may be even more dangerous than before, unless steps are taken to bring about needed changes in attitude and habits of thought. Since about ninety-eight percent of all people incarcerated in the United States will be released sooner or later, it is obvious that in most cases incarceration is at best only a temporary solution of society's problem with an individual. Hence the increasing trend toward the goal of rehabilitation.

Certainly rehabilitation is supported by personalist considerations. Concern for the well-being of persons militates against a backward-looking desire to punish for the sake of punishment. Even deterrence and incapacitation fail to reach forward toward a free and self-fulfilling life. The goal of rehabilitation does imply such a constructive forward look. But how is it to be accomplished?

Some offenders are emotionally disturbed, and their psychological abnormality is at the root of their criminal behavior. They need and should have psychotherapy as at least a part of their treatment under sentence. Unfortunately, psychotherapy has been given a bad name by frequent abuse of psychiatric testimony in legal defense against criminal charges. The theory is that if one was not in one's right mind at the time of the offense, one is not criminally responsible for having committed it. The person therefore may be released as not guilty, with or without some brief treatment.

On the other hand, a judge may order such a defendant to be held in an institution for the criminally insane until declared ''cured'' by psychiatrists. Psychiatry is an art guided by important but inexact science. A psychiatrist may be understandably reluctant to declare a person cured and ready to be released free in the community if that person has been shown to have committed a destructive act. What doctor wants to be responsible for releasing a potentially dangerous person into the community? Probably in serious cases the judge should retain jurisdiction of the court and require periodic review of the case with the defendant and any psychiatrists present for questioning.

As stated earlier, education of youthful offenders is important, and reeducation of older youth and adults in value selection and in marketable skills is important in a large number of cases. Certainly the high regard for persons required by personalist ethics would recommend provision of such educational opportunities. In general, such methods of rehabilitation are used much less in this country than in some others that have great success with them.

Religious conversion followed by religious training often proves highly effective. Clergymen visiting correctional institutions may render invaluable service by providing effective persuasion and opportunity for a new birth in the lives of offenders. Ministers need to be aware that some inmates may try to use them by professing repentance and new beginnings only to get help in winning release. Others will make such a profession honestly enough, but from minds so unstable and easily influenced that the permanence of results is highly uncertain. Nevertheless, it is important that both clergy and devoted lay people should make the effort.

I have witnessed both the beginnings of deeply rooted conversions and professions of repentance that proved unstable. However, I have observed that when some, from whom I have heard confessions and professions of new beginnings with faith, have later been convicted of new crimes, they have invariably been found guilty of much less serious offenses than on prior occasions. Of course, I cannot guarantee that it will always be so, but this has been my experience. On the other hand, some of the most rewarding experiences in my entire ministry have been to receive letters from persons with whom I have shared Christian counsel in prison, reporting years later with gratitude for help given and telling of their present rewarding new life. For me these cases have more than compensated for the disappointments.

There are many cases of moral awakening followed by permanently reordered and useful lives not involving professions of Christian faith. In my larger book on criminal justice I have told of the remarkable ingenuity of Dr. Miriam Van Waters who, as superintendent of the Framingham Reformatory for Women, in Massachusetts, made a regular practice of setting up arrangements to bring about new moral insight and self-reform.[10] Her own motivation was profoundly religious, but her approach to the inmates—whom she called "students"—was not usually in explicitly religious terms.

I observed earlier that in most jurisdictions of the United States little or no attention in criminal justice laws and procedures is given to the victims of crime, other than seeking to use them as witnesses against offenders. Can we rightly say that justice has been done after a crime when no attempt has been made to compensate the victims? I think not.

Could compensation be regularly achieved? Yes. In other times and places victims have been regularly compensated under criminal law. In the ninth century, West Saxon law provided a schedule of monetary payments that had to be paid by offenders to victims for various specified types of injury. Today the law of many widely distributed African tribes requires that convicted criminals and their families make restitution to victims and their families. There have been similar provisions in tribal laws of some

---

[10]For some specifics, see my *Crime and Justice in America. A Paradox of Conscience* (New York: Harper and Row, 1975) 63-64. The Reformatory is now called Massachusetts Correctional Institution-Framingham.

American Indians and the Infugo of northern Luzon, among others. The laws of England require compensation in some kinds of cases today. There is even more emphasis on such requirements in Sweden, Norway, the Netherlands, New Zealand, Poland, and the Soviet Union. While there were once such provisions in the European laws from which those in the U.S. were derived, they have been gradually eroded by increasing proportionate stress on payments to public authorities. Current provisions in Europe are of more recent origin.

The obligation to provide help for victims of crime is clearly implied by our personalist and Christian ethical principle of concern for all persons. The Christian requirement should be especially obvious to anyone who has read or heard the parable of the Good Samaritan. In that parable Jesus did not describe the restitution to a victim by the offender who had injured him, but rather aid or compensation by another who happened to be passing that way. Seeing that Jesus used precisely an instance of aid to a victim of crime to illustrate the meaning of neighborly love, it is strange that we have been so neglectful of provision for such aid through one means or another in most American efforts to do justice after a crime.

It has been found that uncompensated victims of crime tend to commit crimes more frequently than do others. Hence the provision for victim compensation helps reduce crime among persons other than the original offender and those deterred by the offender's having to pay for the wrong done.

We noted that personalist ethics requires concern for the community as well as for individuals. If a victim is compensated, and especially if the aid is provided by payments or labor given by the offender, this helps restore amity and makes possible community including both persons. This, too, is important. But this leads us into another norm of proper criminal justice.

As I have observed, the rate of crime anywhere depends heavily on the strength and inclusiveness of community. The maintenance and well-being of community is also required by the personalist Communitarian Principles. It follows that when the bonds of community have been broken by a crime of one person against others, even if committed by someone who never was really included in the community, one aim of criminal justice must be to restore the community that was disrupted and to make it inclusive of the person who committed the disruptive crime. It is not enough to develop constructive attitudes in the offending individual. Until incorporated into the life of the community, the offender is likely to be a source of trouble again. The longer confined and thus separated from the community, and the more complete the separation has been made by restriction of visitors and of correspondence, the more difficult it will be to bring the offender into an inclusive community.

Mexico, like underdeveloped countries generally, has a high rate of crime. However, the nation has an advanced theory of criminal justice formally governing the policies of what we would here call corrections, though more inclusive in function than here. The name given the system is significant. It is *la Direccion General de Servicios Coordinados de Prevencion y Readaptacion Social,* that is, The General Administration for Coordinating Services of Prevention and Social Readaptation.[11]

The laudable principles of the name given the national department are employed in quite spotty fashion. In most places there are frequent reports of corruption. Local officials also seem often to do much as they please, and local pressures on both courts and the various institutions of corrections exercise further distorting influence. However, some directors of state penitentiaries who are well-educated and honest, and who understand the need for social readaptation, do remarkably good work.

One such director, in particular, Antonio Sanchez Galindo, Director of the Penitentiary Center of the State of Mexico, near Almoloya de Juarez, has achieved a success unequaled anywhere in the U.S. to the best of my knowledge. He has found it necessary to give special training to the guards to prepare for keeping the kind of institution he intends. Having read references to his work and then given myself a crash course in reading Spanish, I read accounts of his work in his own writings and then made a memorable visit to Almoloya. With the indispensable help of John L. Groves of Mexico City, a former student of mine at Boston University, I conversed at length with Mr. Sanchez and toured the center under his guidance.

He does not have an easy task. The majority of inmates have committed crimes of violence. They come from a variety of Spanish and Indian cultures, urban and rural, often with histories of family blood feuds. He must not simply readapt them to former social relations but develop new and better ones.

---

[11]Ibid., 64, 166-67, 172-73.

Included in the program were job training and actual productive work, with earnings divided so as to pay for board and room in the center, make restitution to victims in suitable cases, assist in support of dependents, and provide a small savings account to become available only upon the inmate's release. Since one problem with most incarcerations everywhere is that upon release the inmate has no home, special care is taken to cultivate the relationship of married men with their wives. Both inmates and wives are provided with counseling and medical attention. Then, if both desire it, they are admitted once a week to a private bedroom for a conjugal visit. Before such visits the wife is offered contraceptive assistance, which, I was told, she invariably accepts.

Occasionally, well-behaved prisoners are permitted to visit a special family area with their wives and children, where playground equipment is provided. Near the time of release, inmates are permitted to visit their homes and neighborhoods. In suitable cases, inmates are employed on farms or in industries outside the walls, being picked up mornings and returned every evening. Hence, the outside world is not strange to them when they are released.

Some parts of such programs are used in some states in this country, with good results. The main trouble is that if one inmate on leave outside in such a program commits a crime, there is such a focus of attention on the case and such an outcry against the policy that made the crime possible that public pressure may force an end to the whole program. Overlooked or unknown by the public are the great number of crimes committed by offenders finally released after long close confinement, besides the many crimes committed within the prisons.

Personalist ethics and Christian teachings alike require that the least painful and restrictive means possible be used to control crime. Since such measures as I have been discussing are, in addition, especially effective in bringing criminal careers to an end, certainly all citizens of good will should support them. The measures reflect the sacred worth of the human person and aim toward the recreation of a community of justice and reconciliation.

Communitarian Dimensions of the Moral Laws

Walter G. Muelder

COLLEGE AND SEMINARY

In the Burlington, Iowa, High School the principal, Ray H. Bracewell, who had once aimed for the ordained ministry, counseled me against taking advanced studies in Latin or Greek while in college. The parish ministry did not require these, he argued, for the relevant materials were all available in English translations. I later came to regret following his lead. As a theological school dean and ecumenist, I needed these tools. Another decision also affected my destiny, as I majored in history and studied widely in the social sciences instead of going beyond the junior college level in mathematics and the physical sciences. My minor at Knox College was English literature. I fulfilled the language requirement by taking German, which was spoken in our home, in which I memorized the catechism, in which my father preached, and which became a passport to a year of study at the University of Frankfurt. Though eventually taking a Ph.D. in philosophy, I had but one formal course in philosophy at Knox College, from which I graduated in 1927.

The orientation in history and numerous social sciences reinforced my predilection for social ethics issues, particularly in peace and labor problems. I was a student assistant to Professor Floy Painter at Burlington Junior College while she was writing her doctoral dissertation on Eugene V. Debs. Debs had a favorable standing in our home partly because he opposed America's entrance into World War I. He was, of course, involved in the Pullman Strike of 1894 and organized the Socialist Party of America. In Burlington, railway labor issues were related both to the federal government, which had taken them over in World War I, and to the local scene because of the railroad strike of 1922. This deeply divided the city during my high school years. As for peace, my revulsion to war took the form of an attempt with others to disestablish the ROTC and to argue that it had no place in a Christian college. My reforming zeal was aided and abetted by weekly preparations drawing heavily from *The Christian Century* while serving a two-point Methodist circuit at Gilson and Orange, Illinois. I recall that Kirby Page, Sherwood Eddy, Harry Emerson Fosdick, as well as Tolstoy and Gandhi, fed these sermons. The League of Nations was still a significant institution and, at least once, Fosdick's sermon before the League was featured in Knox's chapel service: ''The Christian Conscience about War'' (1925).

My ambition was to become a professor of philosophy. Armed with Gospel fervor, pacifism, and socialism I came to Boston University School of Theology, where my father had preceded me to study under Borden Parker Bowne. The above concerns have not diminished across the years, but have developed and matured.

In my junior year I enrolled in Psychology of Religion in which a collateral text was James Bissett Pratt's *The Religious Consciousness*. A large part of that book was devoted to mysticism. It spoke to my religious condition and led me to the classics of mysticism and to works like William James's *Varieties of Religious Experience* and Rudolf Otto's *The Idea of the Holy*. The following year the whole panorama of religion in the East and West opened before me in Brightman's course on mysticism. In my first year I also sat under Timothy Tinfang Lew who had us read *China Today Under Chinese Eyes*. For this I had had some preparation at Knox when I participated in an oratorical contest, choosing the topic ''The Chinese Revolution.'' I was asked to repeat the oration at the commencement exercises in 1927.

Systematic study of personalism began the same year. By 1930 I was well grounded, thanks to Marlatt, Cell, Knudson, and, above all, Brightman. Later I was to eke out a graduate student's existence by being, in turn, a fellow and reader for Marlatt, Knudson, and Brightman. I greatly enjoyed chapel services. I helped Glen Trimble run the Socialist Christian Club. The latter, among other things, challenged the compulsory ROTC at the College of Business Administration to debate their disestablishment—and in this we had the support of Professor Brightman. From the beginning of my Boston days, I tried to take as many courses from him as possible.

FRANKFURT AND ERNST TROELTSCH

I had need to get many things coherently together by the end of my seminary years in 1930. But other formative influences were yet to crowd into my formal education, most notably a year at the University of Frankfurt. Here I must mention Tillich, but also Horkheimer, Mannheim, and Werthheimer, one of the leading Gestalt psychologists. Frankfurt was a predominantly Social Democratic city, and it supported its opera and municipal theater well. Here I saw social democracy in action, not as just a minor political party with a soap box demonstration as on Boston Common. Social democracy was in its death throes in Germany as twenty-seven political parties shattered the political and economic scene. Germany was staggering under the shameful sole war guilt clause of the Versailles Treaty and an astronomical indemnity. Inflation and then the world depression hit and millions were unemployed. Hitler, as Einstein was to say, became a cancer on the empty stomach of Germany.

It was while in Frankfurt that I requested Brightman's consent to do my dissertation on Ernst Troeltsch's philosophy of history. This, I hoped, would bring several things into focus: religious idealism, Tillich's religious socialism, Marxism (Troeltsch had been a member of the Weimar Republic cabinet), the religious-historical method, the nature of historical wholes, which had fascinated me after doing a year-long seminar on Hegel and writing on his philosophy of history, and Christian ethics. I was seeking the foundations of a Christian social ethic.

My interest in the philosophy of history was combined with an equally intense interest in history of philosophy. During my ten years of formal higher education I eventually took the grand sweep of Western thought five times, not counting specialized seminars on Plato, Aristotle, Locke and Leibniz, Hume, Kant, Hegel, Fichte, Schopenhauer, Schleiermacher, Ritschl, and Marx. Teaching aspects of Western thought—religious, political, economic, or ethical, not least American movements—has always been congenial to me, though I do not consider myself a specialist. In mid-career my interest in correlating these studies with church history and biblical studies was always for the sake of deepening and developing Christian social ethics. I needed tools, however, that would help me go beyond the Leibniz, Lotze, Neo-Kantian, or even Bowne formulations of personality theory. Perhaps I could find tools and orientation in a study of historical totalities, or Individual Totalities, as Troeltsch called them.

What did Troeltsch contribute to personalism for me in this process? He helped me find the *reality* of social wholes and the conception of person-in-community. He helped integrate the historical materialism of Marx in a larger dialectic of history without repeating the errors of Hegel's philosophy of history and philosophy of right. He confirmed my personalistic rejection of positivism. He challenged me to take seriously Individual Totalities as objects of historical enquiry, acknowledging them as empirically given entities, as wholes of personalistic existence that would require a communitarian redefinition of personal consciousness and a social ethics reconstruction or development.

To appreciate this development we must, therefore, tarry with Troeltsch's category of historical wholes, the Individual Totality. The term *Totality* designates that a *Gestalt* of this type is an empirical object; the word *Individual* signifies its uniqueness, creativity, and the unrepeatability of historical objects, be they epochs, cultural tendencies, peoples, masses, states, classes, or particular persons.[1] An Individual Totality taken as a temporal and developing historical object is found to have the following attributes: (1) *Originality* and *Uniqueness*. These refer to the objective fact that historical social wholes cannot be deduced; they must simply be accepted. Illustrations would be the unique qualities of the Jewish people, Hellenism, the American temper, and the distinctive great personalities like Jesus, Caesar, Paul, Luther, and so on. (2) *Representation* as a characteristic means that historical wholes stand for innumerable details, which must be filled out by the reader who considers these wholes. One grasps these details by such a process of representation, but also through the object under study. In this way religious metaphors make whole ranges of data and

---

[1]Ernst Troeltsch, *Gesammelte Schriften,* 4 vols. (Tübingen: J. C. B. Mohr, 1912-1925) 3:120.

meaning graspable, as Clifford Geertz says much later in his *Interpretation of Cultures*.

(3) Historical wholes are *unities of meaning and value*. Their cohesion is one of meaning and value both for the observer and for the participants. Within larger totalities are smaller units of meaning and value with their own identities while participating in the whole. For example, Methodism within Protestantism and the latter within Christianity, or again, the church-type, the sect-type, and mysticism in Troeltsch's treatment of the church's history of social teachings. He had a pluralistic view of such unities as contrasted to Hegel's statism and absolute monism. Thus Troeltsch reinforced the personalistic principle of organic pluralism.

(4) Closely related to the above is the category of *Common Spirit*. It refers specifically to the relation of the individual and society. The question of the ontological status of common spirit is crucial. Both personalists and Troeltsch combat faulty reification, yet persons participate in the objective empirical reality of many common spirits. Communitarian personalism stresses this participation as requiring communitarian moral laws.

(5) Another dimension of historical totalities is the *Unconscious*. A person is never conscious of the full range of elements that are represented in a totality or in a common spirit. Thus, there are many presuppositions, instincts, and impulses of which a person is not aware, but which, nevertheless, have their effects in and through a person and which influence historical development.

(6) Then, too, there is the factor of *Creativity*. Creativity is located only in personality. Persons are embedded in a superindividual setting from which they draw spiritual life, but novelty arises through persons and becomes causally significant as creativity. (7) Such novelty should be distinguished from the element of *Indeterminism,* or what Troeltsch called *freedom in the sense of the unpredictable.*

In all historical wholes pulsates creative personality. Persons interact with a physical environment and with impersonal, unconscious forces such as Marx identified in the economic order; but personality is the bearer of common spirit and the key to the temporal development of meaning and value. Hence, a further word about development is needed to show how Troeltsch propelled me beyond Bowne, Knudson, and Brightman, who had not wrestled with philosophy of history in a major way.

Development is temporal in a durational sense, is inherently teleological, is fraught with meaning and value, and has a practical interest. Pure contemplation is out of the question. The impartial bystander does not exist. Thus Troeltsch joins Marx and the pragmatists in stressing the concrete unity of theory and practice. Philosophy and science both have a stake in the future; its values are inherent in their modes of inquiry. This perspective was already securely established in my outlook, and later evidence and reflection have only confirmed it. My essays on ''Norms and Valuation in the Social Sciences'' (1950) and ''Theology and Social Science'' (1966) show this interaction of social science with philosophy and theology.

Development denotes a dynamic psychical process that tends toward an end, akin to logical development of a thought. It does not mean universal progress, for it is definitely contingent. It is purposive and temporal and expresses itself within and through the unities of meaning and value and the common spirit of Individual Totalities. It is not the monistic trait of some universal world history. The irrational, individual, accidental, and dysteleological facts of history must be acknowledged. Historical development, in contrast to contemplation, embraces a formative principle—the shaping of future community life according to norms. These norms are universal and ideal.

This long excursus into Troeltsch shows how he influenced my development and helped integrate Marx's historical materialism and his dictum on the unity of theory and practice. At a crucial point, however, I had to correct Troeltsch because he finally surrendered the idea of personality as a *universal* principle and restricted its validity to the West. His historicism went too far, ending in relativism.

My appropriation of personalistic method and principle had made me assert that Eastern religions, philosophies, and cultures also presuppose the person as the agent of his experiences. The experient is the agent, the subject of all theoretical and practical judgments and choices. Bowne showed that superpersonal impersonalism is reductionist as well as is subpersonal naturalism. Brightman's organic personalism provided for relativity without succumbing to relativism.

ENCOUNTER WITH NEOORTHODOXY

No sooner had I digested Troeltsch and become a kind of Troeltschian personalist than I encountered neoorthodoxy. I am sorry that this movement ever happened, though it was a dialectical response to the liberalism and historical relativism that Barthians associated with Troeltsch. Neoorthodoxy made me plain angry because it seemed to beg all the basic questions and to sidestep the painstaking work of epistemology, value-theory, ethics, and metaphysics. Knudson had already exposed the errors in theological positivism in his critique of Ritschl. Biblical positivism is, of course, what Barth intended with his dialectical "No" and its objectivism, which Bultmann later demythologized on existentialist assumptions. In the United States I had some patience with Reinhold Niebuhr's attacks on reformist liberals and sentimental "parlor pinks." I appreciated his Marxism and his realistic appraisal of communism, but I disliked his failure to do his philosophical homework as he put forward a Neo-Augustinian view of persons, politics, and power. Moreover, I rejected his abandonment of pacifism; that is, he seemed to be joining that long line of Christians who are pacifists only between wars. To be a Christian pacifist seemed to me to take pacifist risks during wartime.

Nevertheless, neoorthodoxy forced me to reexamine my assumptions and to respect its role in resisting Hitler and Nazism. I knew, of course, that Niemoeller, the pacifist, also openly defied Hitler. I also acknowledge the constructive role persons like Niebuhr and Bennett played at the Oxford Conference (1937), their contributions to the revival of social Christianity, and their ecumenism in the formation of the World Council of Churches. W. A. Visser't Hooft and others were valiant and brilliant leaders, but one must not forget the non-Barthians like William Temple, J. H. Oldham, Ehrenstrom, and Alivasatos, to mention only a few prior to Amsterdam (1948). Neoorthodoxy pushed theology in a Christocratic direction and tended to regard natural theology and the natural law tradition as alien to biblical theology, thus digging a gulf between reason and revelation, between philosophy and theology, which is only now being bridged.

Two things at stake were the nature of collective wholes and the contrasts between a more pessimistic and more optimistic or melioristic view of human nature. These had implications for such issues as war and peace, violence and nonviolence, and the relation of individual morality to collective egoism and the constructive life of groups, including the possibilities of democratic socialism.

My commitment to socialism in the 1930s was reinforced by the triple team of Ward, Bennett, and Niebuhr at Union Theological Seminary who were actively involved in politics and economic reconstruction. Then, too, the Great Depression made all churches more systematic in their social analyses. As for methods of social change, the Spanish Civil War precipitated a decision as to whether domestic violence was qualitatively different from international war. After wrestling with the Marxist doctrine of class-struggle and observing class violence in Harlan County, Kentucky, I made a firm decision practically to stay in the pacifist fold, a decision that carried me through the Second World War. I emphasize the term *practical decision* because adherence to the method of "moral laws" required that theoretically such issues remain open, particularly due to the Law of Consequences, the Law of the Best Possible, and the Law of Specification. The Law of the Best Possible leads to the practice of compromise in politics. Pacifism requires a continuing examination of the "best" and the "possible" relevant to the actual situation. Taking Jesus Christ as the exemplar of the Law of Personality often helped in making the nonviolent decision when the calculation of consequences was too complex to be decisive.

What of community? In the 1930s the doctrine of the church played an increasingly important role in my ethical reflection. Oxford (1937) said, "Let the Church be the Church!" In other words, let the actual church become and act like the normative Church. Such an imperative appealed to a dimension of prophetic and redemptive community other than the power struggles of collective egoism featured in *Moral Man and Immoral Society.* I now had three challenges: (1) the church's vocation in world history; (2) the Christian conception of human nature; and (3) the right and effective method of social change. These concerns compenetrated during World War II while I was teaching at the University of Southern California and involved in ecumenical action and civic unity affairs.

During that war, I often appealed to vocational pacifism as the proper function of the churches, inasmuch as in the separation of church and state the task of the church is prophetic and not accommodative. In Christian anthropology I criticized Niebuhr's *Nature and Destiny of Man.* In social change issues I adhered to pacifism while making the discovery of thinkers like Gunnar Myrdal, Robert MacIver, and John Elof Boodin.[2] The communitarian conception of human nature became a cornerstone of my developing ethic. I argued, in effect, that personality is a *socius* with a *private*

---

[2]Gunnar Myrdal, *An American Dilemma*, 2 vols. (New York: Harper and Brothers, 1944); Robert M. MacIver, *The Web of Government* (New York: Macmillan, 1947); and John E. Boodin, *The Social Mind* (New York: Macmillan, 1939).

center. Boodin's doctrine of *Social Mind* reinforced what I have said about Troeltsch and historical wholes. Myrdal contributed multiple and cumulative causation and a conception of ranking discrimination and prejudice for the purpose of social policy and strategy. MacIver's sociology of community was later to contribute to the role of self-enforcing values in his treatment of the ubiquity of government and the positive tasks of the state as distinguishable from community. Again Myrdal, like Troeltsch, while affirming much in Marx, went beyond him in outlining plurality in social causation. Moreover, for Myrdal, a benign circle of causation can be set in motion when a vicious circle has been operative. An upward spiral of cumulative causation presupposes and may demonstrate a melioristic conception of social change in contrast to a merely conflictual view of power. Myrdal's meliorism was evident not only in his attitude toward race relations in *An American Dilemma,* but also in his forthright treatment of values and valuation in the social sciences.[3]

Now I had social scientific grounds to supplement my philosophical and theological criticisms of neoorthodox conceptions of persons and collectives. I expressed this melioristic persuasion in my review of *The Nature and Destiny of Man* in this way.

There is a Christian perfectionism which may be called a prophetic meliorism, which, while it does not presume to guarantee future willing, does not bog down in pessimistic imperfectionism. Niebuhr's treatment of much historical perfectionism is well-founded criticism from an abstract ethical viewpoint, but it hardly does justice to the constructive contributions of the perfectionist sects within the Christian fellowship and even within the secular order. There is a kind of Christian assurance which releases creative energy into the world and which in actual fellowship rises above the conflicts of individual and group egoism.[4]

At the time when this was written, Martin Luther King, Jr., was only fifteen years old, but it was later to influence him as a graduate student when wrestling with Niebuhr in relation to nonviolence. Today, one can appeal

---

[3]Myrdal, *An American Dilemma,* vol. 2, appendix 2.

[4]Walter G. Muelder, "Reinhold Niebuhr's Conception of Man," *The Personalist,* 26, no. 3 (July 1945): 292. Reprinted in *The Ethical Edge of Christian Theology* (Lewiston NY: The Edwin Mellen Press, 1983).

to King's career as a further vindication of this view. A communitarian nonviolence is a *relational* synthesis of *duty* and *purpose* through love.

POSTWAR ISSUES AND ECUMENISM

As already indicated, Myrdal's treatment of social causation and Troeltsch's conception of development aided in putting my socialist appreciation of Marx in perspective. Together with my personalistic values, these tendencies helped formulate my essays of "Cumulative Power Tendencies in Western Culture," "Power, *Anomie,* and Personality," and "A Personalistic Critique of Marxism."[5] Here I might point out that most of my writing does not reflect a systematic career plan, but has been responsive often to teaching needs and responsibilities occasioned by understaffed departments and lacunae in the literature of the field in which I was teaching at that moment. This stimulus from the field and the audience was also evident with the development of my responsibilities in the World Council of Churches.

With the consummation of the World Council in 1948, dominated in "Life and Work" by the Idea of the Responsible Society, my thought became more and more absorbed in the social ethics of the church's vocation. Involvement in this and other dialogues interfaced several fronts: preparation for the Evanston Assembly's main theme, "Jesus Christ, the Hope of the World," entailed confrontation with Barthians, Lutherans, and Orthodox; membership in the Faith and Order Commission from 1952 to 1975 required many-sided debates and for seven years special research and case studies on institutional barriers to Christian unity; cochairing the Commission on the Co-operation of Men and Women in Church and Society called for theological reflection, socioeconomic research, and boldness as a gadfly to a male-dominated ecumenical bureaucracy. All this while church and society issues heightened my awareness of the eclectic character of my own discipline and fed my growing commitment to a world "responsible society," including the radical pressures in areas of rapid social change as colonialism yielded to independence in the Third World. The principal ef-

---

[5]The first two were published by the Conference on Science, Philosophy, and Religion, *Conflicts of Power in Modern Culture* (Seventh Symposium, 1947) and *Perspectives on a Troubled Decade* (Tenth Symposium, 1950). The editors were Bryson, Finkelstein, and MacIver.

fect of these manifold dialogues while continuing as dean and professor was (1) to strengthen the explicit theological component in my reflection, (2) to enlarge my commitment to ecumenism, not least after being an official observer at Vatican II (1964), (3) to compel me to do research on women-men relationships prior to the resurgence of women's liberation, (4) to articulate a critical institutional reform in church and university, and (5) to confirm my faith in nonviolent strategy and philosophy of social change. The latter confirmation deepened as Martin Luther King, Jr., applied the nonviolent interpretation of Boston Personalism to the racial struggle and melded it with the spiritual resources of the Black Church, interfaith ecumenism, and the politics of federal constitutional enforcement.

Summarizing now where I stood in the 1950s on a number of issues: (1) affirmation of norms and values as lockstitched in the social sciences; (2) the communitarian nature of the moral subject; (3) agreement with Professor DeWolf in formulating and adding Communitarian Laws to Brightman's system of moral laws; and (4) systematizing a personalist critique of Marxism. This evaluation of Marx was essentially as follows: the strengths include—(1) the dialectic as a principle; (2) his historical approach to science and economic institutions; (3) his repudiation of mechanistic materialism; (4) his repudiation of abstract idealism in favor of the unity of theory and practice; and (5) his critique of ideology. The weak points from a personalistic perspective are: (1) the impersonal and unempirical elements in the dialectic; (2) his tendency to hypostatize categories like class; (3) the tendencies toward scientistic naturalism; (4) his incomplete criticism of ideology; (5) his inadequate doctrine of human nature making the self an ensemble of social relations; (6) his defective philosophy of political order, including the state; (7) his inadequate understanding of the will to power; and (8) his analysis of religion. On the basis of this positive and negative critique of Marx, I challenged personalists to develop a more adequate communitarian unity of theory and practice. About this time I delivered the Lowell Lectures, which were published as *Religion and Economic Responsibility*. One of the chapters was a thorough repudiation of Stalinism and much in Marxism-Leninism. "Socialism from Above" violates what the World Council was later to define as a "just, participatory, and sustainable" society.

Domestically, I declared myself on "Right-to-Work" laws, an issue made acute by the Taft-Hartley Act of 1947. I condemned the laws because "democracy suffers from the anarchy of union insecurity" that they seek. Moreover, "The 'right-to-work' laws are a virtual conspiracy of the crafty, the ignorant, or the misguided to subvert industrial peace, exploit persons' need to work, and deluge the community with industrial irresponsibility."[6] Such laws are the most crass application of the seizure of state power in behalf of "free enterprise" against the true freedom of workers.

In addition to these issues, the hysteria of the McCarthy era required greater attention to civil liberties and academic freedom and their attendant church-state relations. An entirely unexpected dimension of applied personalism was the request from the Commission on the Life and Status of Women in the Church to prepare a paper on its concerns just before the Evanston Assembly (1954). This sociological analysis catapulted me into cochairing the department redesigned as the Department of the Co-operation of Men and Women in Church and Society. Some of my concerns, outlined before full clergy rights were established for women in the Methodist church, are relevant here:

1. An adequate program for the cooperation of men and women in the Church will depend on a profounder Christian vocational ethic than has been prevalent in the Church. This vocational ethic will be oriented not primarily in the work of the ministry but in the total vocational problems of lay persons in our society.
2. The Church has not thus far taken full advantage of its strategic position in society to be a formative influence in molding basic attitudes and values in this field.
3. An abstract Christian idealism regarding the equality of men and women, however true it may be in principle, will not of itself provide the leverage for developing sounder culture patterns in the occupational world.
4. The redefinition of roles and status is as important from the masculine as from the feminine side.

---

[6]*'Right-to-Work' Laws: Three Moral Studies* by an Oblate Father, an Eminent Rabbi, and a Methodist Dean. (Washington DC: International Association of Machinists, 1954, 1955) 43-55.

5. The rich resources of women's talents and spiritual attitudes are often lost to the fellowship of the Church, and to its work in society, by the fact that men define the function of the Church too exclusively in masculine terms. . . . It is important in this connection that the masculine definition of the Church surrender its absolute theological sanction.[7]

When dealing with all these problems from an ecumenical perspective, the encompassing idea was "the responsible society." This middle axiom, first formulated at the Amsterdam Assembly (1948), seemed to gather up the essence of the Oxford Conference (1937), and it appeared to guide reflection for the coming decades. I made it the theme of the University Lecture (1954) and the opening chapter of my major social ethics book, *The Foundations of the Responsible Society*. A middle axiom is a second-order principle that mediates ultimate categories or principles and actual programmatic decisions. It is not as abstract as the highest ideal values, nor as specific as concrete proposals, but it gathers up a whole range of relevant values, gives them dialectical focus, and points a direction or states a guideline for concrete decision making. I found the method of formulating middle axioms to be a useful device in supplementing and applying the regulatory "moral laws." Originally, I planned the "Moral Laws" and the "Foundations" volumes as an integrated single book, but after the manuscript was finished, the publisher feared the costs. Nevertheless, the two belong together, including the chapter "Jesus Christ and Responsible Community," which rounds off the whole with a theological statement.

A special statement on racism and civil rights will indicate their place in my developing social ethics. At Berea College the seal and motto was "God has made of one blood." That the student body and faculty were all white was no fault of the college, but that is a story of itself. Prevented by law from coeducating the races, those of us who taught there were highly conscious of an interracial vocation. Yet, I had an adjustment to make during the civil rights struggle, for as a socialist, I tended to subsume race and

---

[7]"Some Social Aspects of Cooperation Between Men and Women," mimeographed by the World Council of Churches from an address to the Commission on Life and Status of Women in the Church, Lake Forest, 1954.

color under the category of exploitation of classes. In Los Angeles I chaired the Department of Race Relations of the Church Federation; I protested the incarceration of persons of Japanese ancestry; and, when it appeared, I avidly studied Myrdal's *An American Dilemma*. Still, I did not think of racism in distinct structural terms, since both anthropology and Christian theology affirmed but one human race and one human family. Both the doctrines of creation and of redemption are barrierless. Myrdal prompted me, as did MacIver, to take every opportunity to modify what Myrdal called the rank order of discrimination by a strategy of multiple and cumulative amelioration. Hence, I did not approach race as a separable problem until the dynamics of the King crusade made evident the paradoxical character of structural racism—that it is not presently reducible to the class struggle or to the perversities of prejudice and discrimination. It is an Individual Totality lockstitched into the ambiguities of contemporary history. In this respect, as a social ethics issue, race becomes a special kind of issue—and not limited to the history of slavery, Southern Reconstruction, or the land greed of Native Sons of the Golden West.

Sexism, we have come to see, has analogous structural dimensions. One needs to recognize in radical ways that class, race, and sex are not reducible to each other; neither are they completely separable. Unjust discrimination based on these categories violates communitarian personalism. They interpenetrate as structural variables, as well as through psychic processes, at many levels of conscious and unconscious dynamics. To deal with them adequately we should use the tools of differential analysis and of interactive models. Such awareness agitates my applied social ethics a great deal. An ability to assimilate varieties of models has been made easier for me by the study of other institutional barriers to Christian unity.

In retrospect it seems almost axiomatic that the principles of person-in-community, wholeness, and dialectic should demand interactive models of research. Moreover, cultures are complex individual totalities in and through which major changes in one component institution will affect to some degree all other components. A sound interactive model conserves the personalistic principle of organic pluralism and rules out any method that reduces one causal factor to another. At the same time it will be oriented to the ethical principles of the Communitarian Laws, which take this range of empirical data more seriously into account than was done in the era of Knudson and Brightman.

CHARACTERISTICS
OF COMMUNITARIAN PERSONALISM

I must confess to the eclectic character of Christian social ethics in this historical era. The disciplines on which it draws have relative autonomy. And yet, the principle of coherence requires the search for the whole, giving due regard for the dialectical tension among the parts.

Second, the communitarian principle is ecumenical with respect to both space and time, that is, it is social and historical. It affirms solidarism and the constants of the human condition. The search for these constants in theology, philosophy, and science presupposes the priority of personality as the subject.

Third, the Moral Laws as regulatory principles are constant, but their formulation may doubtless be refined. Fourth, all principles are abstractions derived by persons from the concrete metaphysical reality of personal wholeness. Abstract ideals like freedom, justice, participation, sustainability affirm the personality principle while being embodied in changing historical configurations. For example, actual freedom is always concretely historical and subject to the flow of circumstance; yet, it is anchored in the moral constants of person-in-community.

Fifth, Troeltsch's great error was not in his analysis of historical wholes but in his confusion of relativity with relativism. He need not have conceded the metaphysical principle of personality simply because certain cultures and civilizations did not seem to appeal to it or seemed to seek redemption in escaping from it. They only demonstrate it in unique Individual Totalities. Contemporary China and India are as involved in the ethics of ''justice, participation and sustainability'' as are the World Council of Churches and the North Atlantic community.

Sixth, this dynamic formula is a fitting middle axiom for communitarian personalism. Three comments are in order. Since justice is love rationally distributed (love being the highest personality value), justice must concentrate on the property question inasmuch as it has to do with the production, distribution, use, and power related to all scarce values. The presumption of justice is a nisus toward equality consistent with the variables of actual inequality. In the struggle for justice understood as love distributed, the goal and norm are reconciliation.

Participation is also axiomatic in the idea of person-in-community. Participation is the measure of power through decision making. There is very little alienation that participatory power will not overcome. Preparation for, exercise and conservation of, and evaluation of participation are dimensions of both love and justice. Bills of human rights are codes of participation in the service of freedom and justice.

Sustainability is the dynamic equilibrium of God's creation and of human participation in it. It applies to both the ecology of nature and the ecology of social existence. In this respect for nature and society under God, the present generation acknowledges its responsibility for future generations. It means, in harmony with justice and participation and the communitarian moral laws, a democratic socialism understood in generational terms.

Finally, in ultimate terms the highest good for human persons is the adoration of the Objective Good, namely God. Beyond the relative autonomy of social ethics is God, the source and ground of the whole moral order. Since God is personal and human personality is the key to ultimate reality, the quest for the highest good is reverence for personality both human and divine. The moral good for persons participates in the religious good as its source, ground, and goal. The "telos" of personal life is God's will for all human life, which is love. The embodiment of that love of self and neighbor is the Kingdom of God. Though we do not build the Kingdom, we may be said to embody it or to express it interpersonally or in community. One of the vocational embodiments of such normative religious devotion is the Christian Church. The organic pluralism of the historical church is an illustration of embodied communitarian personalism as a servant of world community. This idea of community shows the personalistic ethic to be relational as well as teleological. Communitarian personalism is, finally, theonomous in that human beings are capable of manifesting God, since God's grace penetrates their nature and helps bring them, despite sin and evil, to fulfill God's created design for them.

Reflections on a Philosophical Heritage

John H. Lavely

ARGUMENTUM AD HOMINEM

When I consider the development of my thought, I realize that it takes the form of reflections on a philosophical heritage. My own philosophically articulated thought is my response to the personalist tradition as I came to know it firsthand in Edgar Sheffield Brightman.

I cannot give an account of that response and the reflections in which it is embodied without first recalling the nurture I received at home. This nurture combined deep religious roots *and* liberal intellectual accountability. My father was a graduate of the School of Theology in the post-Bownian era and, after a term on the mission field in China, returned to take a doctorate under Brightman and Knudson. My mother was a woman of superior intelligence, the daughter of a graduate of the School of Theology in the pre-Bownian era. She possessed scholarly competence in Greek and Latin and a gift for interpreting the Bible. She also voted for Norman Thomas every time he ran for president. I was fortunate, therefore, that I never had to work my way through biblical literalism or confront doctrinaire, let alone dogmatic, beliefs in the home. I was also fortunate in that

I was never given the impression that such liberalism lessened or weakened the power and meaning of biblical faith. In short, what I ingested of my parents' intellectual milk was a questioning, historical, critical attitude combined with a sense of the seriousness of the spiritual quest and the importance of responding to human need. Hence, I cannot remember ever going through a conservative, let alone a fundamentalist, stage.

As early as my high school years, I was venturing into the wilderness of theological doctrines and religious arguments for the purpose of pruning dead branches and cutting down rotten trees. But no matter how far I pursued this critique of theology (and I went on with it right through my years at the School of Theology), there always remained the living presence of Jesus of Nazareth. This meant that I had then to undertake the reconstruction of theology, a theology able to account for and to interpret the meaning and message of Jesus. That is, I had to construct my own theological house in which Jesus could live. In the initial stages of this process (which is still going on), I found George Bernard Shaw's preface to his play *Androcles and the Lion* immensely helpful and stimulating. A few years later, Thomas Mann's great work *Joseph and His Brothers* deepened beyond measure my biblical understanding. That was the first time I really understood what was going on in the Old Testament. Of course, Thomas Mann would probably not have spoken to me so powerfully without the background on the Bible provided at home and in the seminary.

During the spring of 1941, my last semester at the School of Theology, I was keeping company with Josephine Magee, also a student at the School of Theology. One of our fellow students went to Josephine and warned her about associating with me because, as he said, "It's well known that John Lavely is an atheist." I was very much surprised and disturbed when Josephine told me of this charge. I thereupon confronted the student, who said he had once heard another student say that I was an atheist. The other student had been a college classmate of mine at Allegheny College, and we had been in a course in philosophy together. It turned out that I had vigorously criticized the traditional arguments for God during class discussion, from which my classmate inferred that I did not believe in God. I was able to convince Josephine that the rumor of my atheism was based on a non sequitur. Not long after that we were married. Nearly forty-four years later we are still happily married, and I am still happily a theist, not without developments in both cases.

The upshot of all this is that I became a philosopher because of the problems that arose for me in the religious arena in which I stood. It never occurred to me that critical inquiry within the religious domain was inappropriate or that it alienated me from the religious enterprise. I have not wanted to be thought of as a theologian if by theologian is meant one for whom some tradition or doctrine is incorrigible or in principle not subject to refutation. Such a conception of theology seemed to me to do a disservice to religion. I could not see that anything that in effect blocked inquiry was intrinsic to religion.

Philosophy of religion, therefore, became for me an uncompromising grappling with problems raised in and about religion. I want to illustrate with reference to one type of problem, one that was decisive for me. I could not identify philosophy of religion with natural theology. The bifurcation between natural theology and revealed theology seemed to me to beg a central question. That is, the dichotomy between reason and revelation already constituted a problem, the resolution of which could not be identified with prior or arbitrary alignment with either reason or revelation. This problem, on another level, confronted me in teaching courses in philosophy of religion. It is what I call the insider/outsider dilemma. The prevailing assumption of most students was (and is) that if you "have religion" (that is, are inside the circle of faith) there is nothing much that can be done to "disprove" it, and if you don't "have religion" (that is, are outside the circle of faith) there is nothing much that can be done to "prove" it. I ask you as I ask myself, how do you deal with this dilemma without simply taking a stand either inside the circle of faith or outside the circle?

EDGAR BRIGHTMAN

It was my relation to Brightman that made the process I have been describing possible insofar as there was anything constructive about it. I had graduated from Allegheny College in 1938 with a major in history and minors in speech, football, and track. It was my father's gentle persuasion that led me to enroll at Boston University School of Theology that fall. I had no call to the ministry: my father lured me by saying that at Boston I could "study under Brightman." Studying under Brightman fulfilled for me every expectation that my father could have had. I took a course from Brightman each of the last five (out of six) semesters at the School of Theology. In the ensuing years, while I pursued a Ph.D. degree in philosophy in the graduate school, of the sixteen courses I took, fifteen were from Brightman. The other was from Harold DeWolf. (Muelder and Bertocci were not yet on the scene.)

I was deeply grateful for the education I received at the School of Theology. Furthermore, almost to my surprise, I came gradually to a commitment to a religious vocation in the church. Following graduation from the School of Theology, I served Methodist churches first in Framingham, Massachusetts, and then in Ligonier, Pennsylvania, from 1941 to 1947. It was only when Brightman recommended me for a teaching position (even though my dissertation was far from done) that I was forced to choose between the pastoral ministry and the teaching ministry. As a result, I went on for four years to teach philosophy at Albion College in Michigan, and in the fall of 1951 I was called back to teach in the philosophy department at Boston University. For thirty-one years I taught in the department, serving two terms as chairperson and frequently offering courses in the School of Theology. I never taught a course on personalism per se until Paul Deats, on his initiative, and I introduced in 1980-1981 "Ethics and Theology in Personalism."

It was Brightman, as I said, who provided the conditions under which my philosophical life grew both as a student and as a teacher. It was his personalism that provided a viable and positive framework within which I could work out my own flexible position. His emphasis on an empirical method and on the tentative/hypothetical character of our best knowledge freed me from the need to battle dogmatic absolutes all the time. And yet, he insisted that every action was an absolute. This was a fruitful equilibrium between theoretical relativism and practical absolutism. Furthermore, he encouraged independence. I did not feel the need to be defensive and engaged freely in vigorous argument with him over some of his views. As a result, there was no pressure to assist in consolidating a final/decisive personalism. I never felt the bandwagon syndrome or the need to "pump" personalism.

It may come as no surprise, therefore, that the three Brightman students who were teaching in the department when he died (in 1953), namely, Peter Bertocci, Richard Millard, and I, consciously collaborated in developing a pluralistic department. We felt that such diversification would be more of a tribute to Brightman than an ingrown, closed, personalistic department. We agreed that it was more important to train philosophers than simply to produce personalists.

In my own case, this policy led me to downplay my own position, perhaps too much. In other words, my development did not come through systematic exposition or elaboration of my personalistic perspective. It came through grappling with the great thinkers in the history of philosophy (in my teaching) and in responding to traditions/movements other than personalism, such as pragmatism and process philosophy, analytic philosophy and existentialism/phenomenology, not to mention confronting Marxism and non-Western religions/philosophies.

Other facets of my experience made their contributions. My acculturation in China 1920-1926, when I was a boy aged four to ten, affected me deeply. I became a pacifist and a member of the Fellowship of Reconciliation at the time in the early 1940s when my classmates like John Swomley and my brother-in-law, John Magee, and I were struggling with the question of whether to register for the draft. From the time I took Brightman's superb course in Principles of Social Philosophy, I have been an avowed democratic socialist. I wrote my dissertation on the Philosophy of History.

Despite these factors, it is still true that my personalism was formed through Edgar Brightman's catalytic and charismatic impact. Consequently, my development conceptually or doctrinally takes the form of refinements, modifications, and even departures from Brightman's position in the context of other influences. My reflections on this heritage will focus on personalism's unfinished business, on my awareness of problems in personalism and of ways to deal with these problems.

UNFINISHED BUSINESS: PROBLEMS/PROMISES

In this section I examine three problems or clusters of problems. The development of my thought does not consist in having solutions to these problems, at least not yet. Rather, my development lies in raising problems and in suggesting some unfinished business for personalists. The prospects for personalism depend on the projects personalists are willing to undertake.

Faith and Reason

The first problem has to do with the interface between religion and philosophy, or, if you will, faith and reason. The classic form in which this issue comes up in the Western tradition is Pascal's "God of Abraham, God of Isaac, God of Jacob, *not* the God of the philosophers and scholars."

Another form in which this issue appears is Thomas Aquinas's proofs of God's existence. "It is necessary," Aquinas argues at the end of the first proof, "to arrive at a first mover, moved by no other; and this everyone understands to be God."[1] There is no argument that the unmoved mover of Aristotle coincides with the God of biblical revelation; it is just assumed. All the other proofs follow the same pattern. Pascal simply rejects the assumption, as does Kierkegaard in his distinction between Religiousness A and Religiousness B.

Although this problem about the interface between religion and philosophy is perennial, it is of special importance for personalists. Why? Because personalists have maintained, I think with virtually no exception, that the God of Abraham, Isaac, and Jacob *is* the same God as the God of the philosophers. Or, to bring out the point more clearly, the living God of the Bible is identical to the Supreme Person espoused by personalistic theists. Indeed, a persistent theme of personalism has been that its conception of God is a better fit with the God of the Bible than is that of traditional Judeo-Christian supernaturalism in its theological form.

Now the question is whether the nexus between philosophy and religion on which personalists have prided themselves is a true knit. I recently became aware of this issue at the 1979 meeting of the Personalistic Discussion Group. In his paper "A Century of Bowne's Theism," Warren Steinkraus spoke of Bowne as a thinker "who has been unjustly neglected," especially in the philosophical community. In his commentary, Erazim Kohak took up the matter of the "unjust neglect" of Bowne. Although I will put my diagnosis of this situation differently from that of Kohak, I am grateful for his perceptive comments. It seems to me that Bowne brought a religious base to his philosophizing, but that, unfortunately, it is hard to see how that religious base informs his position. Consequently, when Bowne "used arguments like bludgeons, beating all who disagreed into submission with blows of relentless logic,"[2] those who stood outside the circle of faith were often simply turned off. At the same time many of

---

[1]Thomas Aquinas, *Summa Theologica,* ed. A. C. Pegis, in *Basic Writings of Saint Thomas Aquinas* (New York: Random House, 1945) pt. 1, ques. 2, art. 3.

[2]Erazim V. Kohak, "The Futility of Argument: A Commentary on Warren Steinkraus's 'A Century of Bowne's Theism' " (presented at a meeting of the Personalistic Discussion Group, 28 December 1979) 1, paraphrasing Steinkraus.

the students who came to the School of Theology with a religious orientation, as they naturally would, found in Bowne's utterances, with their homiletic nuances, an impressive and congenial formulation of their faith. Thus, Boston personalism fertilized itself from within but did not do very well in gaining proselytes from among the pagans, that is, the general philosophic community. This also helps explain why personalism is often called Methodist theology.

I have frequently had students or associates concede that they were personalists when they came to the School of Theology though they did not know it. I vividly recall the theological student who spoke to me at the start of a course in philosophy of religion. He said, "I'm a personalist, and I'm taking this course to find out what a personalist is." Brightman did a marvelous job in raising these preprogrammed personalists to the level of clear intellectual accountability and at the same time addressing the nonpersonalist world. Still, though I have doubtless oversimplified the personalist situation, there remains the problem of the knit between religious roots and its philosophical expression in personalism. This is a problem not just for personalism but for the whole theological world (process theology and liberation theology, for example) unless we capitulate to a permanent split between faith and reason.

What promise is there that the problem of the interface between religion and philosophy can be solved in the personalist perspective? I must say that I have not found a solution in any other perspective and that a solution is much more difficult than might be supposed. I am convinced that the continuity between religion and philosophy can be worked out only in the context of a systematic philosophy of religion.

That is the reason why during my thirty years of teaching at Boston University I have focused on such a philosophy of religion. I have completed about ninety percent of this work. Only one small piece of this comprehensive study has been published. It is called "Faith and Knowledge: Is the Ineffable Intelligible?"[3] I hope to see much more, if not all, of this study published. I would like to call it *Critique of Pure Religion*. The problem is the interface or nexus of religion and philosophy, that is, how to

---

[3]John H. Lavely, "Faith and Knowledge: Is the Ineffable Intelligible?" in John Howie and Thomas O. Buford, eds., *Contemporary Studies in Philosophical Idealism* (Cape Cod MA: Claude Stark, 1975) 116-32.

show the continuity between religion and philosophy and the mutual reenforcement they give to each other. This means, for example, that the philosophical problem of God is not the existence of God. If religion cannot supply any warrant for the existence of God, then there is no way to supply the lack. Since religion's basis for the existence of God turns out to be matter of fact, something that actually happens, a demanding and painstaking analysis of religious dimension is needed. This analysis cannot be carried out without drawing on phenomenology of religion and analysis of religious language. For example, what causes a person to call an experience or event "religious"? What is it about "God" that makes God God religiously? Or what is it about any reality that qualifies that reality as God, that is, as worthy of worship?

But when we have discovered the warrant for the religious assertion or affirmation that God exists we are far from done. For religious claims almost invariably assert not merely *that* God exists but that some particular *kind* of God exists. Here the philosophical problem *is* raised: not whether God exists but about the nature of God, that is, what kind of God exists. Hence, interpretation of religious claims (beliefs) inescapably raises metaphysical issues and poses the conditions under which a religious belief can be justified vis-à-vis other religious beliefs.

Consequently, there is no way to resolve the first problem for personalists without a comprehensive and systematic analysis of religion (that is, the epistemology of religion) and interpretation of religion (that is, the metaphysics of religion).

Reason and Rationalism

The second problem I want to raise has to do with the concept of reason, specifically Brightman's concept of reason. When Brightman's view of reason is mentioned, it is the concept of coherence as the criterion of truth and the emphasis on empirical method we usually have in mind. There is, however, a residue of rationalism in Brightman that I find hard to square with coherence and empirical method. This strain of rationalism can, I think, be documented. In *Person and Reality* he writes, "The validity of logical entailment is an area immune to any force of man or nature or God that may be exerted against it."[4] This appears in the context of an eloquent

---

[4]Edgar S. Brightman, *Person and Reality: An Introduction to Metaphysics,* ed. Peter A. Bertocci, Jannette E. Newhall, and Robert S. Brightman (New York: Ronald Press Company, 1958) 57.

statement about the ultimacy and unchangeableness of the Rational Given, but it is about logic (that is, formal consistency, not empirical coherence) that he makes the most impassioned claims. For Brightman logic had an a priori finality that nothing in this world or the next (or indeed in any conceivable world) could qualify. Although he seemed to subordinate logic to coherence (consistency being only a necessary condition for truth), logic nonetheless appeared to be an independent, if not absolute, principle. How he can square the inviolable Platonic status of logic with the statement in the same section that "The Given is never given by itself"[5] I do not know. To me, logic seems to be a form of coherence. Logic is a human achievement dependent for its sanction on the order it introduces into thinking and communicating. The Law of Identity (A is A) is thus a human resolution that gets its force from the minimum but indispensable level of coherence it formulates. It is normative: if one wants a coherent life, then one ought to be logical or consistent. In short, logic was made by and for persons in response to a need for order.

The concept of coherence, which bulks very large in Brightman's personalism, is, as we have seen, the criterion of truth. Reason is defined as "a logically consistent and coherent method of interpreting experience."[6] Coherence is also a universal principle of value. "True value would be a fully coherent fulfilled desire for a fully coherent object."[7] Bertocci has highlighted an important feature of Brightman's view of coherence by speaking of "growing empirical coherence." The point is worth emphasizing: coherence is a principle for interpreting experience.

The power this principle had for Brightman can be seen in the fact that his "argument" for God consisted in the hypothesis that a personal God provides the most coherent interpretation of all the available evidence; it gives the most adequate explanation of all the facts of experience taken synoptically. Brightman recognized that appealing to or claiming coherence is not as such an argument. Coherence has to be *shown*.

I want to raise some questions about coherence, which may help bring out the source and limits of its power—because it is a powerful principle.

---

[5]Ibid., 56 n. 2.

[6]Edgar S. Brightman, *A Philosophy of Religion* (New York: Prentice-Hall, 1940) 536.

[7]Ibid., 252. Cf. the Axiological Law in Brightman's *Moral Laws*.

I can remember thinking (years and years ago) that Brightman used coherence to justify everything else, but how did he justify coherence? Or to put the question another way, since coherence was the essence of reason, what was the ground of rationality? For a philosopher who staked everything on being empirical, what was the empirical basis of coherence? I didn't really see any phenomenological derivation of coherence unless Brightman simply assumed the Hegelian dialectic. Coherence was closely connected with desire, since for Brightman all value was generically satisfaction of desire and coherence was somehow the highest value (at least as the principle of truth); but what was the connection? In Brightman's analysis of the self, will (activity, purpose) clearly took precedence over desire, since will was one of the three constitutive aspects of person (the other two being rational form and nonrational content) and desire was not mentioned per se. The ambiguity here seemed to me similar to one in Sartre: to be human is *manquer* (to lack) but at the same time "there is no difference between being human and being free."[8]

What is the relation between freedom and desire? It occurred to me that if reason is a method for achieving coherence it must presuppose a need or desire for coherence. If purposive activity was the effort to achieve coherence, then it presupposed a need or desire for coherence. If so, then desire is the prior existential condition without which neither reason nor will is intelligible. Desire is not an act, nor is it a potency. It is an existing condition. Hunger, for example, is not an activity; it is feeling empty. Action is born in the effort to overcome the lack, to satisfy the hunger. So desire is prior to activity, will, freedom.

Reflections like these forced me to the conclusion that desire is the ground of human being. Freedom, creativity, and purpose are born in the endeavor to satisfy desire, in seeking to fill the emptiness within. Many people find desire a disturbing concept. But why take a negative attitude toward that without which no future satisfaction would be possible? Nietzsche says, "I say unto you: One must still have chaos [desire] in oneself to be able to give birth to a dancing star. I say unto you: you still have chaos [desire] in yourselves."[9]

---

[8]Translated from Jean-Paul Sartre, *L'etre et le neant* (Paris: Gallimard, 1943) 61.

[9]Friedrich Nietzsche, *Thus Spoke Zarathustra,* in Walter Kaufmann, trans., *The Portable Nietzsche* (New York: The Viking Press, 1954) 129.

Suppose, then, that desire is fundamental in human nature. Desire for what? There is no way to tell ahead of time. Desire does not tell us what will satisfy. Everything we know about the meeting of need, the overcoming of lack, is a posteriori, after the fact. We cannot even be sure that desire can or will be satisfied. This means that every act is a risk, fraught with the danger that our desire will be frustrated, not fulfilled. Hence, human endeavor is a willingness to make mistakes. It is resistance to the generic fear that action might not bring success, satisfaction, or even survival. In fact, the last act in extreme cases is the catatonic paralysis that reflects the refusal to act for fear desire might be thwarted. Fear of change reflects fixation of desire on some familiar satisfaction or meaning.

So we can only find out in retrospect what fulfills or frustrates. If so, what *do* we find out afterwards about desire? Often, we catalogue types of satisfaction (values) and attribute them to a corresponding set of desires. I want to propose something very different as a theory of desire, something radical, rash, and possibly ridiculous. I remind you that a theory of desire presupposes the continuum of (a) desire, (b) effort, purpose, or activity, and (c) the achievements/failures with their resulting values/disvalues. Let me suggest what led me to entertain and then to take this proposal very seriously.

I was struck by what I will call the unity or unifying motif. In the *Charmides,* speaking of physicians, Socrates says, "the part can never be well unless the whole is well." [10] And in the *Gorgias:* "The artist disposes all things in order and compels the one part to harmonize and accord with the other part, until he has constructed a regular and systematic whole." [11] The epitome of this motif is certainly Hegel's "the True is the Whole." For him, the history of self-formation, concept-formation, culture formation is seen in needing, seeking, realizing wholeness. To be abstract is to be out of connection and that is bad. The dialectic may differentiate itself endlessly and even distort itself, but it is still the same dialectic with its search for the concrete universal.

Coherence (etymologically, sticking together) is a form of this unity motif. It is not merely a sophisticated or technical philosophical principle. Coherence and/or the unity motif are present in ordinary life, prereflective

---

[10] B. Jowett, trans., *The Dialogues of Plato* (New York: Random House, 1937) 1:156.

[11] Ibid., 1:504.

experience. We say, "Something doesn't fit." Or "I've got to get my head together." We don't feel at home unless we have a familiar context. We hang on for dear life to what makes sense to us. One perception is an illusion, but two perceptions are a thing. Three perceptions and we construct a law of nature. Four perceptions disclose ultimate reality. Five perceptions constitute reunion with the One. Consider for yourself the function that myth, language, and institutions perform and the judgment on them if the order and organization they provide break down.

Let me test this motif in the sphere of the higher human values. First, morality. What is character but coherence between my ideals and my actions? Bertocci considers the feeling of obligation an irreducible moral datum. I disagree; I think the feeling of obligation can be analyzed as the feeling that I ought to make my actions coherent with my ideals. This feeling seems to me to presuppose a desire for a unified life. I ought to act in accord with my beliefs *if I want a unified life.* If there is discord between my ideals and what I did, remorse or regret result. I have earlier interpreted logic as a system of coherence in meanings, concepts, and the like. In science we have a synthesis of abstract thought (i.e., mathematics) and sense perception. Scientific knowledge is a joint product, a unity of form (reason) and content (sense). Kant speaks of "modes of knowledge which must have their origin *a priori,* and which perhaps serve only to give coherence to our sense-representations."[12] Art provides a variation on the unity of form and content, on the theme of harmony, and on the coherence of aim and attainment. Religion, in this idiom, is coherent relation to the reality without which (or whom) a person wouldn't seek or find coherence. "The primacy of religious value," as I have said elsewhere, "thus seems to be predicated on the normative principle that maximum fulfillment is maximum wholeness and that such wholeness contributes to and is fostered by relationship to reality. Internal coherence and external relatedness are coordinates for the religious life."[13] The same thing might well be said by someone arguing for the primacy of some other value.

To me the almost irresistible conclusion from this kind of evidence and the proposal I spoke of earlier is simply this: *Person is a matrix of a*

---

[12]Immanuel Kant, *Critique of Pure Reason,* trans. Norman Kemp Smith (New York: St. Martin's Press, 1973) 42 (A2).

[13]Lavely, "Faith and Knowledge," 129.

single basic desire, which I prefer to call a desire for coherence. It can, however, just as well be spoken of as a desire for wholeness, order, harmony, integration, or any one of a number of kindred terms. It is essential to remember that we do not know a priori that a person is existentially a desire for coherence. It *turns out* that fulfillment is a function of some achieved wholeness, that satisfaction is a function of some actual order, that value results from coherence. One must also keep in mind that desire for coherence can never be exhausted in or identified fully with any particular symbol, system, order, no matter how much meaning that symbol or system may at the time have.

It should be apparent by now why I agree with Brightman about the power of the concept of coherence. For me that power is rooted in the nature of person. Coherence is not to be equated with reason or rationality. Rather, reason or rationality is a specification of coherence and like coherence finds its foundation and sanction in the nature of person.

The Person and Anthropomorphism

The third area in which problems come up for me is the concept of the person, and particularly Brightman's concept of the person. I concede that personalism is openly anthropomorphic. Far from seeking to disguise this fact, personalists flaunt the personal model before the world boldly and unashamedly. Is the person able to bear the weight of supporting, Atlas-like, the personalistic worldview?

Brightman defines a person as "a complex unity of consciousness, which identifies itself with its past self in memory, determines itself by its freedom, is purposive and value-seeking, private yet communicating, and potentially rational."[14] Two pervasive traits of personal experience should be mentioned. One is *privacy:* that is, experience is always "first-personal." The second is *self-transcendence:* experience always refers beyond itself, expressing and reflecting transaction with its environment. Self-transcendence is the most important trait; it expresses the unifying function of personal experience by building up internal connections, and it solves the problem of the egocentric predicament by establishing external

---

[14]Edgar S. Brightman, "Personalism (Including Personal Idealism)," in Vergilius Ferm, ed., *A History of Philosophical Systems* (New York: The Philosophical Library, 1950) 341. Cf. *A Philosophy of Religion,* 350.

relations. It is the executive of both domestic and foreign affairs. Thus, we start with privacy and end with relationships.[15]

Whatever I may think of the details of his analysis of self or person, I am one with Brightman in being an unregenerate anthropomorphic. Knowledge is person dependent, a function of persons. As Kant says, "We can know *a priori* of things only what we ourselves put into them."[16] If so, a nonhuman point of view is not open to us. No ecstasy enables us to step outside the human condition.

I draw two conclusions from the person-dependent character of our knowledge, neither of which I will more than barely state. First, all human knowledge is tentative; no knowledge is incorrigible. Therefore, the anthropomorphic theme has to be balanced by an agnostic theme. Second, the process of knowing cannot be taken seriously unless knowing is a function, an achievement, of centers of being. Hence, at the very least this is a pluralistic universe, peopled with persons. The most important area in which Brightman's avowed anthropomorphism operates is in his use of the personal model or analogy as the basis for his hypothesis about the existence and nature of God as a person.

There are problems, however, with Brightman's concept of person. One problem is that Brightman identifies person with conscious experience not only phenomenologically but also ontologically. As a result person turns out to be equated with mind in a roughly Cartesian sense. I have heard Brightman insist emphatically that a person's body is no part of his or her mind. I think it is clear, therefore, that a person's real being is exhaustively identified with mind and that the body is an external environment on which the mind intimately depends. I have lately come to think that person refers to an ontological identity that encompasses body and mind in one reality. Body and mind are thus both abstractions, partial differentiations of a more fundamental reality. It is to this more fundamental

---

[15]By privacy I mean, not a Cartesian ego or a Leibnizian windowless monad, but the existential field of lived awareness. For more detailed treatments of his analysis of self/person, see Edgar S. Brightman, "Personalistic Metaphysics of the Self: Its Distinctive Features," in William Ralph Inge, ed., *Radhakrishnan* (London: George Allen & Unwin, 1951) 287-304; *A Philosophy of Religion*, 346-61; *Person and Reality*, 255-79.

[16]Kant, *Critique of Pure Reason*, 23 (Bxviii).

reality that I apply the term *person,* and I see no reason why an identity of mind and body cannot be adapted to personalistic uses.

A second problem with Brightman's concept of person is a certain asymmetry between divine person and human person.[17] I am not denying that there are differences between human and divine personality.[18] The divine person is uncreated and creates other persons, in both respects being a unique person. But Brightman also says that *"the divine person has,* in contrast with man, *no body and especially no nervous system."*[19] We have just seen that a human person is in external relations to his or her body. What Brightman means in the above quotation is clearly that God is not dependent on or in external relations to some nonpersonal order of being. What is overlooked is that the entire natural order (what on the human level is analogous to the body) is an objectification of the divine activity and is a dimension *within* God. We thus have the following anomaly: the human person (being *really* nonspatial mind) is more spiritual than God, who is in some sense the unity or identity of nature and spirit (or body and mind). Not only the temporal but also the spatial is an intrinsic dimension of the divine person. In this sense, it is quite legitimate to speak of nature as God's body or behavior, provided it is not viewed as external to the divine being. In my opinion, this conception of God is a more adequate concept of person than is Brightman's concept of human person. The conception of the latter should be modified to make it more like that of the divine person. The result would be that the human person is the microcosm of the macrocosmic divine Person. Just as the order of nature is a dimension within the divine Being so the body is a dimension within the human person. All real relations are thus social.

Another symptom of this asymmetry is seen in the preference Brightman gives to the temporal order of experience in contrast to the spatial order of experience. In *Person and Reality,* he writes, "All experience is . . .

---

[17]See L. Harold DeWolf, "A Personalistic Re-examination of the Mind-Body Problem," *The Personalist* 34 (Winter 1953): 15-24. I think DeWolf offers only an incomplete solution to Brightman's problem; see especially pages 23-24. I am glad to acknowledge that DeWolf makes a comparable point on pages 19-20.

[18]See Brightman's discussion of these in *A Philosophy of Religion,* 364-69.

[19]Ibid., 366.

temporal. But it cannot be said analogously that all experience is spatial. . . . It is unempirical to say that all experience is spatial in the same sense in which all experience is temporal.''[20] Is it true that the experience of ''here/there'' (space) is less fundamental than the experience of ''now/ then'' (time)? I wonder, to use Kant's language, whether the form of outer sense (space) is really less intrinsic than the form of inner sense (time). If our experience were ever totally devoid of a dimension of transaction with an environment (that is, a spatial dimension), would we not be monads without windows? A modification of Brightman's view such as I am proposing would thus give a more consistent account of spatial order, an order that has created problems for most idealists.

The last and most serious problem I want to raise brings into question the very availability for metaphysical purposes of the concept of person, or, in Kantian language, its possibility. I refer to this as the opaqueness of person. I came upon this difficulty years ago in trying to work out the conditions that would make it possible to have any metaphysical position, any defensible worldview. I saw that the only point at which I had direct, first-hand access to reality (something real) was my own existing, reality in my own case. I saw too that the primary, if not the only, root-metaphor, analogy, or model I had available for understanding other reality (building up a world hypothesis) was person, meaning by *person* here simply the something existing in me.

But even if one accepts this premise (that person is inescapable metaphysical model), I began to see a difficulty: thinkers who purported to use this model came up with very different views of reality. I suddenly saw that I would have to take much more seriously Descartes's question, ''*What then am I, I who am certain that I am?*''[21] I clearly am myself—whatever that is. I am myself, but can I know myself? I at last came to the alarming and, for a personalist, embarrassing conclusion that though person is unavoidable, it is somehow ineluctable, elusive, evasive. It is the fish no net can catch. Or, to use another metaphor, we never see that which casts the shadow. Perhaps we can never know that which we need to know in order

---

[20]Brightman, *Person and Reality,* 41.

[21]René Descartes, *Meditations on First Philosophy,* in Elizabeth S. Haldane and G. R. T. Ross, trans., *The Philosophical Works of Descartes,* 2 vols. (New York: Dover Publications, 1955) 1:150.

to know anything else. If the notion of person as such is inscrutably opaque and even vacuous, perhaps personalists have erected an altar to an unknown god (unknowable person). Mystery, thy name is person.

I kept this embarrassment to myself for a long time for fear my fellow personalists would throw me off the Boston University Bridge into the Charles River if I disclosed something intrinsically incommensurate about person, just as the Pythagoreans are said to have thrown Hippasus of Metapontium overboard for revealing the secret of the incommensurable, "that some geometric quantities cannot be expressed in terms of whole numbers."[22]

But now I have a suggestion that is, I think, worth exploring. We have a tendency to dissociate the person as a private, inner experience from the person as manifest or objectified form. If we isolate the former, the person becomes an elusive "nothing within," to use Dr. Donald Dunbar's locution. If we reduce the person to his or her outward manifestations, the person is dehumanized. The problem, however, is not that the real person is either inner experience or outer expression alone. Just as person is not either mind or body but encompasses both, so the paradox of person is the ambiguity and the mystery of the complex or continuum of inner experience and outer expression. In the dialectic of spirit (person), to use Hegel's language, infinite inner content and finite outer form are concretely interdependent. Separate, each is utterly abstract. All forms are limited expressions of the infinite content. No forms will ever exhaust the inexhaustible content, but without some form the content is nothing.

Thus, instead of having the person polarized between inner experience and outer expression, we have the person as a continuity, beginning in amorphous desire and achieving the radiant and complex unities of paradigm persons. On this basis a person is an indefinitely open-ended reality, indescribably rich and diverse, both incurably perverse and yet infinitely promising. I am not sure whether this dialectical or functional approach solves the problem about the use of the concept of person as a metaphysical model. In the concluding section, however, I opt for the possibility of a personalist metaphysics.

---

[22]C. S. Kirk and J. E. Raven, *The Presocratic Philosophers* (Cambridge: Cambridge University Press, 1957) 231 n. 3.

IS A PERSONALIST METAPHYSICS POSSIBLE?

To this question I answer: "Yes, with three provisos." First, that the conditions under which any metaphysics is possible can be specified, including the conditions under which judgments as to the truth or falsity of a metaphysical hypothesis could be made. In my judgment, as long as the context of every problem is all there is, as long as transaction with "the world" goes on, some metaphysical perspective is virtually inescapable, even though no metaphysical position will ever be completely satisfying. The distinctive metaphysical question is, *What kind of reality* could do what has been done? "Reality" is a name for whatever "does" (accounts for, explains) what has been done or happens. What we want to know is *what kind* of being or process or reality it is.

In the Shorter Logic, Hegel says, "All things have a permanent inward nature, as well as an outward existence. . . . Their essential and universal part is the *kind;* and this means much more than something common to them all."[23] That is, kind does not mean merely type but nature.

That brings me back to the question: Is a personalist metaphysics possible? I again answer: Yes, if, second, person is a center of "kind-ness." That is, if person is a model or analogy of what it means to be a kind of reality and if its "kind-ness" is not insurmountably opaque, personalism may be the most promising of metaphysical options. Whether we have made or can make any progress in dealing with the mystery of the model, I leave at the moment undecided.

Let me repeat the question once more: Is a personalist metaphysics possible? Yes, if, third, persons find sources of reinforcement in their transaction with their total environment. In this sense, functioning as persons in response to reality may be more significant than trying to plumb the elusive depths of our nature. I want to illustrate my point by referring to two magnificent moments in the Judeo-Christian tradition.

The first of these is Moses' original encounter with YAHWEH on Mt. Sinai. The record of Moses' experience is a powerful expression of the ideal of a personal or living God. It is a peak in the development of the con-

---

[23]William Wallace, trans., *The Logic of Hegel,* Part I of *The Encyclopaedia of the Philosophical Studies* 2d ed., rev. (London: Oxford University Press, 1904) 47.

sciousness of God as personal. It is not enough for Moses, however, that God has disclosed the divine and delivered the divine's commission.[24] Moses needs to be convinced; he is not initially disposed to yield, in spite of the fact that he is overwhelmed.

> Then Moses said to God, "If I come to the people of Israel and say to them, 'The God of your fathers has sent me to you,' and they ask me, 'What is his name?' what shall I say them?" God said to Moses, "I AM WHO I AM." And he said, "Say this to the people of Israel, 'I AM has sent me to you.' "[25]

At first glance, God's answer to Moses may seem to be no answer; it may even give the impression of overbearing domination, shouting him down as it were. This is very wide of the mark. How could a person "name" (in an ultimate ontological sense, which is what Moses asks for) himself or herself? What is like unto a person except another? If someone asks me to "name" myself, I can reply, "know thyself." He or she may say, "This is what I wanted you to help me learn." I can then say, "You (and I) were made in the image of God." We are thus back with Moses: What is the image of God, the "name" (nature) of God? Since there is no God but God, how could God answer other than I AM WHO I AM? That is, there is no other analogy for personal being than *itself* (that is, an I-self). There is no other God unto whom God may be likened. Hence, God's "name" is nothing less and nothing more than the existing center naming *it*self, a Thou identifying *it*self in dialogue. (The limits of ordinary language are ironically reflected in the usage of *itself* to refer to I-self or Thou-self in the preceding sentences.)

The second moment is articulated in the New Testament faith that "God was in Christ reconciling the world to himself,"[26] that is, in the doctrine of the Incarnation of God in Christ.

What does it mean to say "God comes on earth to dwell"? *Cur deus homo?* What makes it possible to affirm that "God was in Christ reconciling the world to himself"? The whole "mystery of grace" is predicated on one conviction: that God is a person, that God has realized the divine

---

[24]See Exodus 3:1-12 (RSV).

[25]Exodus 3:13-14 (RSV).

[26]2 Corinthians 5:19 (RSV).

purpose in a child, and that in the best of persons we find the most of God. Thus, the premise and proclamation of the Incarnation is that only a person of holy love could do what God has done in Christ. Only a reality analogous to Christ could bring Christ into being and sustain him in being what he was. To say that Christ is the supreme revelation is to affirm that God is a person filled with holy love. If we do not exchange the precious and mysterious meaning of personal existence and personal relations for the coinage of substances and essences, then the Incarnation makes sense. What is meant in confessing that God was in Christ is that God and Christ are the same kind of being, persons, and that there is a closeness, both in nature and in meeting, between God and human being (Christ) not credible on any other basis and more "real" than Moses or anyone else had heretofore grasped. When Jesus says, "He who has seen me has seen the Father,"[27] it is doubtful that he is asserting that he is ontologically identical with God. He is rather saying something like: I cannot tell you anything more about God than by being my (best) self. That is, there is no other analogy for God than a person at his or her best and the best analogy is the best person.

Thus, for personalism, person is the only kind and the name of the Person is kindness.

---

[27]John 14:9 (RSV).

Conflict and Reconciliation in Communitarian Social Ethics

Paul Deats

I have now taught "Ethics and Theology in Personalism" three times, each time doing additional reading and learning. As I listened to and about Boston Personalists in the lecture series out of which these essays came, I at times wondered if I did not have a very disadvantaged childhood and youth, although, thank goodness, I did not know it at the time. Unlike many of my predecessors, I did not come from a parsonage family; I did not follow in my father's footsteps to study philosophy at Boston University; I even came very late to Boston and to personalism. It is time now to acknowledge my indebtedness to Boston Personalists, to affirm my identification with the tradition, and to put into the record the open questions and revisions that seem appropriate.

I discovered I was a Boston Personalist after I was thirty years old, when I began doctoral study at Boston University and a decade after I finished Union Theological Seminary. It was for me a discovery and a refinement of my own developing thought, not a conversion experience. Insofar as I had read or heard "personalist ideas," I did not make the explicit connection to a philosophical system.

It was some comfort to me to learn (in 1984, not 1952) that Borden Parker Bowne had only decided to call his philosophical theory "Personalism'' in 1905, when he was almost sixty years old and had been on the Boston University faculty almost forty years.[1]

No one had coerced or even sought to persuade me to acknowledge that I had been a ''closet personalist'' and to go public. I simply lived and studied in an atmosphere in which personalism was prevalent, if not dominant. I had one course under Edgar Sheffield Brightman (his Whitehead seminar), had Walter G. Mueder as my major professor, and studied with or knew Peter Bertocci, Harold DeWolf, Paul E. Johnson, John Lavely, and S. Paul Schilling—all of the third generation of Boston Personalists.

LIFE

I have come a long way, not just two thousand miles, from the small segregated town in Texas, where almost everyone was either Methodist or Baptist, and where I grew up; but, in an equally strong sense, I have never left home. I have no desire to repudiate that from which I have come, in terms of my family. The sense of solidarity I first experienced in my home and in parts of that Texas town has simply been extended, culturally, ethnically, and religiously.

My maternal great-grandfather founded the town. My father brought milk cows into the county in the 1930s. He was an active lay leader in the Methodist church (South!); and the men in that church organized ''The P. K. Deats Sunday School Class'' in recognition of his work. At the time this lecture was given, my eighty-nine-year-old mother was proudly presenting to the community performances of her granddaughter's Indian Dance Company, including a wild frenzy devoted to Kali, the Hindu goddess. There must have been a stir when that small troupe joined my mother in morning worship.

In high school I was a charter member of the Future Farmers of America, fed out a baby beef, and became labeled in *The Southern Farmer* as ''the South's Boy Orator.'' I confess that my oration opened with a ringing declaration that ''If our country were invaded by a foreign enemy, we would rise to a man to defend it.'' I should also confess that I did not write the

---

[1]See Francis J. McConnell, ''Bowne and Personalism,'' in Edgar S. Brightman, ed., *Personalism in Theology* (Boston: Boston University Press, 1943) 21-39; *Borden Parker Bowne: His Life and Philosophy* (Nashville: Abingdon Press, 1929).

oration and that the foreign enemy attacked was soil erosion. I went to an agricultural junior college, became a major in the ROTC and wrote in the only paper I remember a stinging refutation of Harry Emerson Fosdick's sermon "The Illusion of Using Evil to Defeat Evil." The one theological instruction I received came from a tough army sergeant who told us as we traveled to San Antonio to parade, "Boys, I'll go to hell for you, I'll come to hell after you, but I won't go to hell with you."

I was torn between the law and the ministry and decided to go to Southern Methodist University and enter the ministry. I met my future wife's father, who was the dean of students, when I was called into his office for fighting in the dorm. To my knowledge he never held that against me when I asked if I could marry his daughter, Ruth Zumbrunnen, or during our marriage. I became a pacifist from my experience in the Student Christian Movement and in Highland Park Methodist Church (Dallas) under the preaching of Marshall T. Steele.

When Ruth and I were married in September of 1941 we went at once to Union Theological Seminary in New York City, where we faced Reinhold Niebuhr in classes as the United States was drawn into the war. By invitation we were in the nearby Japanese Methodist Church the night before Pearl Harbor; and Ruth's job working for the District Superintendent gave me the opportunity to drive for the rice distribution to the then unemployed Japanese waiters, house servants, and gardeners huddled together in closed restaurants.

I wrote my thesis on "John Wesley's Social Message" and returned to Texas to work at the Wesley Foundation at the University of Texas, where there were five thousand Methodist students, with many in the ROTC. We had as a speaker a returned missionary from Japan, whose comments were reported in the *Daily Texan* on Monday under the headline "Japs Are Human Too." That brought an early morning call from the ROTC captain protesting that such talk interfered with the war effort.

In 1948 several of us led a Service of Repentance for the Draft and other Warlike Acts, which brought a series of attacks in the *Dallas Morning News* and my eventual dismissal (after three years). After the first attack, my father, who did not agree with my pacifism, called to say he had several thousand dollars and was ready "to sue the pants off them." The other issue leading to my being fired was the desegregation of the Texas Methodist Student Movement, as well as my support for Norman Thomas for president.

In 1951, ten years after our first venture to the East for theological education, Ruth and I moved East again, this time to Boston with three daughters. Here I encountered Muelder, Brightman, DeWolf, Schilling, and Paul Johnson, as well as Glen Trimble, as I was exposed to the systematic study of Marxism and racism, and to personalism. I also was able to study sociology and cultural anthropology in the Harvard Department of Social Relations.

Ruth and I had agreed we would return to Texas in three years, when I finished my Ph.D. in Social Ethics. However, in 1954, when I was awarded the degree and we became parents of a son within a month, I was invited to stay on in the School of Theology to teach religion in higher education and social ethics. I adjusted slowly to this for I am not by temperament an academic. Yet I have now spent almost fifty years in the academy, as student, campus minister, and teacher. My only real temptation to leave came when a delegation urged me to run for Congress, just before Father Drinan entered politics.

I have learned from my distinguished teachers and from a large and varied group of students, many of them now distinguished themselves. But I have learned at least as much from our own family, with their diverse commitments and careers, and from our sabbatical leaves in Africa in 1962, in England in 1968-1969, in Latin America in 1978, as well as from such ecumenical meetings as the World Council of Churches conference in 1966 and from the experience of four of us from Boston University working with Martin Luther King, Jr., in St. Augustine, Florida, in 1964.

CONTINUITIES WITH PERSONALISM

Personalism was never imposed on me by any teacher. In fact, I had to inquire on my own, learning much especially after I initiated the seminar on "Ethics and Theology in Personalism" in 1980 and persuaded John Lavely to be coteacher and personal tutor. My pilgrimage to conscious self-identification has been mainly without torment, a gradual self-awareness of who I am. I identify more with the philosophical stream of Brightman, Muelder, Schilling, McConnell, and Lavely than with the more explicitly theological stream of Knudson and DeWolf (although the separation itself is probably alien to personalism). Let me outline my indebtedness. I am especially appreciative of four themes or foci—the centrality of personality, the commitment to reason, the attention to the problem of evil, and the articulation of the moral laws.

First, I have found congenial and illuminating the central place accorded to *the human person* and to personal experience of *purpose* and of *value* in philosophy, metaphysics, and ethics. As I will suggest later, there have been tendencies in some personalist writing toward individualism. However, the developing mainstream since Muelder persuaded Brightman to explore *social* philosophy has been the more organic conception. The human person has been seen not as an isolate, but as coming to self-awareness and a sense of identity in a community of persons, bound together by value commitments and in purposive activity.

Second, perhaps because of my encounter with Reinhold Niebuhr's "crisis theology" and my ministry on a university campus, I welcomed personalists' refusal to surrender in the face of attacks on reason, especially from theologians, keeping reason in dialectical tension with faith, countering charges of "rationalism" by the appeal to emerging empirical coherence. I continue to find this understanding of the faith/reason dialectic enriched by H. Richard Niebuhr's interpretation of faith as faithfulness—trust in God and loyalty to God's purposes, which seems to be consistent with personalism.

Third, the resolute attention given to the problem of good-and-evil has been important to my life, my ministry, and my theology. I especially affirm the courage of some in the tradition to face the full implications of choosing in favor of goodness over power in interpreting God's creating and judging and redeeming activity. This should be restated choosing to interpret power in terms of purpose and goodness rather than yielding to force and coercion as central. I do not see this as denying the importance of power and conflicts of power in liberation themes made central by feminist, black, and Latin American theologians.

The idea of a self-limited and thus finite God, less than omnipotent, is no obstacle to my loyalty and worship. A former student, Glenda Yoder, wrote that omnipotent power (if indeed, such power even exists!) seems inherently alienating. Power is at least potentially good, and the problem with omnipotent power is that it leaves others powerless. Powerlessness is what is evil and what corrupts the holders of excessive power.

In a recent paper,[2] Bishop Jack Tuell focuses on two passages from Brightman's *Person and Reality*.

> There is nothing worthy of worship in power as such; only the power of the good is adorable, and it is adorable because it is good rather than because it is power. God is the goodness in the universe. If there is power for evil, it cannot be the will of God.

A few pages later Brightman closes his discussion of the "Given" in this manner:

> God's control of the Given means that he never allows the Given to run wild, that he always subjects it to law and uses it, as far as possible, as an instrument for realizing the ideal good. Yet the divine control does not mean complete determination; for in some situations the Given *with its purposeless processes* constitutes so great an obstacle to divine willing that the utmost endeavors of God lead to a blind alley and *temporary defeat.* At this point, God's control means that *no defeat or frustration is final,* that the will of God, partially thwarted by obstacles in the chaotic Given, finds new avenues of advance and forever moves on in the cosmic creation of new values.

Tuell then refers to a letter in the *Los Angeles Times* of 6 November 1982 by Process Theologians John B. Cobb, Jr., and David Ray Griffin. In replying to an article about God's power over evil, they write that the key issue is not God's weakness but "the *kind* of power that should be attributed to a deity." They contrast the image of power as the external and coercive exercise of force by one object upon another with another image of power as an attractive presentation of options, persuasive, evocative of a "self-determining response." Then they argue that the problem of God's relation to power is usually posed in terms of the first image.

> People want to know, therefore, why God does not snatch a child out of the way of a backing car, stop a bullet that is about to kill an innocent person (or stop the finger that was about to pull the trigger), or prevent the operation of the Nazi death camps. Superman is pictured as doing

---

[2]"Personalism, Existentialism, and Process Theology Revisited," unpublished, 1984. The quotations are from *Person and Reality: An Introduction to Metaphysics,* ed. P. A. Bertocci, J. E. Newhall, and R. S. Brightman (New York: The Ronald Press, 1958) 336, 342 (italics added).

things like that. If God is even more powerful than Superman, why does God stand idly by? We would despise Superman if *he* did so.

Cobb and Griffin insist that this is the wrong image of power. They think of God as having the power

> to evoke order out of chaos, life out of inanimate matter, consciousness and then self-consciousness out of mere life, love and concern for justice out of hate and indifference, global consciousness out of tribalism, and a resurrected life beyond death.

They go on to note "the power to discover the basic laws of the universe."[3] However, they do not spell out, in this brief letter, the aspect of power implicit in "the laws of the universe." There is a power in God's judgment that is not vindictive, or punitive or arbitrary, but that operates through humans, exercising their freedom, breaking themselves and injuring others in violating the moral and physical law-abidingness of the universe.

Fourth, as an extension of this discussion, I have learned from Brightman, McConnell, Muelder, and Schilling, as well as from my own reflection, that even the conception of God must yield to moral criticism. Even so, human life must yield to moral criticism and must be guided by moral principles or laws. Here I have learned from Brightman's original formulation of, and especially from Muelder's additions to, the Moral Laws. Muelder's comments on "Moral Law and the Human Predicament" take human sin and error seriously into account.

> To speak of responsibility is to acknowledge that men are often irresponsible. To stress norms means that men violate them. To seek the good society means that men live in imperfect and unjust societies. To command obedience to moral law means to acknowledge the facts of disobedience and immorality.

The "pervasive human predicament" includes moral dilemmas of choice and raises theological issues, to which I will turn shortly. Muelder acknowledges that sin, disloyalty, and the fear of death go beyond faith

---

[3]Cobb and Griffin's letter to the editor appeared in the *Los Angeles Times* of 6 November 1982, sec. 2, p. 2, in reply to John Dart's "God's Power over Evil Questioned," ibid., 19 October 1982.

and reason as well as beyond philosophy and theology; they are religious questions, relating to how humans struggle with the ultimate issues of life.[4]

Some critics have objected that the complicated method of the moral laws lies beyond the capacity of most persons and is probably impossible for even the gifted all the time. Here I have been helped by Muelder's comment that he does not begin life *de novo* each morning. He carries or embodies a structure of commitments, loyalties, and moral principles—even habits, which enable him to act with seeming spontaneity in a given situation. It is at this point that the moral law ethic comes closest to an ethic of character. Bertocci helps with his definition of character as "the willingness to discipline one's self by one's own ideals."[5] Character refers to persisting expectations of a person's behavior, to trustworthiness in maintaining commitments.[6] Such an acknowledgement opens the question of how such a person of character and habit knows when a character requires reorientation and loyalties need reexamination.

OPEN QUESTIONS—AND TWO NEW MORAL LAWS

However presumptuous it may be for a bare initiate to suggest not only open questions but even revisions of the moral laws, let me be presumptuous, relying on Brightman's insistence that the method itself requires continuing revision. I introduced with considerable tentativeness these questions in November 1979 in my "Conviction, Conflict, and Consensus in Ethics," when I was installed as the Walter G. Muelder Professor of Social Ethics. For that occasion I prepared a one-page summary of the Moral Laws. I still cannot account for the error that had the "Law of Social Devotion" read the "Law of Social *Deviation*." I am sure that my mentor suspects the error was not typographical but characterological. He may be correct.

Muelder has a strong understanding of the social nature of personality

---

[4]Muelder, *Moral Law in Christian Social Ethics* (Richmond VA: John Knox Press, 1966) 56-58.

[5]Peter A. Bertocci, *The Person God Is* (New York: Humanities Press, 1970) 133.

[6]Bertocci, *The Goodness of God* (Washington DC: University Press of America, 1981) 97, 108-109.

and of the organic character of society, but as I read the communitarian laws, I do not find sufficiently explicit the full range of "participation in the community." Even in the moral laws, the focus is on the moral agent making up his/her own mind. How does the moral agent discover that the mind is made up wrongly and requires change? How does participation and conflict not only contribute to the group, but enable the agent to learn how to make up and change his/her mind? How does one do justice both to integrity and to consensus? Recognizing convictions and working through conflict to consensus are neglected but necessary components of an adequate ethic.[7]

Our moral experience includes the experience of conflict, whether we seek to deny or avoid that conflict or we face it head-on. We also make mistakes, wrong choices, and not only mistakes but choices that are evil in intent as well as in consequence. And our most perplexing moral decisions come as we face dilemmas, conflict within ourselves, or with other persons, or among groups. So I here attempt a trial formulation of two further moral laws, which may not fit precisely following Mueld's list, which may require reordering the last few laws.

The Law of Conflict and Reconciliation

All persons, in their own lives and in the life of groups to which they belong, ought to accept conflict in the course of seeking to formulate and achieve the ideals of personality and of community, and to work through conflict—with others, "friends" and "enemies" alike—toward consensus, justice, and reconciliation. Conflict appears to be inescapable in human experience, despite our efforts to gloss over it, especially in religious groups. McConnell wrote an essay entitled "Progress through Conflict" in which he notes that Jesus faced conflict, and he holds that "conflict has a legitimate place" in human progress.[8] He tells a marvelous story of Bowne himself engaging in conflict, verbally thrashing a missionary for mistreat-

---

[7]Deats, "Conviction, Conflict, and Consensus in Ethics," *Nexus 59* (Boston University School of Theology) 23, no. 2 (Summer 1980): 11.

[8]"Progress through Conflict," in William K. Anderson, ed., *The Minister and Human Relations* (Nashville: General Conference Commission on Courses of Study, The Methodist Church, 1942) 75.

ing an Indian.[9] McConnell obviously approves. He also holds that the effort "toward the reconciliation of men . . . moves often through such definite and dynamic statement of the truth that it may force men to take opposing sides."[10]

Conflict involves coercion and restraint. It is H. Richard Niebuhr who reminds us that the restraint of sinners is always by sinners and never by saints and that restraint must always be aimed at reconciliation.[11] My own inclination (or personal commitment) is to make nonviolent resolution of conflict a moral law, but that would turn an essentially teleological ethic into one of duty (or at least insert a duty). Nevertheless, I am sure that the burden of proof is against violence, especially in a nuclear age.

The Law of Fallibility and Corrigibility

All persons ought to expect to make—and suffer others to make—mistakes, and even intentional misdeeds, as well as to experience failure and defeat, without being overcome or losing hope. When mistakes are recognized, and repentance expressed, and forgiveness asked, the way is open for resources, human and divine, to be available. McConnell insists that such repentance can and should be collective as well as individual.

I am reminded of Richard C. Cabot's contentions regarding agreements, or what we would call commitments. For him the moral life consists in making and clarifying one's agreements, in keeping those agreements, and in improving agreements in line with the purposes of the first agreements. Thus, in the revising we are to be guided by the moral laws we first used to shape the moral life.[12]

Some may think I have trespassed beyond philosophy and into theology, at least religious experience. Personalism recognizes few, if any,

---

[9]"Bowne and the Social Questions," in E. C. Wilm, ed., *Studies in Philosophy and Theology* (New York: The Abingdon Press, 1922) 141.

[10]*Living Together: Studies in the Ministry of Reconciliation* (New York: The Abingdon Press, 1922) 72-73, 81.

[11]H. R. Niebuhr, "Man the Sinner," *Journal of Religion* 15, no. 3 (July 1935): 280.

[12]Richard C. Cabot, *The Meaning of Right and Wrong* (New York: Macmillan, 1936) 19-46, with the summary on 35.

"No Trespassing" signs. Our human experience of the grace of forgive-ness has much to do with correcting the "inner consequences," even if the outer ones are beyond remedy, of our wrong choices. Grace can operate so that persons and communities are not always prisoners of their past.

I append to this chapter my own revision of the Moral Laws.

THE MORAL LAWS
IN THE TRADITION OF BOSTON PERSONALISM*

A. Formal laws: "How ought we to choose?"

1. Logical law: All persons ought to will logically, that is, each per-son ought to will to be free from self-contradiction and to be con-sistent in his or her intentions.

2. Law of Autonomy: All persons ought to recognize themselves as obligated to choose in accordance with the ideals they acknowl-edge. Or: Self-imposed ideals are imperative.

B. Axiological laws: "What should we choose?"

---

*Note on sources: This articulation of a moral law conception of ethics was first stated by Edgar Sheffield Brightman in *Moral Laws* (New York: The Abing-don Press, 1933; now available as a Knaus Reprint Edition). The derivation of the Moral Laws from experience is found on pages 81-96. Brightman formulated the first eleven laws on pages 98, 106, 125, 142, 156, 171, 183, 194, 204, 223, and 242. He wrote that the normative science of ethics should seek universal laws "by a method which renders subsequent criticism and improvement possible" (page 31).

The Communitarian and Metaphysical Laws were developed by L. Harold DeWolf and Walter G. Muelder. The present formulation is taken from Muelder, *Moral Law in Christian Social Ethics* (Richmond VA: John Knox Press, 1966), with the restatement of Brightman's laws found on pages 61-112, the Commu-nitarian Laws on pages 116-19, and the Metaphysical Law on page 124. DeWolf's formulation of "General Principles of Moral Decision" is found in his *Respon-sible Freedom: Guidelines to Christian Action* (New York: Harper and Row, 1971) 144-78.

The Laws of Praxis were formulated and the system revised to incorporate them before the Metaphysical Law by Paul Deats in the lecture "My Debt to Bos-ton Personalism," on 17 April 1984.

3. Axiological law: All persons ought to choose values that are self-consistent, harmonious, and coherent, not values that are contradictory or incoherent with one another.

4. Law of Consequences: All persons ought to consider and, on the whole, approve the foreseeable consequences of each of their choices.

5. Law of the Best Possible: All persons ought to will the best possible values in every situation, hence, if possible, to improve every situation.

6. Law of Specification: All persons ought, in any given situation, to develop the value or values specifically relevant to that situation.

7. The Law of the Most Inclusive End: All persons ought to choose a coherent life in which the widest possible range of value is realized.

8. Law of Ideal Control: All persons ought to control their empirical values by ideal values.

C. Personalistic laws: "For whose sake should we choose?"

9. Law of Individualism: Each person ought to realize in his or her own experience the maximum value of which he or she is capable in harmony with moral law.

10. Law of Altruism: Each person ought to respect all other persons as ends in themselves and, as far as possible, cooperate with others in the production and enjoyment of shared values.

11. Law of the Ideal of Personality: All persons ought to judge and guide all of their acts by their ideal conception (in harmony with the other Laws) of what the whole personality ought to become both individually and socially.

D. Communitarian laws: "In what social context shall we choose?"

12. Law of Cooperation: All persons ought, as far as possible, to cooperate with other persons in the production and enjoyment of shared values.

13. Law of Social Devotion: All persons ought to devote themselves to serving the best interests of the group and to subordinate personal gain to social gain.

14. Law of the Ideal of Community: All persons ought to form and choose all of their ideals and values in loyalty to their ideals (in harmony with the other Laws) of what the whole community ought to become, and to participate responsibly in groups to help them similarly choose and form all their ideals and choices.

E. Laws of Praxis: "How shall we respond to conflict and defeat?"

15. Law of Conflict and Reconciliation: All persons, in their own lives and in the lives of groups to which they belong, ought to accept conflict in the course of seeking to formulate and achieve the ideals of personality and of community, and to work through conflict—with others, "friends" and "enemies" alike—toward consensus, justice, and reconciliation.

16. Law of Fallibility and Corrigibility: All persons ought to expect to make—and suffer—mistakes, failures, and defeat, without being overcome by these experiences or losing hope. When mistakes are made, and repentance is acknowledged, and forgiveness asked, the way is opened for resources, human and divine, to be made available.

F. The Metaphysical law: All persons ought to seek to know the source and significance of the harmony and universality of these moral laws, that is, of the coherence of the moral order.

Index

 *The Boston Personalist Tradition*

Interior typography designed by Alesa Jones
Binding designed by Margaret Jordan Brown
Composition by MUP Composition Department

Production specifications:
    text paper—60-pound Warren's Olde Style ∞ ™
    endpapers—Gainsborough Sand
    cover (on .088 boards)—Holliston Kingston # 35408
    dust jacket—Printed one color, PMS 483 (burnt umber), on Gainsborough Sand